FORMER NAVAL PERSON

By the same author:

CONVOY ESCORT COMMANDER

MARITIME STRATEGY

Former Naval Person

Winston Churchill and the Royal Navy

VICE-ADMIRAL SIR PETER GRETTON
KCB, DSO, OBE, DSC (rtd.)

CASSELL . LONDON

CASSELL & COMPANY LTD
35 Red Lion Square, London WC1
Melbourne, Sydney, Toronto
Johannesburg, Auckland

© *Sir Peter Gretton, 1968*
First published 1968

S.B.N. 304 93160 8
Printed in Great Britain
by Cox & Wyman Ltd.,
London, Fakenham and Reading.
F.668

CONTENTS

DA
566
.9
C5
G74

Contents

ILLUSTRATIONS

ACKNOWLEDGEMENTS

I wish first to acknowledge my gratitude for the gracious permission of Her Majesty the Queen to use materials in the Royal Archives. For much help in the selection and use of the papers, I am indebted to the Librarian, Mr Robert Mackworth-Young, and his staff.

The late Mr Randolph Churchill was especially kind in allowing me to read many of the proofs of his current biography of his father and to make use of some material therein.

I also wish to thank those who allowed me access to their archives, books, letters or papers, and who also in many cases granted copyright permission: the British Museum (Jellicoe Papers); the Bodleian Library and Mr Mark Bonham Carter (Asquith Papers); the Public Record Office; the Admiralty Library; Commander William Staveley (the Sturdee Papers); the late Captain Lionel Dawson, RN; Admiral J. H. Godfrey; Admiral of the Fleet Lord Mountbatten; Mrs Frewen (Frewen Diaries); Lord Fisher (Fisher Papers); Lord Beatty (Beatty Letters).

Gratitude is also due to Captain L. C. Creswell, RN, Admiral Sir Gilbert Stephenson, Rear-Admiral C. D. Howard-Johnstone and Admiral Sir William James for help and advice.

In addition, I trespassed on the time and patience of many people who read some or all of my chapters and gave invaluable criticism, advice and suggestions. The final judgements are, of course, my own responsibility.

Professor Arthur Marder read every chapter, and was generous in advice and encouragement and in the use of material from his own books. Mr David Cox of University College, Oxford, and Commander John Owen also read the whole book. Sir Desmond Morton, Air Chief Marshal Sir Arthur Longmore, Admiral Sir William Davis, Vice-Admiral Sir Geoffrey Barnard, Sir Eric Seal, Captain S. W. Roskill, Mr Robert Rhodes James, Lord Salter, Mr Martin Gilbert, Vice-Admiral T. Baillie-Grohman, Captain George Oswald, RN, Captain John Ellerton, RN, the late Commander Malcolm Saunders, Captain R. H. Johnson, RN, and Captain R. D. Franks, RN, all read one or more chapters.

I am also grateful to the authors and publishers of the following works for permission to reproduce copyright material:

The Hon. Randolph S. Churchill, *Winston S. Churchill*, Vols. I and II (Heinemann)

David Lloyd George, *War Memoirs* and Letters (Sir Max Aitken and Beaverbrook Newspapers)

Kenneth Young, *Churchill and Beaverbrook: a Study in Friendship and Politics* (Eyre & Spottiswoode)

Sir Winston Churchill, *The World Crisis* (Odhams Books)

Lady Violet Bonham Carter, *Winston Churchill as I Knew Him* (Eyre & Spottiswoode and Collins)

W. S. Chalmers, *The Life and Letters of David, Lord Beatty* (Hodder & Stoughton and A. P. Watt & Son)

The Journals and Letters of Reginald, Viscount Esher (Nicholson & Watson and A. P. Watt & Son)

Admiral of the Fleet Lord Cunningham of Hyndhope, *A Sailor's Odyssey* (Hutchinson and A. P. Watt & Son)

The Papers of Admiral Sir John Fisher, Vol. II (The Council of the Navy Records Society, London)

Brasseys Annual (William Clowes & Son)

The Navy (The Navy League)

Navy League Annual (The Navy League)

Robert Rhodes James, *Gallipoli* (Batsford)

Lord Moran, *Winston Churchill: the Struggle for Survival, 1940–65* (Constable)

Professor E. L. Woodward, *Great Britain and the German Navy* (Oxford)

Sir Arthur Longmore, *From Sea to Sky* (G. Bles)

D. Samson, *Fights and Flights* (Ernest Benn)

Admiral Sir Edward Bradford, *Life of Admiral of the Fleet Sir Arthur Knyvet Wilson* (Murray)

Admiral Sir Percy Scott, *Fifty Years in the Royal Navy* (Allen & Unwin)

Lord Hankey, *Supreme Command in the World War* (Allen & Unwin)

Charles Morgan, *The Gunroom* (Black)

Dudley Sommer, *Haldane of Cloan: His Life and Times, 1856–1928* (Allen & Unwin)

Donald McIntyre, *Wings of Neptune* (Peter Davis)

Bell Davies, *Sailor in the Air* (Peter Davies)

The Naval Memoirs of Admiral of the Fleet Sir Roger Keyes (Eyre & Spottiswoode)

Major-General J. L. Moulton, *The Norwegian Campaign of 1940* (Eyre & Spottiswoode)

Sir Winston Churchill, *Great Contemporaries* (A. D. Peters)

Admiral Sir William James, *The Eyes of the Navy* (Methuen)

Admiral Sir William James, *A Great Seaman: the Life of Admiral of the Fleet Sir Henry F. Oliver* (Witherby)

Acknowledgements

Admiral Mark Kerr, *Prince Louis of Battenberg, Admiral of the Fleet* (Longmans)

Admiral Duncan, *The Earl of Camperdown* (Longmans)

The Autobiography of Richard Burdon Haldane (Hodder & Stoughton)

Admiral Sir Reginald R. S. Bacon, *The Life of Lord Fisher of Kilverstone* (Hodder & Stoughton)

Lieutenant-General Sir Adrian Carton de Wiart, *Happy Odyssey* (Cape and E. P. S. Lewin & Partners)

Admiral Sir Dudley de Chair, *The Sea is Strong* (Harrap)

Admiral Sir Lewis Bayly, *Pull Together!* (Harrap)

Sir Winston Churchill, *Marlborough: His Life and Times* (Harrap)

Sir Winston Churchill, *Savrola* (Longmans)

Sir Winston Churchill, *London to Ladysmith via Pretoria* (Longmans)

Barbara Tuchman, *August 1914* (Constable)

Philip Goodhart, *Fifty Ships Which Saved the World* (Heinemann)

Lord Cork and Orrery, *My Naval Life* (Hutchinson)

General Sir Frederick Maurice, *Haldane, 1856–1915* (Faber)

C. W. Nimitz *et al.*, ed., *Triumph in the Atlantic* (Prentice-Hall)

Lionel Yexley, *Our Fighting Seamen* (Stanley Paul)

The *Daily Mail*

Crown copyright material is reproduced by permission of Her Majesty's Stationery Office

Finally I should like to acknowledge my indebtedness to two books which were published after the manuscript was delivered but have been most useful during proof-reading: Geoffrey Bennett's *Charlie B.* (Peter Davies) and Donald McLachlan's *Room 39* (Weidenfeld & Nicolson).

*. . . I drafted during the afternoon of May 15 my first
message to President Roosevelt since I became Prime Minister.
To preserve the informality of our correspondence I signed myself
'Former Naval Person', and to this fancy I adhered almost
without exception throughout the war.*

WSC, The Second World War, II, p. 22.

INTRODUCTION

This book devotes much space to the problems of the Royal Navy; this is essential if the impact of Sir Winston Churchill on the service is to be properly measured, but the temptation to delve too deeply into naval questions was not easy to resist. Similarly, Churchill's character was so fascinating, his life so full and his interests so wide that it was tempting to dwell on parts of his career not directly relevant to the Navy, and particularly on the political events which preceded his arrival at the Admiralty in 1911.

Consequently, I may be accused of concentrating exclusively on either Churchill or the Royal Navy; certainly I am well aware that such balance as I have achieved will not satisfy everybody. But I am a naval officer putting forward a professional naval judgement on the outcome of Churchill's long and intimate contacts with the service, both in Government and in Opposition. Whatever the result, I have found the task one of absorbing interest, which has brought great enjoyment.

In my account of Churchill's time in office before and during the First World War, I am confident that all the important sources of information about the events and dramas of those days have been tapped. The judgements I offer are therefore based on the full evidence—which does not mean they will always be right.

In describing Churchill's impact on the Navy between the wars and during the Second World War, however, one finds a different situation. The events of the war are fully and brilliantly recorded in the official history,* and because of the capture of many enemy records the official historians have a unique knowledge of the plans, appreciations and actions of both sides. In addition there is available a wealth of individual histories and biographies, besides Churchill's own books.

But there are large gaps in the pattern of the individual histories. Neither Admiral Sir Dudley Pound nor Admiral Sir Tom Phillips were able to give their own story of events. Thus:

---

* *The War at Sea*, Vols. I–III, S. W. Roskill, HMSO, 1954–61. The official historian of the Second World War at sea, unlike his predecessors, Corbett and Newbolt, was able to resist official pressure to paint a brighter picture than events deserved or to omit unfortunate episodes.

'We have been told what was done, but not always why it was done and who was responsible for causing it to be done.'

Until the official papers, the minutes of meetings, the letters to and from Commanders-in-Chief and other sources are available the full story cannot be obtained. I would not claim, therefore, that the last four chapters are complete; but I believe that they will show how Churchill revitalized the Admiralty in 1939 and that they will enable a valid comparison to be drawn with his achievements some twenty-five years earlier.

1

FAMILY BACKGROUND AND EARLY LIFE

This history takes a great deal of pains to make the Duke of Marlborough's extraction very ancient. This may be true for aught I know. But it is no matter whether it be true or not in my opinion. For I value nobody for another's merit.

SARAH, DUCHESS OF MARLBOROUGH

. . . it is well to notice how early a strong, masterful character develops. How much can parents really do? One would think that the future lay in their hands. . . . Is it not . . . wonderful how comparatively powerless they so often are?[1]*

WSC

WINSTON SPENCER CHURCHILL played a great part in shaping the Royal Navy of today. When, in 1911, he became First Lord of the Admiralty for the first time, he concentrated, with rare zest, his vast energies and prolific imagination on a service which he knew needed reform. His contacts with Admiral Fisher and with Lord Haldane, among others, must have convinced him of the urgency of the need for change. He arrived with a record of opposition to large defence estimates and a reputation gained in the social services, the labour exchanges, national insurance and prison reform; yet in his first three years at the Admiralty he spent over eight months afloat, mostly in the official yacht *Enchantress*, which he turned into a mobile office and from which he directed the affairs of the Navy. Very soon after taking up his post he had become fascinated by the work, which absorbed almost all of his time and energy, and his colleague Lloyd George complained at this time that 'Winston is less and less in politics and more and more absorbed in boilers'. For Churchill's own part, the magic of the Navy soon overpowered him and he became a willing prisoner. 'Who can fail to work for such a service?' he wrote after the Naval Review at Portland in 1912; and certainly his days and nights were filled with thought and discussion about the ships

---

* Superior figures throughout text refer to source notes, p. 320.

and the men who manned them. But he was not mesmerized, and succeeded in retaining a sense of proportion which is well illustrated by his reply to the senior officer who criticized one of his proposals on the grounds that it was against naval tradition: 'Don't talk to me about naval tradition. It's nothing but rum, sodomy and the lash.'

Despite a temporary aberration in the mid-twenties when, as Chancellor of the Exchequer, fighting for economies, he savagely cut the cruiser-building programme, he never forgot his attachment to the Navy, which grew deep emotional roots. These roots deepened during his period as First Lord at the beginning of Hitler's War, and I will always remember his dismay when in 1952, as Prime Minister, he was forced finally to agree to the appointment of an American admiral as Supreme Commander of the NATO command in the Atlantic.

It is easy to imagine his pride and satisfaction when observing—from another world—the superb bearing and perfect precision of the naval gun-carriage crew which drew his coffin from Westminster Abbey to St Paul's on 4 February 1965.

How did Winston Churchill acquire this interest in and affection for the Navy? We read of his ambitious games with toy soldiers which absorbed much of his playtime as a child, and we know of his devotion to Blenheim Palace, where he was born, and of his deep pride in the deeds of his ancestor, the great soldier-duke. But, although there is a record of Winston as a child visiting a naval exhibition and being impressed by beautiful models of guns and ships, there is no other mention of boats, ships or the sea in the accounts of his childhood. Once his father had decided that his son did not possess the ability for the Bar, the Army was the only obvious alternative, and no one seems even to have considered a naval career.

The list of his reading while he was a cavalry subaltern at Bangalore, immersing himself in books in order to make a new, self-propelled start to his education, includes no accounts of great naval battles or lives of sea commanders. There is no evidence that in his youth he knew much about the great Duke's sailor brother, Admiral George Churchill, who was a most effective 'Chief of Naval Staff' to the Lord High Admiral, Prince George of Denmark, during the Wars of Queen Anne,

This knowledge was to come later, when he was working on his masterly biography *Marlborough: His Life and Times.**

In any case, although Admiral George Churchill served with great distinction in Whitehall, he was never able to fly his flag at sea, and his career lacked the glory of his famous brother's. Indeed, there are incidents in it not creditable to the family—some historians have ignored them, though Winston never concealed the facts—and the Admiral was once confined in the Tower of London for extracting money from the captains of the merchant ships which he was escorting in trade convoys. There was little here to attract a young man to a life at sea.

Several of his Spencer relations had served at the Admiralty as First Lords, but this might have influenced him towards a political career rather than towards the Navy. No. There is little in his family history to lead to an interest in naval matters, and if we look back even farther than John, Duke of Marlborough, we find the first Sir Winston fighting in the Royalist army in the Civil Wars.

The most diligent searcher after naval influence on the young Winston Churchill cannot do better than recall that his father, Lord Randolph, met Jennie Jerome for the first time at a ball on board the cruiser *Ariadne,* lying in Cowes Roads. Perhaps from this stems the hidden motive which led his son, happily for the Navy, so eagerly to espouse its cause and to shape its fortunes.

Winston Churchill went to the Royal Military Academy, Sandhurst, in September 1893, after twice failing to pass the entrance examination and after much cramming in London. Introduced almost for the first time to educational activities which interested him, he did well and passed out high in his class. He was greatly attracted by history and English.

Lord Randolph died in January 1895, just before his son joined his first regiment, the 4th Hussars, and Winston was now on his own, though loyally supported by his mother. Finance became a serious problem, for Lord Randolph had never been wealthy and had not accumulated capital,

---

* Harrap, 1933–8.

spending every penny of his income and more, while Jennie's trust from her father was not large.

In those days, young officers in the cavalry were allowed much leave, in Winston's case for most of the winter months; and being short of money after the expenses of the summer polo season, Winston Churchill embarked in November 1895 on his well-known trip to Cuba as a war correspondent. Again, there is little of interest from the naval or maritime side of his life, and he does not appear to have much enjoyed the crossings of the Atlantic or the trip from New York to Cuba, the verdict on the passage to New York in the *Etruria* being that he hated the sea and the ship. However, when he was in New York, *en route* for Cuba, he was taken to the Brooklyn navy yard, where he was much impressed by the sailors and said to his host, 'Anglo-Saxons make the best seamen.'

Liner passages, which he was to endure many times again, were to his impatient nature a waste of time—a vacuum in a life into which he planned to cram so much action: he was obsessed by Lord Randolph's early death and often referred to his belief that he also would die young and must therefore achieve his ambitions early.

In the late summer of 1896 he sailed with his regiment for India, and was soon stationed at Bangalore. The story of how he determined to complete an education which was deficient in almost every aspect except that of the writing of English has already been mentioned. Military history, philosophy, economics, politics, all figure in the subjects which he devoured; naval history seems outstanding only by its absence.

But he was unashamedly determined to see action, to get his name well known; for he looked ahead to the political life which he knew must come, and he hoped for the acquisition of a campaign medal or two to decorate his uniform. He succeeded in getting attached to the Malakand Field Force as a correspondent for a newspaper, mixing his duties, as he was to do again, with some useful fighting. This was in 1897, but in 1898 he failed to get an attachment to the Tirah expedition, owing to a prejudice, natural in modern eyes but less so in the nineteenth century, which frowned on serving officers acting as war correspondents and criticizing their senior officers in the reports which they sent home to their papers. His book on the Malakand Field Force,* though widely read and well reviewed, did not help his quest for further diversions from regimental duty, for he was as ready to criticize strategy as he was tactics and he was often right. In a twenty-four-year-old subaltern this was considered precocious, to say the least, and some of his seniors were very angry indeed.

He was finding Army life extremely expensive—he was able to take three months' home leave in the summer of 1897 after only nine months abroad—and his writings were beginning to earn more than his Army pay. His mother could afford to give him only a small allowance, and he soon decided that he must leave the Army and devote himself to politics, with his writing as his principal means of support.

So accordingly, after the failure to get a job with the Tirah expedition, and with Disraeli as a precedent, he determined to use the remaining months of regimental duty in writing a political novel. *Savrola* was completed in a remarkably short time—only a few months—and though Winston later begged his friends never to read the book, it was a successful first novel and much can be learnt about the character, ambitions and ideas of the author from its pages. The book is fascinating in many ways, but in the context of this study the most interesting feature is the description of the Admiral in command of the fleet of the fictitious state of Laurentia, who plays an important role in defeating the revolution.

These men who live their lives in great machines become involved in the mechanism themselves. De Mello had lived in warships all his days and neither knew nor cared for anything else. Landsmen and civilians he despised with a supreme professional contempt. Such parts of the world as bordered on the sea he regarded as possible targets of different types. With equal interest he would burst his shells on patriots struggling to be free or foreign enemies on a hostile shore or in his native town. As long as the authority to fire reached him through the proper channels he was content; after that he regarded the question from a purely technical standpoint.[2]

---

* *The Story of the Malakand Field Force*, Longmans, 1898.

Where, I wonder, did the young Churchill acquire this remarkable view of senior naval officers? It may have been at the house of his mother or during visits to friends, or it may have been through reading articles in magazines and the newspapers. Whatever the source, it is evident that he looked upon admirals as hard, competent but unimaginative men, devoted to their profession and somewhat isolated from the world; men who obeyed 'lawful' commands in a spirit of unquestioning obedience which might ignore justice or the moral issues of right and wrong.

The other feature of great interest in the book is the young author's conviction that warships would always prevail against forts. Despite some damage inflicted by the forts manned by the rebel forces, the fleet succeeds in entering the harbour of the capital of Laurentia, and thus helps significantly to bring the rebellion to an end. Perhaps the bombardment of Alexandria in 1882 by a British fleet had left its mark on his mind, because for many years after the battle accounts of the victory over the Egyptian forts were popular in the Press of the country; accounts in which the captain of the battleship *Inflexible*, Captain John Fisher, subsequently First Sea Lord, played a prominent part.

It is tempting to speculate about the effect of this youthful impression of the ships-versus-forts problem on the attitude in 1915 of the First Lord of the Admiralty to the passage of the Dardanelles. I think that, from all accounts, it was the rapid submission in 1914 of the forts in Belgium to the fire of the new German howitzers which was the greatest influence on his judgement, but, consciously or unconsciously, memories of *Savrola* may also have played their part.

The book completed, he returned home on a second spell of leave. The London Season in the summer of 1898 was a full one, and he was busy in the political as well as the social field. Much of the time, however, was spent in long and frustrating efforts to join General Kitchener's expedition in the Sudan, for there was stubborn opposition in many circles and Kitchener himself was determined that this youngster would not be given the opportunity to criticize senior officers again. Even a plea from the Prime Minister, with whom Winston

Churchill had discussed his book on the Malakand expedition, failed to move Kitchener. But the War Office was becoming irritated by the General's independence: the Adjutant General observed that Kitchener was Commander-in-Chief of the Egyptian Army, not the British Army, and so Winston Churchill was attached to the 21st Lancers and ordered to join them at once. He arrived in Cairo just in time for the advance on Khartoum and took part in the famous cavalry charge at the Battle of Omdurman which he later described so vividly in *The River War*.*

He was only in the Sudan for one month, but this period covered the most important phase of the expedition, and the subsequent book, which achieved immediate and well-deserved success, gives a comprehensive account of the campaign as a whole. Naval references are, not unexpectedly, few, and mainly confined to the work of the gunboats on the Nile. Here he came across, unknowingly, an officer with whom he was to work very closely in later life, for David Beatty, on the eve of the big battle, threw a bottle of champagne to the thirsty-looking soldier on the river bank! Such a gesture cannot have failed to imprint a most favourable impression of naval officers as a whole on the mind of the young Churchill.

There is also a reference in the book to the cruiser *Scout*, whose landing-parties were used with success to deal with disturbances in the harbours of the Sudan coast. The vividness of his recollections of these times is shown by an incident fifty years later, when he was resting in the South of France after the labours of Hitler's War, and visited one evening the destroyer *Cheviot* lying in Monte Carlo harbour. On arrival at the gangway, he looked at the ship and said, 'This is no destroyer, Captain, this is like a cruiser of the *Scout* class.'

One of the results of the publication of *The River War* was an intensification of the dislike and distrust felt by Kitchener for the young author. The General's callous conduct in Khartoum after the battle of Omdurman was censured in very clear terms, and the great man did not like it; changes in the second edition did little to heal the wound. It was many years

---

* Eyre & Spottiswoode, 1899.

7

before the breach between the two was filled, and even then there was doubt about the finality of the friendship. I believe that the episode left an aftermath of suspicion in Kitchener which was to have far-reaching effects during 1914 and 1915.

But, to return to the narrative, it was now time to complete the last stages of the transition from the life of a soldier to that of a politician and writer. He rushed back to his regiment in India, took a successful part in the final of the inter-regimental polo tournament, which was won by the 4th Hussars, and then left the regiment and India for ever. After visiting Lord Curzon, the Viceroy, he travelled home in the spring of 1899, completing *The River War* on board ship. He also broke his journey for a few days in Egypt, where he was able to obtain some more facts about the campaign and also to persuade Lord Cromer, the Agent and Consul General in Egypt, to advise him on many aspects of the book.

He arrived home in May, promptly left the Army and made his first entry into politics in the famous Oldham by-election of June 1899. He had published three successful books: two on military expeditions and one novel. He had met a large number of important and influential people, some of whom had become friendly and others hostile. He had also—and this was essential if he was to make a successful entry into politics—gained a reputation as a precocious and ambitious thruster. The first part of his career was over and he was ready to take on any task which would advance him in his new profession. Opportunity was close at hand, and he was quick to grasp it.

2

THE APPRENTICESHIP, 1899–1911

The night was chilly. Colonel Byng and I shared a blanket.
When he turned over I was in the cold. When I turned over I
pulled a blanket off him and he objected. He was the Colonel. It
was not a good arrangement.[3]

wsc. At Spion Kop. 1899

It is easy for an individual to move through those insensible
graduations from left to right, but the act of crossing the floor
is one which requires serious consideration. I am well informed
on the matter for I have accomplished that difficult process not
only once, but twice.[4]

wsc

I asked the question, 'What will happen then?' 'My dear
Winston,' replied the old Victorian statesman, 'the experiences
of a long life have convinced me that nothing ever happens.'
Since that moment, as it seems to me, nothing has ever ceased
to happen.[5]

wsc

June 1899–July 1900

W INSTON CHURCHILL'S first election attempt was
unsuccessful. He stood at Oldham in a by-election
caused by the death of the Tory member, and his
fellow candidate in this two-member constituency was Mr
J. Mawdsley, a trade-unionist of socialist leanings. This ill-
matched pair was defeated, and Winston's political career had
started badly. But he had found some weaknesses, one of
which was his lack of knowledge of the lives, conditions and
feelings of working-class men and women. He did not wait
long to fill this gap in his political education.

Other matters, however, were soon to divert him from his
political aims. Shortly before the outbreak of the Boer War
the *Morning Post* appointed him its war correspondent in
South Africa, and only two days later he was aboard the
Dunottar Castle bound for the Cape. Among the passengers
was General Sir Redvers Buller, the new Commander-in-Chief,

accompanied by his staff, and the new correspondent was able to discuss military affairs on passage.

Winston Churchill's activities in South Africa are well known and have often been described; especially the incident of the armoured train at Chievely, his capture by the Boers and his escape. He then saw action at Spion Kop, having persuaded General Buller to give him a commission in the South African Light Horse; he accompanied Ian Hamilton on his march to Pretoria and he was present when the British Army took the city on 5 June 1900.

By then, he was sure that the rest of the war would consist of a painful and undramatic process of 'mopping up', so he sent off his last dispatch to the *Morning Post* and sailed for home, reaching London by the end of July.

It had been a stirring experience which had brought him to public notice, and his escape, especially, had made him a hero; his political chances were much improved, particularly as one of the British mining engineers who had helped him to evade recapture came from Oldham. It is worth examining also its effect on his reputation amongst those in high places on the one hand and on his contacts and relations with the Navy on the other.

His *Morning Post* dispatches were brilliant, but he never hesitated to criticize the High Command or the Government, and this did not endear him to the majority of his superiors. Lord Roberts was very unfriendly and tried to restrict his activities, though with little success. Winston also strengthened his friendship with Ian Hamilton—a friendship which was to lead to the fateful and tragic collaboration over the Dardanelles campaign.

He achieved his ambition of a reputation for physical courage, despite some malicious political attempts to brand him as a coward which led to a successful action for libel. There is ample evidence of his coolness and determination during the armoured-train affair, and in several other actions observers record his exemplary conduct under fire. Captain (later Admiral Sir Percy) Scott, commanding the *Terrible*, which with the *Powerful* had provided most of the Army's long-range artillery for the war, writes: 'Mr Winston Churchill

10

displayed great gallantry . . . and I have always thought that his gallantry might have been rewarded. He was a civilian, it was his business to run away, and he could have done so, but he stayed to fight. As a rising man, however, he had many enemies and instead of getting a decoration, he had to bring a libel action against some of his defamers.'[6]

Winston was evidently struck by Percy Scott's inventive genius and ability to get things done, and he paid tribute to him in his war dispatches.* He was impressed by the determination of the naval contingents in the war never to be defeated by any call on them and their ability to achieve the impossible —and in his book *London to Ladysmith*† he writes:

> The Artillery were asked if guns could be brought up Spion Kop and maintained there. The reply was: 'No, if they could reach the top, they would only be shot out of action.' Two long range naval twelve pounders, much bigger than the field guns, had arrived. The naval lieutenant said that he would go anywhere or have a try anyhow and if he got to the top, he would either knock out the Boer guns or be knocked out. That was what he wanted to find out . . . the contrast in spirit was very refreshing.[7]

Even in the armoured train at Chievely the gun was naval and was manned by ratings from the *Tartar*, one of whom was mentioned in dispatches, so that Winston can have been in no doubt as to the considerable contribution made by the Navy to the Army's fire-power. His meetings with Percy Scott and his knowledge of Scott's achievements in providing guns, mountings, ammunition and crews for the Front, often against the opposition of the Admiral at the Cape and without any technical help except for that of the ships' artificers and the resources of the Durban railway workshops, must have impressed themselves on his mind. In later years he backed Scott in the many battles that obstinate genius fought with the Admiralty, and during the war he advised Balfour to appoint Scott as officer-in-charge of the air defence of London, where his ability to improvise and to cut red tape was used to good effect.

---

* *Morning Post*, 7.3.1900.
† Longmans, 1900.

On the other hand, Winston had been very critical of the senior army officers, whom with few exceptions he considered unimaginative and unenterprising to the point of criminal folly, and these opinions must have swayed him in the battles over 'Mr Brodrick's Army' which were to follow only two or three years later.

Finally, I think that this campaign, the last to be fought in which the horse was a major factor, confirmed him in some of those concepts of war on land which were to bring trouble later when applied to operations at sea. In his *Ian Hamilton's March*,* for instance, there is a graphic description of the Yeomanry advancing on their horses in line abreast, 'each independent but the whole simultaneous,' which I find ominous, for it portends those sweeps for submarines which were such a useless feature of operations at sea in two world wars.

August 1900 – December 1905

Following a dissolution of Parliament in September 1900, there was a General Election, and on 1 October Oldham was one of the first constituencies to poll. This time Winston had all the advantages of his popularity as a war hero, and his running mate was more suitable, a stockbroker called Crisp. But the result was close and Winston and the leading Liberal got in, while Crisp and Runciman lost by only a few hundred votes.

After the election, he set about stabilizing his finances. *London to Ladysmith*, *The River War* and *Savrola* were all doing well and *Ian Hamilton's March*, which was published in October 1900, was an immediate success. He then set about a very ambitious lecture-tour of North America and England, with the object of putting a substantial sum in the bank, and by February 1901 he had secured some ten thousand pounds, which he entrusted to the care of Sir Ernest Cassel. He was ready to start his career in the House without financial worry.

He launched his parliamentary life in a maiden speech on

---

* Longmans, 1900.

18 February. The main theme of the speech was a plea for compassion for the Boers, which was not a policy which attracted the approval of his Tory leaders, and this feature of his back-bench speeches was to become common. An opportunity to distinguish himself soon came, when in the spring of 1901 the Secretary of State for War, Mr Brodrick, produced a plan to expand the Regular Army. He maintained that owing to the South African War 'we have by accident become a military nation and we must endeavour henceforth to remain one'.

This was a splendid opportunity for one nurtured on Lord Randolph's views of the necessity for economy in defence expenditure on the one hand and of the pre-eminence of the Navy in the defence of the British Empire on the other. His attacks must, I believe, have gained an additional zest from the fact that Brodrick had been Under-Secretary of State at the War Office in 1886 when Lord Randolph had resigned in protest against swollen military expenditure; his resignation being to his surprise accepted by Lord Salisbury.

Winston first put down an amendment which deplored the continual growth of expenditure on the Army to the detriment of naval development, But he withdrew it in favour of the official opposition motion, which he supported effectively during the subsequent debate.

The most telling part of his speech referred to the Navy:

> The only weapon with which we can expect to cope with great nations is the Navy. I confess I do trust the Navy. . . . Without a supreme Navy, whatever military arrangements we may make, whether for foreign expeditions or for home defence, must be utterly vain and futile. With such a Navy we may hold any antagonist at arm's length and feed ourselves in the meantime, until, if we find it necessary, we can turn every city in the country into an arsenal, and the whole male population into an army.
>
> The superiority of the Navy is vital to our national existence. This has been said before. No one will deny that or thank me for repeating the obvious. Yet this tremendous army expenditure directly challenges the principle. . . .
>
> There is a higher reason still. There is a moral force which as the human race advances will more and more strengthen and

protect those nations who enjoy it. . . . We shall make a fatal bargain if we allow the moral force which this country has so long exerted to become diminished, or perhaps destroyed for the sake of the costly, trumpery, dangerous military plaything on which the Secretary of State for War has set his heart. (*12 May 1901*.)

There is an almost uncanny vision into the future in this speech, and it put in more eloquent terms the conclusions which a subcommittee of the Committee of Imperial Defence arrived at after much deliberation in 1912.

This direct opposition to Government policy was not popular with his superiors, but he did not waver in his views and set out to conduct a campaign of speeches and articles designed to attack 'Mr Brodrick's Army'.

The following extract from an article in the *Daily Mail* of 18 June 1901 indicates the line he took. It is additionally interesting because the proprietor, Northcliffe, did not agree with his views and refuted them in a leading article. Churchill maintained that:

We must endeavour to make this accidental military status permanent. Why? The course of our history, the geography of these islands, the character of their people show that the Empire which it is our duty to maintain is essentially commercial and marine. No empire in human records has owed less to military strength. The greatest battles we have ever won were in point of numbers fought mainly by foreigners. The finest commanders we have produced led aliens to victory in greater numbers than their own countrymen. India was conquered by a Company which employed five sepoys to one white soldier. Australia never heard the tramp of war. The Cape was picked up by a navy for a navy. Only in America were considerable military forces employed, and of what avail was that when a foreign combination had established even naval equilibrium? No people have gained more freedom from the danger and burden of standing armies than the British.

. . . What is the very least we can do, having regard to our own safety? . . . We require, first of all, the finest Navy in the world. In order that the Navy can move freely about the seas, we must have frequent coaling stations. . . . Then comes the Army. We want a regular Army, first, to supply our great garrisons and coaling stations abroad; secondly, as a training school at home;

thirdly, as the backbone of civil power; and, lastly, to hold the land defences of this island, or for a foreign war with Europeans, and we ought not to raise troops for either purpose.

Thus started a period of opposition to party policy which continued until he left the Tories in 1904.

Lord Salisbury resigned in July 1902 and A. J. Balfour, a friend whom Churchill much admired, became Prime Minister, but though this delayed the rupture it did not prevent it. After a period of 'prodding' with the 'Hooligans', a ginger group within the party, he finally broke on the issue of protection with which Joseph Chamberlain nearly split the Tory Party, and he crossed the floor on 31 May 1904.

He was now completely free to resume his attacks on the Government from the Opposition benches, which he proceeded to do with unequalled venom and persistence. In December 1905 Balfour resigned, Campbell-Bannerman formed a government, and Winston Churchill, after refusing the post of Financial Secretary to the Treasury, became Under-Secretary for the Colonies. He knew that a South African settlement must be achieved and he believed that he was best qualified by experience of the country and its problems to bring it about. Moreover, the Minister, Lord Elgin, would be in the Lords, and there would be much important business to be carried through the Commons.

Minister of the Crown

This is a convenient opportunity, before discussing Churchill's work at the Colonial Office, to recall that from March 1902 to November 1905 he had been writing the biography of his father.*

It is fascinating to reflect on the parallel political paths which father and son took in turn—and Winston was writing the book at the time when he took the ultimate step which Lord Randolph never faced: crossing the floor—but these thoughts have no place in a narrative of this nature.

Much can be learnt from the biography, however, of his early opinions on strategy and defence policy, as well as on

* *Lord Randolph Churchill*, Odhams, 1952.

politics, and its study is indispensable if Winston's later attitudes to the naval ship-building programmes are to be understood.

The three main topics which bear directly on my subject are
Lord Randolph's convictions, first, that the safety of the
country must depend on the Navy and that swollen expenditure on the Army was wasted; secondly, that the Suez
Canal, useful as it might be, must not be regarded as vital to
the security of the Empire; and, thirdly, that administration
of the Army and Navy should be amalgamated at the top. I
have already shown how Lord Randolph's views provided the
basis for his son's arguments in the battle with Mr Brodrick—
Winston himself described it as 'lifting again the tattered
flag I found lying on a stricken field'—and for the rest of
his life he was to persist in his determination to avoid a large
standing army. Later, it was the Air Force as well as the Navy
which he wished to maintain and strengthen at the expense of the military machine, but the principle remained
unchanged.

As to the Suez Canal, Lord Randolph seemed to have the
gift of looking ahead as far as 1941. He said:

> You will be told that Egypt is the high road to India. . . . This is a
> terrible and widespread delusion. . . . The Suez Canal is a com-
> mercial route to India and a good route too in time of peace; but
> it never was and never could be a military route for Britain in
> time of war. In time of war there are no well marked high roads. . .
> The path of Britain is on the oceans. . . . You must avoid as your
> greatest danger any reliance on transcontinental communication
> where at any time you have to encounter gigantic military hosts.[8]

It now seems to be unfortunate that Mr Eden did not read
these words before dispatching the Suez expedition of 1956.

On the third topic, defence administration, Lord Randolph
was well ahead of his time. To the Hartington Commission of
1890 he proposed that the Army should be led by a Captain-
General and the Navy by a Lord High Admiral, while the
responsibility for estimates and for the supply of both services
was to be vested in one man, the Secretary of State for the
Army and Navy. Thus Lord Randolph forecast the Ministry of

Defence many years before its formation, and his son was able to become the first effective Minister of Defence in 1940.

I cannot doubt that the writing of the book by a back-bencher unencumbered by any administrative responsibilities must have had the same effect on his later policies as did the production of the biography of Marlborough in the thirties on his conduct of the Second World War.

In the General Election of January 1906 Winston, despite the opposition of the Suffragettes, was returned triumphantly for one of the Manchester seats, taking full advantage of the Liberal landslide. At the Colonial Office, his main work was devoted to the settlement with South Africa, a settlement which, because of its clemency to the Boers, was hotly criticized by the Opposition, but lasted long enough to gain South African support in two world wars and the guarding of the Cape route to the East which is, somewhat tenuously, maintained today by the defence agreement with a Government which has cut all formal ties with the British Commonwealth.

He did good work in office and was made a Privy Councillor in May 1907. In April 1908 Campbell-Bannerman resigned and Asquith reconstructed the Government. After turning down the Admiralty on the grounds that it was not, at the time, an important department—'not something one could do anything with'—Winston became President of the Board of Trade, a post in which he would be able to work closely with his ally Lloyd George, who became Chancellor of the Exchequer, on the problems of social reform.

However, one of the most interesting features of his first two and a half years of office had been his meeting with the First Sea Lord, Admiral Sir John Fisher, in April 1907. The two men, one old, one young, had much in common and they formed an immediate close friendship. Lady Violet Bonham Carter records that after turning down the Admiralty in favour of the Board of Trade Winston met Fisher, who asked him what post he was to get. When he was told that Winston had turned down the Admiralty he was horrified, and so beguiled Winston with pictures of how the two of them could rule the waves together that he persuaded him to go back to

Asquith and ask him to reconsider. But it was too late: McKenna had been appointed.[9]

Fisher was anxious to educate this rising young politician into the ways of the Navy, or rather into Fisher's ideas on the Navy, and well did he succeed. 'When I returned to my duties at the Colonial Office,' Winston said after one meeting, 'I could have passed an examination on the policy of the Board of Admiralty.'[10] He was wisely increasing the scope of his knowledge in preparation for a widening political career.

It is interesting to speculate whether Fisher disclosed that in December 1905 the Tory Foreign Secretary, Lord Lansdowne, had authorized talks between the French and British military staffs, and that his Liberal successor, Grey, had in January 1906 continued the practice; though he did not inform the Cabinet, presumably because he feared that the pacifist wing, led by Lloyd George, would have objected.* Fisher disagreed violently with the plans which emerged from these staff talks, and it seems to me improbable that he did not discuss them. He was not averse to indiscretion at any time if he thought it advanced his cause.

Fisher also succeeded in enlisting Winston's support in his great battle with Lord Charles Beresford, and by his reasoning and his enthusiasm he converted Winston wholeheartedly to his cause—a fortunate turn of events for the Navy. This feud between two of the most senior and distinguished officers in the Navy, and the dissensions which rent the service as a result, will be discussed further in the next chapter.

The important point to note is that from 1907 to 1911, except for the occasions when the old sailor broke off relations because of Winston's attitude to the Navy's ship-building programme, Winston was in close touch with Fisher, and he

---

* The Prime Minister, Campbell-Bannerman, apparently did inquire of Grey whether the Cabinet should not be informed when he learnt of the previous Government's commitments. But Grey, when asked in later years, could find no trace of a reply to the Prime Minister's question in his papers, and thought that the matter had been forgotten. He blamed the Cabinet inexperience—'the rest of us with the exception of Asquith had never been in a Cabinet before'. And, of course, there was then no efficient Secretariat.

18

was therefore able to keep abreast of naval and military affairs, despite his differing ministerial posts. And, of course, when he became First Lord in October 1911 he immediately sent for Fisher and used him as an unofficial adviser.

Because of his promotion to Cabinet rank, Winston was forced to fight a by-election in April 1908, and was defeated. But he was soon re-elected by Dundee, which he represented for many years.

During his time at the Board of Trade, he concentrated on social questions, such as unemployment insurance, hours of work, pensions and health. He reorganized the Port of London, he introduced the eight-hour day in the coal-mines, he set up minimum-wages boards and he established, with the help of a young economist called Beveridge, the system of labour exchanges which still retains its main features today.

Similarly, when he was made Home Secretary in February 1910, after the General Election which brought the Liberals back to power with a reduced majority, he concentrated, as much as he was able, on prison reform.

But this anticipates the future. During his periods of office two main problems dominated the political scene and took up an increasing share of Winston's time, thoughts and energies. The first was Home Rule for Ireland, and the constitutional crisis which arose from the Government's determination to create enough peers to override the veto of the House of Lords —a veto which had been imposed on the Liberal budget proposals. The second was defence, and the growing power and menace of Germany, which increasingly threatened British security.

Home Rule, with its attendant difficulties, requires little attention in this work except to remind the reader how much it dominated political life and how great were the passions it aroused. Winston's attitude to Home Rule and to the constitutional crisis explains much of the hostility which faced him from his old party, the members of which thought that he was betraying his class and did not hesitate to say so in the most violent language.

The second great problem deserves separate attention. The menace of Germany was heralded by the Navy Law of 1898, which Tirpitz introduced soon after he rejoined the Imperial Navy Office from a cruiser command in the Far East. Up to 1898 the military power of Germany had been recognized and even admired in this country, but it had not been feared. As soon as it was clear that Germany was determined to challenge British naval pre-eminence, however, there was a rapid change of outlook. Backed by a strong navy, the German Army became a potential danger to this island.

Consequently, the common peril in Europe forced France and Britain together, despite years of hostility and despite conflicting policies overseas which threatened, at Fashoda for example, to break up the new *entente cordiale*. Centuries of conflict had to be forgotten before the friendship could become firm, and events were to show that the alliance would be always uneasy. But German militarism sowed the seeds of its own destruction by driving the two old enemies into each other's arms.

Anglo-German naval rivalry—the approach to war

It was in 1901–2 that the Admiralty became seriously concerned about the German naval threat. The Navy Law of 1898 had been followed by that of 1900, which had much increased the potential strength of the German Navy—a strength which can be broadly summarized. By 1920, when the programme would be completed, there would be a Battle Fleet of 34 battleships, 8 armoured cruisers and 24 smaller cruisers; a Foreign Fleet of 3 armoured and 10 smaller cruisers, and a Reserve Fleet of 4 battleships, 3 armoured and 3 smaller cruisers. Destroyers and submarines were to be provided on a generous scale.

By November 1902 the 1898 programme had been steadily and efficiently implemented, and all reports on the German Navy spoke of the excellence of its materials and personnel. So Selborne, then First Lord, circulated a paper to the Cabinet which included the warning:

The naval policy of Germany is definite and persistent. The Emperor seems determined that the power of Germany shall be used all the world over to push German commerce, possessions, and interests. Of necessity it follows that the German naval strength must be raised so as to compare more advantageously than at present with ours. The result of this policy will be to place Germany in a commanding position if we ever find ourselves at war with France and Russia, and at the same time to put the Triple Alliance in a different relative position to France and Russia in respect of naval strength to that which it has hitherto occupied. Naval officers who have seen much of the German Navy lately are all agreed that it is as good as can be.

He followed this up with a further paper:

The more the composition of the new German fleet is examined the clearer it becomes that it is designed for a possible conflict with the British fleet. It cannot be designed for the purpose of playing a leading part in a future war between Germany and France and Russia. The issue of such a war can only be decided by armies and on land, and the great naval expenditure on which Germany has embarked involves a deliberate diminution of the military strength which Germany might otherwise have attained in relation to France and Russia.[11]

The Board had come to this conclusion mainly because of the physical features of the German ships, which indicated clearly that they were designed for a North Sea battlefield.

During the Admiralty's awakening to the German threat, Winston was busy attacking Mr Brodrick's plan to expand the Regular Army, and was using his father's old arguments that it was upon the Navy alone that the security of the country depended. There is no evidence, however, that he was aware at the time of the Cabinet concern over the German threat—his relations with his political leaders were poor—and there is little if any mention of Germany in his articles and speeches.

Public awareness of Germany's naval programme followed gradually on the Admiralty warning to the Cabinet. In 1903 Erskine Childers's *Riddle of the Sands,** which forecast a German invasion, was published, and in Germany novels which predicted war with England were popular. The newspapers on both sides joined in, and by the end of 1904 there was much talk of the inevitability of conflict.

The *entente* with France, which was confirmed formally in

* Sidgwick and Jackson.

April 1904, took time to produce results, and its progress was checked by situations like that in the Russo-Japanese war when each of the parties supported a different side. But the Moroccan crisis, the most acute phase of which lasted from March to July 1905, greatly strengthened the *entente* and caused the possibility of war with Germany to be constantly considered by the Committee of Imperial Defence. As Balfour put it three years later:

> Personally I was one of those who was most reluctant ever to believe in the German scare. But I cannot now resist the conclusion that every German thinks that 'the enemy is England'; that while the more sober Germans admit to themselves that they will never be able to deal single-handed with the English navy, the German Staff and, what is much worse, the German nation, have ever before them the vision of a time when this country will find itself obliged to put out its utmost strength in some struggle with which Germany is not at all connected, and that then the opportunity will come for displacing the only Power which stands between it and the universal domination of Europe, or hinders the establishment of a colonial Empire.[12]

In the winter of 1904–5, there was a war scare in Germany. It was caused by a coincidental combination of events—the concentration of British naval strength in Home Waters, some bellicose articles in the British newspapers, and, in particular, a tactless statement by the Civil Lord, Arthur Lee, on 3 February 1905 that in a war with Germany the Royal Navy 'would get its blow in first, before the other side had time even to read in the papers that war had been declared'. There seemed to be a real fear of what modern jargon would call a 'preventive war', and in November 1905 the Emperor partially mobilized the Fleet and summoned his Ambassador from London.

All this led to a reconsideration of the two-power standard in capital ships which, having been designed to deal with a hostile combination of France and Russia, was becoming increasingly out of date owing to the growing strength of the German Navy and the open hostility of Germany towards Britain.

So the two-power standard became a two-power standard

with a margin, and the Admiralty recommended that a margin of ten per cent over the combined naval strength of Germany and Russia should be maintained. Later on, after the Russo-Japanese war had showed that the Russian Fleet could not pose a serious threat, the combination of Germany and France was considered to be the yardstick. The United States Navy was never considered a potential enemy and did not enter into the calculations.

At the end of 1905, the building programme for capital ships was considered by the Conservative Government, which, just before it resigned, had laid down a policy of building four large ships (battleships or battle-cruisers) each year, to be added to the Dreadnought and three Invincibles already authorized.*

The new Liberal Government accepted the programme in principle, and it was approved by Parliament; but the radical wing led by Lloyd George demanded a reduction, and the Admiralty was persuaded to agree to the inclusion of only three ships in the 1906–7 programme,† and only two in that of 1907–8,‡ with a proviso that if the Hague Conference did not succeed in obtaining agreement on the reduction in naval armaments a third ship could be added.

This decision, announced in July 1906, produced a minor Navy scare, led by the Tories and supported by the Tory newspapers, but neither the Admiralty nor the Government was worried and both stuck to the programme.

Winston, as a junior minister, had attended the Prussian Army manœuvres in September 1906 as a guest of the Kaiser, and had come away with the conviction that his host did not want war with England. He strongly supported, therefore, the Government proposals for a reduction in the naval programme, but the Hague Conference, ending in the late summer of 1907, achieved nothing, and the third ship of the 1907–8 programme

---

* *Dreadnought, Invincible, Inflexible, Indomitable*; all laid down in 1906 or earlier and completed by the end of 1908.

† *Superb, Temeraire, Bellerophon*; all laid down in 1907 or earlier and completed by the end of 1909.

‡ *Collingwood, St Vincent*; both laid down in 1908 and completed by the end of 1910.

was duly laid down.* The failure of the conference strengthened Germany in her determination to continue to build a great navy and the inevitable outcome—Armageddon—was drawing closer and closer.

The amendment to the 1900 Navy Law was published on 18 November 1907 and approved by the Reichstag in February 1908. Often known as the '1908 Law', it authorized an acceleration of the building programme. The annual rate of production of new and replacement capital ships was increased from three to four. In addition, the 'large cruisers' of the 1900 Law were to become battle-cruisers.† The effect of this would be that, by 1920, instead of 34 battleships and 20 large cruisers‡ there would be 58 battleships and battle-cruisers.

The accelerated German programme produced more alarms in the Press, but neither Fisher nor the Government took any notice and the 1908–9 programme, announced in December 1907, contained only one battleship and one battle-cruiser§ as well as orders for smaller cruisers, destroyers and submarines, and was described as 'very modest'. But even this proposal produced a crisis in the Cabinet. Lloyd George led the attack, with the strong support of McKenna and other ministers, and demanded that the battleship should be cut out, but after much talk of resignation on both sides the main features of the programme were approved in the spring of 1908. Fisher was furious, and a row ensued in the course of which he was informed by Lloyd George that Lord Charles Beresford was ready to take over from him if he resigned—information not likely to improve relations between the two admirals. Winston was aware of the quarrel and tried to reconcile Fisher and Lloyd George.

Shortly afterwards the Prime Minister, Campbell-Bannerman, resigned and Asquith took over; Churchill became a

---

* *Vanguard*; laid down in December 1909 and completed in June 1910.
† *Blücher* was an example of the large cruiser, and no more of the type were built. Sunk at the Dogger Bank action, she was slow and weak.
‡ Navy Law of 1900 as amended in 1906.
§ *Neptune, Indefatigable*; both laid down in 1909 and completed in 1911.

Cabinet Minister and McKenna relieved Lord Tweedmouth at the Admiralty. Winston at once joined Lloyd George in raising opposition to the plan to include four capital ships in the 1909–10 naval programme.*

But events throughout 1908 combined to strengthen the hand of those who wished to increase the rate of ship-building. King Edward VII's visit to Germany was disappointing in its results and did nothing to relieve tension between the two countries. The Kaiser made some extremely provocative remarks, there was agitation in the Press of both sides, and the British Government failed to get any agreement on a reduction in naval armaments. The German attitude is illustrated by an extract from a report of remarks by Tirpitz to the British Naval Attaché in Berlin:

> Here is England, already more than four times as strong as Germany, in alliance with Japan, and probably so with France, and you, the colossus, come and ask Germany, the pigmy, to disarm. From the point of view of the public it is laughable and Machiavellian, and we shall never agree to anything of the sort. . . . I am prepared to acknowledge that it is a correct religious aspiration, but not practical for people who live in the world. We have decided to possess a fleet, and that fleet I propose to build and keep strictly to my programme.[13]

After joining the Admiralty, McKenna quickly dropped his ideas on naval economy and became a convinced and eloquent advocate of Admiralty policy. The Prime Minister confirmed in the House the intention of maintaining a two-power standard, but this did little to satisfy public opinion. Then, in the autumn of 1908, came the Casablanca Crisis, during which France and Germany brought Europe near to war.

Viscount Esher† noted in his diary on 5 November: 'I have never known a more anxious day. I was at the Defence

---

* *Colossus, Hercules, Orion, Lion.*
† Esher was an unusual character who wielded considerable political influence from behind the scenes. He was well received in Court circles and also friendly with politicians of both parties. His most important public post was his membership of the Committee of Imperial Defence.

Committee for many hours. . . .' And on 12 November: 'On Saturday last it looked like war. . . . [the French] never asked or attempted to inquire whether we were going to their assistance. In point of fact, Asquith, Grey, and Haldane had decided to do so.'[14]

In the wake of the Casablanca Crisis, the Admiralty prepared its programme for 1909–10. Owing to reports of the acceleration of German ship-building, the known expansion of German capacity to manufacture guns and turrets and the increased speed of German shipyard construction, the Board persuaded McKenna to ask for six big ships instead of the planned four. The Government agreed to this proposal, subject to there being no reduction in the tempo of the German programme, and Metternich, the Ambassador, was so informed before the end of 1908.

During the summer of 1908, Winston had been busy attacking the Army Estimates. He had taken McKenna's place on the Cabinet subcommittee on the War Office, and he quickly submitted a memorandum which proposed reductions on the grounds that the Army was too large and expensive.

There was now a confrontation between Haldane, the War Minister, and the Churchill/Lloyd-George team, which Haldane won with the help of a counter-memorandum refuting Churchill's arguments and including a sinister but apparently disregarded reference to 'treaty obligations which may compel us to intervene on the Continent'. There seems to have been no discussion of this very important matter.

Undeterred by his defeat, Winston delivered a strong pacifist speech at Swansea on 15 August 1908. He denied any suggestion of a growing antagonism between Germany and England and deplored current warnings of the German menace. He repudiated the idea that war was inevitable—there was nothing to fight for except tropical plantations and scattered coaling-stations. 'Germany has nothing to fight about, no prize to fight for, no place to fight in, and we rejoice as a nation in everything that brings good to that strong, patient and industrious German people.'

This speech made the King very angry, and he got Grey, the Foreign Secretary, to rebuke Winston for his indiscreet interventions in foreign policy. But this was only the preliminary skirmishing before the battle for the 1909–10 estimates which commenced in the Cabinet in December.

Churchill wrote in *The World Crisis* some years later: 'I was led to analyse minutely the character and composition of the British and German navies, actual and prospective. I could not agree with the Admiralty contention that a dangerous situation would be reached in the year 1912. I found the Admiralty figures on this subject were exaggerated. I did not believe that the Germans were building Dreadnoughts secretly in excess of their published fleet laws.' He reached the conclusion that four ships would be enough and that the extra two demanded by the Admiralty should be considered in relation to the programme of 1910, i.e., put off till next year.

It looked as though the 'little-navy' faction would win, for on 19 December Lloyd George was able to report in a letter to his brother: 'Two very important Cabinets on Navy Estimates. Winston and I fought McKenna, Morley supporting me and Grey. We have won. We have checked him for the moment at any rate. It looked three days ago as if he would ruin my financial plans by his extravagant demands. That danger is, I believe, over.'[15] But these forecasts of victory were premature, and the battle continued in January and February 1909, with many threats of resignation from both sides.

Lord Esher gives a vivid description of the tension:

Winston wanted me to tell Jackie [Fisher] that though as fond of him as ever, he would quit office rather than agree to six Dreadnoughts: that there was no bluff about this, and that the Government would break up. Next day he hunted me all day, and finally I met him and Lloyd George at the Board of Trade. . . . We discussed the whole position. I am bound to say that they are both attractive personalities. They take difference of opinion so well. Lloyd George, in his heart, does not care a bit for economy, and is quite ready to face Parliament with any amount of deficit and go for a big Navy. He is plucky and an Imperialist at heart if he is anything. Besides, he despises the stalwarts on his side. Winston is timid and combative. Lloyd George—though he takes no trouble—picks up the whole case very adroitly. Winston works tremendously hard but gets involved in subtleties. Lloyd George realizes that in 1912 we shall be in danger of having hardly a *one* power naval standard. Winston cannot see it. I pointed out to them that the great majority of the country is against them. That nobody goes into detail, and that six Dreadnoughts—whether rightly or wrongly—stands for sea supremacy. To resign upon the point would ruin them. No one has ever resigned with personal triumph on a negative policy. They really would have betrayed their trust. All this they took admirably. Lloyd George, I am sure, agreed: Winston trembles, and would walk over a bridge, but his *amour propre* demands one. The question is, can it be found?[16]

But Esher was too scornful. Winston in his search for economy was thoroughly testing an Admiralty case which he would not accept without further proof. He was helped by Admiral Sir Reginald Custance (Lord Charles Beresford's adviser) and by Sir William White (former Director of Naval Construction), and he had some formidable arguments from these opponents of the Dreadnought design. It is extremely puzzling to find Lord Charles on the one hand encouraging the Tories in their attack on the Government for ignoring the German menace and in their demands for a large Navy, and on the other hand feeding Winston with ammunition with which to fight the whole Dreadnought building programme. It seems that Beresford was blinded by his hatred of Fisher. However, throughout the controversy Fisher was in turn feeding Garvin, the editor of the *Observer*, with secret information, and so there seems to be little to choose between Fisher and Beresford when the question of ethics is considered.

During the height of the struggle, Winston published a letter to his Dundee constituents which questioned the whole basis of the Admiralty case and 'exposed four cardinal errors' in Government policy.[17] The first was, that the naval strength of a country could be measured in ships rather than men and guns; the second, that fleets could be built and augmented in secret; the third, that the two-power standard depended on numbers alone; and the fourth, and most fundamental, that any profound antagonism existed between England and Germany. This was unusual behaviour for a Cabinet Minister, but it must be seen as a sincere attempt by one dedicated to the improvement of the conditions of the common man, which he believed could only be achieved through economies in Government spending on defence forces, already more than large enough for a reasonable safety margin. The Army had had its attack and now it was the Navy's turn. He did not question the need for a powerful Navy—as he had indeed questioned the need for a large Army; what he questioned was the need for such a big programme and the arguments about German strength which led up to it.

Meanwhile the Admiralty, emboldened by the Press agitation, had determined to ask for eight ships in 1909–10. ('We want eight and we can't wait!') Again there was a round of anxious Cabinet discussions. On 24 February, it seemed that McKenna had lost. But by the next day Grey and Asquith had added their weight to the increased programme. On 25 February 1909 the decision was taken which Winston described. 'In the end, a curious and characteristic solution was reached. The Admiralty had demanded six ships; the economists offered four; and we finally compromised on eight. However, five out of the eight were not ready before the "danger year" of 1912 had passed peacefully away.'[18]

The compromise included the agreement that four Dreadnoughts* should be laid down in 1909–10, and that a further four ships would be ordered in the same period but that their keels would not be laid until after 1 April 1910.† At the time there was still a slight doubt, certainly in the minds of Winston and Lloyd George, as to whether these further four ships would count as part of the 1909–10 programme or whether they might take their place in the next year's programme, thus maintaining a rate of only four ships each year. However, by midsummer the Austrian Navy had embarked on a serious Dreadnought building programme, to be followed in turn by Italy, and all opposition was dropped. On 26 July 1909 McKenna announced that the four further (or contingent)

---

* *Colossus, Hercules, Orion, Lion*; all laid down in 1909 and completed before 1912.
† *Conqueror, Thunderer, Monarch, Princess Royal*; all laid down before the end of 1910 and completed in 1912.

ships would be built 'without prejudice' to the 1910–11 programme. The economists had conclusively lost, and twelve ships were ordered in two years.

Winston was quick to try to repair his fences with Fisher, who had resented the use of Lord Charles Beresford in the argument and had broken off relations during the height of the crisis. But his efforts were unsuccessful, as this extract from a letter from Fisher to Winston shows:

> I appreciate your kind motive in writing me your long letter of today's date. I confess I never expected you to turn against the Navy after all you had said in public and in private. (Et tu Brute!) I am sure that you won't expect me to enter into any discussion with you, as there can be only one exponent of the Admiralty case—the First Lord. As to lack of foresight on the part of the Admiralty, the Sea Lords expressed their grave anxiety in a memorandum presented to the First Lord in December 1907. The Cabinet ignored that anxiety and cut down the estimates. You want to do the same again. We can take no risk this year—last year we did. We felt then that there would be time to pull up—the margin is now exhausted.
>
> I reciprocate your grief at our separation, I retain the memory of many pleasant duets.

However, Fisher evidently harboured no real resentment, for in a letter to the King, who was always interested in his views, he said: 'I think I am most disappointed in Mr. Haldane, who has been a terrible Judas. Lloyd George and Winston Churchill, bad as they were, fought out in the open. They said that they would resign if more than four ships—McKenna asked for six and we have got eight!' And in another letter to Winston he added: 'I think that it would be quite lovely to call the four extra Dreadnoughts: No. 1 "Winston", No. 2 "Churchill", No. 3 "Lloyd" and No. 4 "George". How they would fight! Uncircumventable.'[19]

Winston, for his part, was downcast at the failure of Lloyd George and himself. He often harked back to the experiences of Lord Randolph in the quest for economy in defence spending, with the unspoken implication that perhaps he should himself have resigned. But he made clear, in a speech at Manchester on 23 May 1909, that he would continue the fight.

The Naval Estimates have risen by three millions this year. I regret it, but I am prepared to justify it. There will be a further increase next year. I regret it; but within proper limits necessary to secure national safety I shall be prepared to justify it; but I hope that you will not expect me to advocate a braggart and sensational policy of expenditure on armaments. I have always been against that as my father was before. In my judgement a Liberal is a man who ought to stand as a restraining force against an extravagant policy.

Lloyd George on the other hand accepted defeat, but determined not to allow his schemes for pensions and sickness benefit to go by the board. Accordingly he drafted the toughest budget of modern times in order to raise the necessary money, and the struggle with the House of Lords now entered its final and most serious stage.

In retrospect, Winston took a more resigned view of the events of the great naval scare. While he was sure that his facts had been right, he had been wrong in his judgement of the broader issues, as he wrote later.

In the light of what actually happened there can be no doubt whatever that, so far as facts and figures were concerned, we were strictly right. The gloomy Admiralty anticipations were in no way fulfilled in the year 1912. The British Margin was found to be ample that year. . . . But although the Chancellor of the Exchequer and I were right in the narrow sense, we were absolutely wrong in relation to the deep tides of destiny. The greatest credit is due to the First Lord of the Admiralty, Mr McKenna, for the courageous and resolute manner in which he fought his case and withstood his party on this occasion. Little did I think as this dispute proceeded, that when the next Cabinet crisis about the Navy arose, our roles would be reversed: and little did he think that the ships for which he contended so stoutly would eventually, when they arrived, be welcomed with open arms by me.[20]

There were two by-products of the naval scare—first, an increase in the interest taken in navies by the countries of the British Empire; and secondly, the virtual abandonment of the two-power standard.

A widespread feeling had developed that the United

Kingdom was bearing more than its fair share of the increasing burden of naval armaments. The dominions and colonies received the same protection from the Royal Navy as did the home country, yet their contribution was very small indeed. As a direct result of this, the battle-cruisers *Australia* and *New Zealand* were laid down in 1910 and completed in 1912 at the expense of these two dominions. In Canada, there was much fruitless discussion which was to provide difficulties for Winston when he later became First Lord, and in Malaya the Princes of the Federated States also considered a contribution, which was subsequently to take the form of the battleship *Malaya*, laid down in October 1913. The two battle-cruisers and the battleship thus paid for by the dominions and colonies were supplementary to the United Kingdom building programme. They were inclined to be either included or left out in the many comparisons of big-ship strength between the Royal Navy and the German Navy which were produced on both sides of the North Sea, depending on what point of view the compiler of the tables of strength supported!

Another by-product of the scare, the abandonment of the two-power standard, was not publicly admitted at the time, though Admiral Jellicoe, when Controller of the Navy in April 1909, had suggested that it be replaced by a sixty-per-cent superiority in capital ships over Germany. This proposal was accepted by the Board, though apparently the Cabinet was not informed and it was not until 28 March 1912 that the First Lord, Churchill, announced the new standard publicly.

As a final aftermath, Winston himself seems to have changed his attitude. On 5 November 1909, as President of the Board of Trade with all the facilities of his department to draw on, he ordered an investigation into the financial situation of Germany, with particular reference to her ability to pay for an increasingly expensive naval programme. The conclusion of the experts was that Germany was financially over-strained in many directions, that taxation was at its limit and that Germany's credit had fallen to the level of that of Italy. Nevertheless, the borrowing powers of the German Government were probably unlimited.

Winston ended his report by saying that there were two

courses open to the German Government—to soothe the internal situation or to find an escape from it by external adventures. '. . . One of the two courses must be taken soon, and from that point of view it is of the greatest importance to gauge the spirit of the new administration from the outset. If it be pacific, it must become markedly pacific, and conversely.' His comment on the report was: 'That is, I think, the first sinister impression that I was ever led to record.'[21] This may be an exaggeration, but nevertheless it seems to me that it marks a watershed in his political career, when any wishful thinking about Germany had had to be discarded and when, deep in his mind, he realized that a conflict could not be avoided.

Preparation for Admiralty

After this digression to describe the great battles over the ship-building programme, which ended in the defeat of the Lloyd-George/Winston-Churchill team in the spring of 1909, it is necessary to return to Whitehall.

On 23 November 1909 the House of Lords rejected the budget, which called for considerable tax increases, by a large majority. After much anxious discussion with the King, it was decided to postpone the drastic course of creating peers until the will of the people had been tested by a General Election.

In the election of January 1910 Winston Churchill was re-elected for Dundee by a large majority, but the Liberals in the country as a whole lost many seats. The Tories and Liberals were almost exactly equal; so the Labour Party and the Irish Nationalists were henceforth to dictate policy. Asquith offered Churchill the choice of the Chief Secretaryship of Ireland or the Home Office. After much thought the Home Office was chosen, and the move was announced on 15 February 1910. The post carried with it, as had the Board of Trade, a seat in the Cabinet. Moreover, by custom, the Home Secretary made a daily report of the proceedings of Parliament to the Sovereign; Churchill performed this task with gusto and Sir Sydney Lee records that his Disraelian prose delighted the King.[22]

However, in the account of the Naval Estimates debate of 14 March 1910 he was unable to disguise his misgivings at the indifference of members to the swollen expenditure, and he contrasted the passivity with which huge sums were voted with the excited controversy of 1909.

The First Lord of the Admiralty [McKenna] is now reading his annual statement. A year ago this was the subject that electrified Parliament. Today the naval issues are no less important, and the expense far greater. Yet so fickle is the House of Commons, so ready always to discard the old love for the new, that the chamber is half filled, and the members (including your Majesty's servant) are off to the House of Lords to hear Lord Rosebery move the first of his resolutions. There does not seem any danger of difficulty arising upon the naval programme or the money votes.[23]

Three days later, he reported on the continuation of the debate, and his views on Lord Charles Beresford are worth quoting.

The debates upon the Naval Estimates have followed the course which Mr. Churchill indicated in his letters last week as probable. The discussions have been lifeless and enormous sums of money and vast programmes of construction have been agreed to with an almost cataleptic apathy. The central feature of these important but sluggish proceedings has been the collapse of Lord Charles Beresford. Mr. Churchill has rarely been more impressed with the efficiency of the House of Commons in reducing outside reputations to a more modest compass than in this case. Lord Charles has spoken with good manners and good humour. He showed to advantage all the personal qualities of his family in genial and breezy modes of speech. He was received with great respect and sturdy cheers by the Conservative party. His opponents heard him without the slightest dislike. He failed utterly to make any impression in any quarter of the House. As a Fleet Commander he may deserve his widespread popularity, as an orator, he may retain it, but as a naval statesman his hour has struck.
One of his arguments to which Mr. Churchill was forced to listen was to the effect that, although Great Britain might be three times as strong as Germany, that fact proved nothing because we 'had so much more to guard'. This theory carried to its full extent would seem to require us to have a supreme fleet in every part of

the globe at once; whereas the sea is all one, the command of the sea wherever gained is effective everywhere, and the whole fortunes of the war pass into the hands of the power that secures victorious decisions from the great naval engagements—upon which all our preparations should be concentrated. . . .[24]

Meanwhile Fisher, who had retired in January 1910, had been made a peer, so that the two old antagonists were now both at Westminster, where Beresford represented Portsmouth North. Sir Arthur Wilson had become First Sea Lord and was setting to work to heal the dissensions in the Navy caused by the long feud. Relations between Fisher and Winston remained cool, despite the latter's efforts. A letter from him in March 1910 says: 'I was truly *delighted* to get your letter. I stretched out several feeble paws of amity, but in vain. I like you very much indeed, and I am only sorry that the drift of events did not allow us to work together. Your elevation to the peerage was a source of real pleasure to me, and was a partial recognition of the great services you have rendered to British naval supremacy.'[25] But this warm communication had no effect, and Fisher refused a social invitation shortly afterwards, reporting to a friend: 'I did not accept—wiser not, I thought; the King would have had a fit!' Again, in July 1910, Fisher writes: 'Lloyd George and Winston are at their old game on the Navy, Winston gushed and asked me to lunch. I said I was *engaged* to McKenna, which I think he saw was neat!'

Winston was Home Secretary for only twenty months, but he added to his reputation with his handling of a series of tense and difficult situations.

On 6 May 1910, King Edward VII died suddenly. The accession of the new Monarch delayed but did not alleviate the constitutional crisis over the powers of the Lords, which was for over a year to dominate the minds of politicians of both parties. On 28 November 1910 Parliament was dissolved so that the Liberals could again seek a mandate for the Parliament Bill. Winston was returned for Dundee with another large majority, but in the country as a whole the balance remained steady.

While the debate on the Lords raged in Parliament, the international scene was darkening, and on 1 July 1911 the

Agadir Crisis broke. In the spring France had sent an expeditionary force to Fez, to protect French lives endangered
by the rising against the Sultan of Morocco. This move was
clearly the prelude to the annexation of Morocco, and the
Germans, whose ambitions in these parts had been shown at
the Algeciras Conference, were not slow to react. The gunboat
Panther sailed for Agadir, and the crisis was on.

The reason for this move was given as the protection of
German interests and nationals, but the real motives were
deeper and more ominous. The main object seems to have been
to secure a bargaining-point which would produce concessions
in other colonial areas if France were to annexe Morocco. But
Germany did not show her intentions at once.

In Britain, there were fears that the Germans wished to
seize a port on the African Atlantic coast, and though the
Board of Admiralty was not worried by this it was emphatic
that Germany must not get a foothold in the Mediterranean.

France was extremely alarmed at the new signs of German
aggressive behaviour, and there was much diplomatic activity
in the capitals of Europe. On 21 July Lloyd George made his
famous Mansion House speech warning Germany of the
dangers of the situation and of the policy of the British
Government. The crisis immediately became more tense, and
on 25 July Grey told Lloyd George and Churchill that he had
'just received a communication from the German Ambassador
so stiff that the Fleet might be attacked at any moment. I have
sent for McKenna to warn him.'

After some hard bargaining between Germany and France,
the crisis subsided in October, followed by an agreement
which was signed in early November by which Germany
recognized a French Protectorate in Morocco in return for a
slice of the French Congo.

But there were some important side-effects in Britain. The
apathy of the Admiralty, as it was described by Hankey,
Secretary of the CID, was strongly criticized, and it was said
with some justification that the Fleet had not been ready for
war. At the height of the crisis the Atlantic Fleet had been at
Cromarty and the Home Fleet dispersed between Portland,
Berehaven and the three Home Ports. The First Sea Lord

had been so sure that nothing would happen that he had gone off shooting in Scotland.

Churchill says of these times: '. . . practically everybody of importance and authority is away on his holidays. . . . I cannot help feeling uncomfortable about the Admiralty. They are so cocksure, *insouciant* and apathetic, so far as one can judge from all that one sees and hears.'[26] The situation thoroughly alarmed Hankey, who wrote:

> What a chance for our friends across the water! Supposing the High Sea Fleet, instead of going to Norway as announced, had gone straight for Portland, preceded by a division of destroyers, and after a surprise night torpedo attack had brought the main fleet into action at dawn against our ships without steam, without coal, and without crews! Simultaneously another division of destroyers might have gone for the Atlantic Fleet at Cromarty, leaving only the Berehaven Division and the scattered remnants of the 3rd and 4th Divisions to deal with.[27]

This period, too, was the occasion of the clash between Winston and the Admiralty over the question of the guarding of the naval cordite magazines at Chattenden and Lodge Hill. It started at a garden party at Downing Street, when the Chief Commissioner of Police warned Churchill, in answer to a question, that a few determined Germans could easily overpower the small force of police on guard. It ended with the magazines being protected by soldiers, readily provided by Haldane, after the senior Admiral present at the Admiralty in the absence of McKenna and Wilson had refused to provide marines.

Another result of the Agadir Crisis had been an awakening of Winston's interest in military matters, which had lain dormant for some years. He was given the run of the War Office by Haldane, and there he made an intensive study of the situation in Europe, helped by General Henry Wilson, the able Director of Military Operations, whose clear mind and sharp wit initially attracted Winston. But he did not come under any spell.

> I thought that the General Staff took too sanguine a view of the French Army. Knowing their partisanship for France, I feared the wish was father to the thought. It was inevitable that British

military men, ardently desirous of seeing their country intervene on the side of France, and convinced that the destruction of France by Germany would imperil the whole future of Great Britain, should be inclined to overrate the value of the French Army and accord it brighter prospects than were actually justified. The bulk of their information was derived from French sources. The French General Staff were resolute and hopeful. The principle of the offensive was the foundation of their military art and the mainspring of the French soldier. Although according to the best information, the French pre-war army, when fully mobilized, was only three-fourths as strong as the German pre-war army, the French mobilization from the ninth to the thirteenth day yielded a superior strength on the fighting front. High hopes were entertained by the French generals that a daring seizure of the initiative and a vigorous offensive into Alsace-Lorraine would have the effect of rupturing the carefully thought out German plans of marching through Belgium on to Paris. These hopes were reflected in the British General Staff appreciation. I could not share them. I had therefore prepared a memorandum for the [C.I.D.] which embodied my own conclusions upon all I had learnt from the General Staff.[28]

This memorandum forecast with uncanny accuracy the course of a Franco-German war. Churchill predicted that, by the twentieth day, the French would have been driven off the line of the Meuse and fallen back on Paris and the south, but that by the fortieth day the Germans would have overreached themselves and that the opportunity would come for a 'decisive trial of strength'.

He advocated sending the Regular Army to France. Four divisions on the outbreak of war, two more when the naval blockade was effectively established; six divisions from India and one from South Africa were to arrive in southern France by the fortieth day. He pleaded that these divisions should not be thrown into action piecemeal, but be assembled near Tours, where, by the fortieth day, they would become an important factor in events. He also proposed to embody the Territorials on the outbreak of war and to raise 500,000 men for Home Defence by a compulsory levy as well as by calling for volunteers.

General Wilson received a copy of this memo, with which he

evidently disagreed.* But it was carefully read by the members of the Cabinet and their advisers, and on 23 August 1911 Asquith called the famous meeting of the CID to which he invited both Lloyd George and Churchill. This meeting is described in some detail in the next chapter; here it is enough to say that, as a result of the evident differences between the Admiralty and the War Office over strategic plans, the Prime Minister determined on a change of First Lord. He wanted naval plans co-ordinated with War Office plans and he believed that a naval war staff must be set up for this purpose. McKenna had set up a War Council in October 1909, which was intended to consider strategic problems and war plans. But, rather than a true war staff, this was a face-saving device, found necessary to appease the demands of the subcommittee of the CID which had investigated Beresford's charges against the Admiralty.† Its duties were purely advisory and it met only on the invitation of the First Sea Lord. As both Fisher and Admiral Wilson believed that war plans were best developed in their own brains and left there undisturbed by advice or ideas from anyone else, it is not surprising to find that the Council met seldom and achieved little when it did.

In considering the supersession of McKenna, it is interesting to find that Lord Charles Beresford believed that the change was the result of a letter he had written to the Prime Minister at the height of the crisis, in which he complained about the unreadiness of the Fleet for war and begged that no dispatch should be sent to the German Government which 'inferred that we intended to fight' until the Fleet had been reorganized.

---

* In his diary for 15 August, General Wilson records that he was sent for by Haldane and found the CIGS, Sir William Nicholson, in the room. 'Haldane said that he had had a useful dinner last night of Asquith, McKenna, Grey and Churchill. He had told these ignorant men something of war, with the result that Asquith arranged for a special meeting of the CID for tomorrow week. Haldane and Nick came down to my room and I showed them my map. This was a revelation. Later on Winston Churchill came over to my room. . . .' Wilson added: 'Winston had put in a ridiculous and fantastic paper on war on the French and German frontier which I was able to demolish. . . .'
† See p. 49.

He feared that 'the Germans might come over at night, catch us, causing a frightful debacle'.

There is no evidence that this assertion was correct, and it is clear from contemporary papers that it was the reorganization of the Admiralty rather than that of the Fleet which worried Asquith, who did not believe that McKenna was the right man to carry out the far-reaching reforms needed—reforms which would have to overcome the obstruction of the First Sea Lord and most of his colleagues.

But the question of who should be the successor was much more difficult to decide, and there are numerous accounts, not all consistent, of the train of events which was to follow.

There is no doubt that after the meeting on 23 August Haldane told the Prime Minister that he could not 'continue to be responsible for military affairs unless we have sweeping reform at the Admiralty'.[29]

Haldane followed this up with a letter in which he said:

You have recognised that the position disclosed at the meeting of the C.I.D. on August 23rd is highly dangerous. By good fortune we have discovered the danger in time, but had war come upon us last night as it very nearly did, the grave divergence of policy between the Admirals and the Generals might well have involved us in disaster. The fact is that the Admirals live in a world of their own. The Fisher method, which Wilson appears to follow, that war plans should be locked up in the brain of the First Sea Lord, is out of date and impracticable. Wilson's so called plan revealed an ignorance of elementary military principles which is startling. I have after mature consideration come to the conclusion that this is, in the existing state of Europe, the gravest problem which confronts the Government today and that unless it is tackled resolutely I cannot remain in office. . . . I am determined that things at the Admiralty shall not remain any longer as they are.

Asquith took all September to ponder over the problem of a successor to McKenna, for, although he liked and admired him, he did not believe he could push through reform because he was 'in the pocket of the Admirals'. Moreover, McKenna himself opposed the idea of a naval staff, and considered it an attempt to apply to the Navy a system designed primarily for the Army.

An obvious choice for First Lord was Haldane, who had successfully reformed the War Office, had set up an efficient General Staff and was certainly not in the pocket of the generals! But Haldane had been a very vocal critic of the Admiralty and would not have been well received there. It was very important to try to get at least the passive co-operation of the admirals. Winston may have fought the big Dreadnought programme, but he had always supported the idea of a strong Navy and was clearly both interested in and informed about defence matters generally. Both men were anxious to get the post and each considered himself best qualified for it.

On 30 August Winston, while on holiday in Somerset, had sent a letter to Grey in which he suggested political action in conjunction with France and Russia to guarantee the frontiers of Belgium, Holland and Denmark. He had ended by saying:

> . . . I am not at all convinced about the wisdom of a close blockade, and I did not like the Admiralty statement. If the French send cruisers to Mogador and Saffi, I am of opinion that we should (for our part) move our main fleet to the north of Scotland into its war station. Our interests are European, and not Moroccan. The significance of the movement would be just as great as if we sent our two ships with the French.

It seems probable that Grey, as requested, showed this letter to the Prime Minister. Moreover, Lloyd George favoured Churchill, and Haldane was in the House of Lords. Maybe all these factors helped sway the decision which Asquith took in Scotland, after inviting both the contenders to his house for a confrontation early in October.

Winston describes what happens thus:

> Mr. Asquith invited me to stay with him in Scotland. The day after I had arrived there, on our way home from the Links, he asked me quite abruptly whether I would like to go to the Admiralty. He had put the same question to me when he had first become Prime Minister. This time I had no doubt what to answer. All my mind was full of the dangers of war. I accepted with alacrity. I said 'Indeed I would'. He said that Mr. Haldane (he was Lord Haldane by then) was coming over next day and we would talk it over together. But I saw that his mind was made up. The fading light

of evening disclosed in the far distance the silhouettes of two battle ships slowly steaming out of the Firth of Forth. They seemed to be invested with a new signficance to me.[30]

Haldane wrote of his confrontation next day with Winston:

I told him that his imaginative power and vitality were greater than mine, and that physically he was better suited to be a War Minister. But at this critical moment it was not merely a question of such qualities, the Navy and the public had to be convinced, and they would be most easily convinced of the necessity of scientific preparation for naval war by someone who had already carried out similar preparations with the only Service in which they had been made or even thought of. I was satisfied that in all probability I could accomplish what I wanted within twelve months, and if he would look after the Army during that time, I would return to it and he could then take over the Admiralty . . . Churchill would not be moved and Asquith yielded to him. . . . I parted from him at Archerfield in a very friendly spirit. For not only did he agree about the necessity of a scientific war staff for the Navy, a staff which would study battle plans and also the types of ships and guns but he made me a proposition. If I would withdraw my insistence on going to the Admiralty to fashion the war staff there on the lines which had been followed in the Army, he declared himself prepared to ask me to come over to the Admiralty and to sit with him and the Admirals and fashion the new staff with them. With this proposal I closed. It was the best I could do under the circumstances.[31]

Asquith announced his decision formally to Haldane in a letter of 10 October, and gave the need to have the First Lord in the Commons as the dominant factor.

They [Knollys and the King] entirely agree as to the need of a change at the Admiralty. The idea of your removal there was naturally very attractive to me, and, as you will readily believe, all my personal prepossessions were and are in its favour. The main, and in the long run the deciding, factor with me, in a different sense, has been the absolute necessity of keeping the First Lord in the Commons. We shall have to encounter there our own Little Navy men, the experts, such as they are, of the official opposition, and, as our plans develop, the spokesman of the disgruntled Admirals and the old class of naval specialists. The position can, I am convinced, only be adequately held by a Minister who can speak with full authority, not merely as the head of a department, but as the person primarily responsible for the new policy.

Haldane took this unwelcome decision extremely well, and was friendly and co-operative to his new colleague, with whom, from the War Office, he was to work so closely. As he wrote in a letter soon after the change: 'Winston is full of enthusiasm about the Admiralty and just as keen as I am on the War Staff. It is delightful to work with him.' Haldane's biographer comments wisely that:

> Although Haldane was eager to go to the Admiralty himself, once the die was cast and Churchill appointed he was anxious to help his friend and colleague in every possible way. This was typical of Haldane and refreshing to find in political life, which produces all too little evidence of altruism.[32]

McKenna was informed on 16 October and was upset and angered by his removal. He tried to get the move deferred on the grounds that his health would not allow him a change of office in the middle of a Parliamentary session. But, after some hesitation, Asquith insisted on an immediate transfer, particularly as this was the time when the Admiralty Estimates for the coming year were prepared.

Before he left, McKenna made one final and unsuccessful attempt to convince Asquith that the strategy of sending troops to France immediately on the outbreak of war with Germany was unsound, and also that the continuance of the Anglo-French staff talks was dangerous, as it encouraged the French to provoke Germany in the conviction that we would support them whatever the circumstances. But there was no mention of the burning question of a naval war staff in the record of the conversations, and it seems probable that McKenna never realized that this was the issue which had lost him his appointment.*

---

* For example, McKenna's biographer, his nephew Stephen, dismisses the naval-war-staff issue as unimportant, and stresses the differences over the strategy to be adopted in war as the cause of the move from the Admiralty.[33]

On 23 October 1911 McKenna and Churchill exchanged offices, and the 'four most memorable years of my life' (as Churchill wrote in 1921) had commenced.

But before recounting the events of these four years, it is convenient to examine the condition of the navy which Winston Churchill inherited, so that the reader will have a clearer view of the problems which he was to find.

3

THE STATE OF THE NAVY IN 1911

*In reality, the British Navy at the end of the nineteenth
century had run in a rut for nearly a century. Though
numerically a very imposing force, it was in certain respects
a drowsy, inefficient, moth-eaten organism.*[34]

ARTHUR MARDER

THE sailing Navy had remained basically unchanged for
two or three centuries. Certainly from the time of the
Stuarts until the Napoleonic Wars there had been little
difference in the ships and few changes in the methods of fighting. Guns had improved a little, but battles were still fought at
a range of a few hundred yards, and at Trafalgar boarding was
still the ultimate tactic. Better indeed to capture an enemy
ship than to sink it, for then it becomes an addition to your
own strength.

Then, in the second quarter of the nineteenth century, came
the steam engine, and from that time change necessarily
became the order of the day; an order which is still maintained
today. The breech-loader replaced the muzzle-loader; oil
succeeded coal; the mine, the torpedo, the submarine and the
aeroplane revolutionized naval warfare. But there was no
period of consolidation. The mass of officers scarcely realized
that a revolution had already occurred in the Navy, and they
resisted change. They had nostalgic memories of mast and
sails, of undisputed naval supremacy, and of a service with the
highest standards of seamanship, smartness and cleanliness.
The new weapons and the new methods demanded different
standards in different fields of endeavour. Many naval officers
feared, mistakenly, that concentration on, say, the accuracy
of gunnery would bring a deterioration in standards of smartness, and they resented the time spent on weapon-training.
There was also a human reaction against the need to learn new
skills and to adapt the training of both officers and men to the
demands of the new Navy. The reader will hear again of the
astonishing accuracy of so many of Admiral Fisher's forecasts
for the future, but it is of interest to quote now the words of
one of his disciples who wrote, with his approval, in 1905: 'If

45

the Navy is to be abreast of the times, it must be turned inside out every fifty years, and the personnel reconstructed from the very foundation.'[35] The steam engine had, in about the 1860s, started one reconstruction; by 1910 Jackie Fisher had achieved many badly needed changes, though not everything for which he wished. Today, the training of the electronic-brained, jet- or nuclear-propelled Navy is again being reshaped, as foreshadowed almost exactly by the Fisher-Selborne reforms of 1902.

But whereas, in 1968, reform, change and innovation are generally welcomed, even by the older officers, in 1910 every move was bitterly opposed. Only an explosion, followed by a brilliant creative engineer, could provide the new structure needed. Fisher provided the explosion, and Winston Churchill became the creative engineer; with the result that a modern service, materially prepared for war, was created just in time for 1914. But the change in thought and outlook required to operate the mass of new material took longer to produce, and here can be found the weakness of the Royal Navy in 1911 and, to a lesser but still serious extent, at the outbreak of war in 1914.

Stragegy and war plans

It will already be evident that it was the realization that the war plans of the Admiralty were unco-ordinated with those of the War Office, which led Asquith to replace McKenna with Churchill, armed with instructions to form a Naval War Staff.

But Asquith should have not been surprised to discover that the Army and the Navy had unrelated war plans with conflicting aims. During the crisis of 1905–6 over the Moroccan question the War Office, with the approval of the Committee of Imperial Defence, planned, in the event of war with Germany, to send an army of 100,000 men to France. The First Sea Lord, Admiral Fisher, would have none of it. 'He doubted the military capacity of the French, expected the Germans to beat them on land, and saw no purpose in ferrying the British Army over to be included in that defeat.'[36] (He was full of an amphibious operation in the Baltic.)

Fisher was secretive about his war plans and preferred private arrangements with the Commander-in-Chief of the Channel Fleet, Admiral Sir Arthur Wilson.[37] There can be no doubt that Fisher often thought of a 'preventive war' against Germany, the rise of whose navy he viewed with alarm and whose ambitions were only too clear to him. He mentioned this possibility on two occasions to King Edward, whose reactions were extremely unfavourable, and in 1905 the First Lord and the Prime Minister were invited, very informally, to consider the possibility of a sudden attack on the German Fleet. But their response was frigid and the possibility was never considered part of Admiralty policy.

Again, in December 1908, when the French were on the brink of war with Germany and demanded that the British prepare to send an army of 100,000 men to France, Fisher agreed sulkily that he could transport them across the Channel safely, but, when asked by Asquith to explain his views, launched into a diatribe against an act of 'suicidal folly' and again urged the Baltic scheme of a landing in Pomerania.

The war scare subsided, erupted briefly in the Casablanca Crisis of 1908, and finally flared dramatically again at the time of Agadir in 1911, to bring with it a new First Lord and the prospect of action to prepare co-ordinated plans.

Much of this confusion would have been avoided if the CID had been effective. The committee had first been formed in 1902 and had become a permanent institution by 1904. It replaced a Defence Committee, which had been composed only of politicians and had seldom met. The new body included among its members the political and the professional heads of the services, and was served by a staff which recorded decisions in minutes, collected information and prepared memoranda. The task of the committee was defined as 'obtaining and collating for the use of the Cabinet all the information and expert advice required for shaping national policy in war, and for determining the necessary preparation in peace'. The Prime Minister was Chairman and the decisions reached were highly authoritative, Cabinet approval proving a formality in practice.

Some ministers disliked the committee because it increased

the prestige of both the Prime Minister and the ministers who were permanent members; some senior officers, in both the Admiralty and the War Office, feared that the committee would take over their functions. Fisher was one of these, and his opposition was increased by his dislike and distrust of generals. General Sir John French thought that 'he is liable to resent any participation by the Army in national defence! He regards them as Marines, pure and simple' (and therefore under his own control). Sir Arthur Wilson, in his time, was equally hostile, maintaining that the Committee had no business meddling with the planning of naval and military operations. It seldom met and its decisions, as Lord Esher wrote, were 'treated as the amiable aberrations of a few well-meaning but harmless amateur strategists'.

Back in 1902, Prince Louis of Battenberg, who had recently been serving in the Naval Intelligence department of the Admiralty and therefore knew the current state of war plans, had written in reply to a request for remarks by Fisher (then Commander-in-Chief, Mediterranean):

> The impression I gained from the study of the subject [strategy] in its earlier stages was that although a mass of information had been collected and classified as regards foreign stations, it represented chiefly the views of the several Commanders in Chief rather than the views of their Lordships. There seemed on the whole a disinclination on the part of the Admiralty to lay down for guidance any precise plan of action. . . .[38]

He recommended that 'possible operations should be worked out by the senior officers abroad, of course, based on broad lines of policy laid down by the Admiralty and the whole finally approved by them', and he also urged that the First Sea Lord should be given a naval assistant to help him with war plans—a proposal which was quickly implemented.

Naval plans for war

While despite numerous scares of war there were no co-ordinated national plans, the state of naval war plans was equally chaotic. When Lord Charles Beresford brought a series of charges against the Fisher administration to the attention of the Government in 1909, the only charge which received serious consideration was that concerning war plans. The Committee of Inquiry which was set up was a subcommittee of the CID and was chaired by the Prime Minister. After many sessions and much expert evidence, in August 1909 it reported, *inter alia*, that:

> In connection with the question of War Plans it should be mentioned that Lord Charles Beresford attributed many of the Admiralty's alleged shortcomings to the absence of a proper strategical department.
> The First Lord of the Admiralty furnished the Committee with a résumé of the steps which have recently been taken to develop a War Staff at the Admiralty, and indicated further advances in this direction which are in contemplation.[39]

But little was done.

A war course had been started at the Naval College in 1904, and in 1908 Fisher added to its duties the investigation of problems sent to it by the CID and the Admiralty. But it worked in comparative isolation and achieved little in this field. Admiral Dewar, then a commander and a natural rebel, wrote that in 1911 and 1912 the President of the College discouraged thought, that officers below flag rank were considered incapable of having, or putting forward, constructive ideas, and that the study of history was frowned on.[40] 'The Admiral must be right' appeared to be the college doctrine, though where the Admiral was supposed to learn his business was not clear.

A dominant factor which overshadowed all others was the change in the assessment of which country was the potential enemy; this change had become agreed policy in the first decade of the twentieth century. For very many years France had been considered the most probable foe, and war plans, fleet dispositions and the location of bases had been arranged accordingly. Thus a new outlook had to be acquired—an outlook which surveyed the waters to the north and east rather than to the south. These changes added many complications to the work of planning.

Ever since the coming of the steamship, a battle had raged

between two schools of strategic thought. One, fostered in military circles and known as the 'bolt-from-the-blue' school, believed that invasion of this island was perfectly feasible, and consequently that a large standing army and many defensive forts were needed to protect the country. The other, the 'blue-water' school, supported—though not always as firmly as would have been expected—by the Navy, was convinced that the Fleet could deal with anything except minor raids or hit-and-run bombardments, and was content that the British Army should be sent overseas. This controversy bedevilled planning for many years and, although apparently settled more than once, arose again and again. In 1908, a subcommittee of the CID examined the question closely, and agreed, *inter alia*, that:

1. . . . so long as our naval supremacy is assured against any reasonably probable combination of Powers, invasion is impracticable.
2. . . . if we permanently lose the command of the sea, whatever may be the strength and organization of the home force, the subjection of the country to the enemy is inevitable.
3. . . . our army for home defence ought to be sufficient in number and organization not only to repel small raids, but to compel an enemy who contemplates invasion to come with so substantial a force as will make it impossible for him to evade our fleets.
4. . . . to ensure an ample margin of safety such a force may, for purposes of calculation, be assumed to be 70,000 men.[41]

In July 1909 the Prime Minister finally gave approval to these conclusions and the matter was formally closed. (But it was re-opened in 1913.)

The main object of any naval plan was to defeat the enemy Fleet, and there was much discussion as to the best way to achieve this. Traditionally, strategy had been based on the close blockade, which had been perfected in the Napoleonic Wars, when frigates were stationed close off the main enemy ports and were able to warn the Fleet cruising off shore of any enemy movement. But the steamship, the mine and the torpedo had, in the opinion of many naval thinkers, made close blockade impossible by the turn of the century and the development of the submarine had confirmed their judgement.

But in 1911 the policy had not changed:

> The present War Plans provide for the blockade of the Heligoland Bight by the 1st and 2nd Destroyer Flotillas, supported by the 1st, 2nd and 3rd Cruiser Squadrons, with the principal object of (a) preventing raiding expeditions leaving German ports in the earlier stages of hostilities; (b) preventing the German Fleet putting to sea without the British Commander-in-Chief knowing it, and when it is known to be at sea, conveying him such information as to its movements as will enable it to be brought to action by the British Main fleet.[42]

Commerce destruction

The throttling of German seaborne trade was a feature of all war plans from 1905 onwards, and, whether carried out by close or distant blockade, was considered to have the advantages not only of causing economic damage to Germany but also of forcing the German Fleet to come out and offer battle. The importance of Belligerent Rights was by now again fully understood in the Admiralty, and the doctrine of the Freedom of the Seas firmly rejected.

Capture of German overseas bases

Despite the importance attached to the stopping of enemy seaborne trade, and also, of course, to the protection of British shipping, little thought was given to the capture of German colonies from which trade was to be conducted and from whose bases commerce-destroyers, whether warships or armed raiders, could operate.

Protection of British shipping

During the early years of the twentieth century there was little argument on the importance of maintaining the flow of supplies to Britain from overseas in war. The destruction of the enemy's main Fleet, and hence the acquisition of command of the sea, was clearly the first aim. The defence of shipping against enemy raiders which evaded our ships and squadrons was to be achieved by one of three possible methods—convoy,

E

patrolling of trade routes, or stationing of cruiser squadrons at focal points. Convoy was rejected almost unanimously, for a variety of reasons which appear incomprehensible to the modern reader, and by 1911 the system of prescribed trade routes along which cruisers would patrol had been rejected in favour of the dispersion of trade and the stationing of cruisers at focal points. Under this system, it was hoped, the enemy would have difficulty in finding his victim and would be forced towards the focal points where he would be detected and destroyed.

Combined operations

The War Office believed in a continental strategy in which the Army was to bring maximum aid to the French at the out-break of war. The Admiralty, on the other hand—and they had many lessons of history behind them—supported a maritime strategy, and did not consider that the help which the British Army could bring in France was on a scale worth sending. They believed that the Army was a 'projectile to be fired by the Navy' at targets in the rear and on the flank of the enemy, designed to cause the maximum dislocation with the minimum effort.

But, unfortunately, the admirals could not agree amongst themselves on the targets. Fisher favoured a landing-area on the Pomeranian coast, ninety miles from Berlin, while Admiral Wilson wished to seize both Heligoland and an island off the coast of Schleswig-Holstein as bases for the torpedo craft and submarines engaged in the close blockade of Germany.

The objections to both schemes were formidable. How could the Fleet pass into the Baltic, whose entrances were narrow, easily defended and easily mined? And, once inside, how could the Fleet be kept supplied? Given the extended system of rail communications in Germany, how could a British Army limited to 100,000 men deal with the vastly superior forces which could quickly be brought to oppose it? As to the capture of one of the Frisian Islands, the naviga-tional difficulties were immense, the islands were heavily defended; when captured, they would still be within gun-range of the mainland, and the prospects of establishing an operational base there seemed remote. Moreover, the German High Seas Fleet was based close by, and any battle which was fought would be under conditions most unfavourable to the British Fleet.

The differences on strategy between the War Office and the Admiralty were sharply outlined in the CID meeting of 23 August 1911, the political effects of which have already been mentioned. The minutes give a full account, and Marder has made an excellent summary.[43] It is necessary here only to give a few of the salient points.

The contrast between the presentations of the two strategies was startling. General Wilson, speaking from a carefully prepared brief, illustrated by suitable maps, described detailed plans to transport the British Army to France and deploy it there. Admiral Wilson spoke from no brief; he had no staff to prepare one and Admiralty plans, in any case, were locked in his own head. His description of his proposals for naval action in war was singularly unconvincing. All were based on the close blockade and the need to seize forward bases off the German coast, and he appeared to ignore the advent of submarines and mines. He also mentioned that the Navy might find it necessary to enter the Baltic, but he did not seem clear why and how it should be done.

Under cross-examination by the soldiers, by the Foreign Secretary and by Churchill, he failed utterly to convince his audience and the meeting broke up in confusion, with the military plan holding the field. Nothing daunted, Admiral Wilson proposed to the War Office, immediately after the meeting, the formation of a mobile force of some 6,000 infantry to assist the naval Commander-in-Chief, but the reply was firmly negative and political changes soon brought fresh ideas to the Admiralty.

Tactics

Until this time—1911—the only naval actions which had been fought under modern conditions had taken place during the Russo-Japanese War of 1904–5, and although the lessons of the war had been carefully studied the great discrepancies in technical efficiency between the two navies made comparisons unreliable and firm conclusions difficult to deduce.

The history of tactical doctrine in the Royal Navy had been chequered. Whereas strategic thought retained a sense of continuity which had been nourished by Pitt and Dundas, Anson and Barham, and fostered by Fisher, tactics had been comparatively neglected except by admirals of genius at widely separated intervals.

In his letter to Fisher in 1902, which has already been mentioned, Prince Louis wrote:

> May I add a word about tactics, that is, battle tactics? How much can be prescribed and how much left to the Admiral? At present, we are in a fog but ideas are beginning to take shape. Given your ships and their peculiarities, and the especial diposals of armaments, and assuming that the gun is the weapon, surely there must be some one formation and some definite relative positions to maintain with reference to the opposing fleet which promises better chances of success than any other. If we can find this out, should it not be adopted and Admirals directed to stick to it?
>
> In view of the few opportunities afforded our Admirals in gaining practical experience in this, is it right to leave a new Admiral an absolutely free hand and to ignore the results of the patient labours of others who have gone before?[44]

It seems astonishing that such a situation could exist; clearly much thought and much experience were needed before some sound doctrine could be produced.

A study of naval history shows clearly that when overmuch importance was attached to the contents of the Fighting Instructions and to patterns in signal-books, initiative dwindled, constructive thought became atrophied and centralization of command rigid. The fruits of such conditions were uniformly disastrous, and resulted in either defeats or inconclusive battles. Only when initiative by junior officers was encouraged came such victories as Quiberon Bay in 1759, the Battle of the Saints in 1782, the Glorious First of June in 1794, the Nile in 1798 and Trafalgar in 1805. I think that the most vivid illustration of a healthy attitude to Battle Orders is found in the story of one of Duncan's captains at Camperdown in 1797. 'Captain Inglis of the *Belliqueux*, 64, had neglected to make himself a complete master of the signal book and on the morning of the battle found himself more puzzled than enlightened by it. At last, throwing it upon the deck, he exploded, "Damn the bluidy book, up with the helum and gang in the middle of them." [45]

In fact, success in battle seems to have varied inversely with the size of and importance attached to the Fighting Instructions, and as a sidelight on the question I believe that one blessing, probably undeserved, for the Navy in the Second World War was that the Fighting Instructions in use in 1939, being based on a conflict of the type of Jutland, were utterly irrelevant to the war in progress and were never opened.

In 1911 every senior officer lacked experience of modern war. The years of peace had built up a picture of admirals with almost divine infallibility. Rigid battle orders were issued before every exercise, describing every move in detailed sequence. Decentralization was forbidden, initiative frowned on, and 'follow the Admiral's motions' or 'wait for the Admiral's orders' were the guiding rules. Many, probably all, of the failures of the First World War may be traced to this stultifying attitude.

Admiral Dewar writes of 'the quadrille-like movements which took the place of real tactical exercises', and complains of the paucity of thought devoted to tactics at the Naval War College, describing how, as a member of the staff, he determined to make a thorough study of the problem based on historical analysis. But he received little support for his work and his main conclusion, that 'single line' fettered the Commander and that a more flexible concept was needed, was extremely unpopular and treated as heresy. [46]

It is also clear that tactics were not practised enough at sea, and that weapon-training was given too great a share of the available time. Admiral Lord Charles Beresford said in 1902 that he was now fifty-six years old, with one foot in the grave, and he had tactically handled three ships for five hours in his life and that was a great deal more than some of his brother admirals. Moreover, weapon-training and tactics were un-co-ordinated.

Probably the main reason for these weaknesses was the growing ascendancy of the material school in the Navy of the day. In 1911 the technical revolution started by Fisher when he became First Sea Lord in 1904 was still being consolidated. Too much stress was laid on technical efficiency in weapons, too little trouble devoted to finding the best ways of fighting these weapons in war. The theorist was distrusted, the practical man was supreme; and officers like Custance, Richmond, and Dewar, who read much and thought deeply about tactical problems, were ignored. It was said that: '. . . officers who made any real study of war from the point of view of Staff work were regarded as cranks or lunatics, hunters of soft jobs; and the gin-and-bitters school were quite content to be left to the guidance of their splendid but not always highly trained instincts.'[47]

The dogma of the single line had banished independent thought and naval tactics had degenerated into a deadly game of follow-my-leader.

Personnel

In assessing the state of the Navy in 1911, I have relied on many different sources. A great service like the Navy presents a different picture to different observers. In particular, the enthusiast and successful officer is inclined to linger over the best qualities while forgetting some of the worst. Conversely, the bitter or disappointed man, who may not have gained the promotion which he thinks he has deserved, is apt to dwell on the weaknesses and abuses of the service and to leave out any reference to the features which attract the admiration of the world. I have therefore tried to balance each quotation of opinion with another from an opposing school of thought—to compare the conformist with the rebel, and the materialist view with that of the historian.

Most naval officers in the first decade of the twentieth century came from the middle classes. Many were from naval and military families, or the sons of country gentlemen, parsons and professional men. There were a few members of the nobility, and of course the career of the Prince of Wales (later George V), who was brought up as a naval officer, brought the service into close relationship with the Monarchy.

The life of the naval officer did not encourage the dilettante or the man who wished to spend a few agreeable years in the service before retiring to his country estates. The duties were arduous, and family life was broken by very long absences. Officers spent many years at sea without serving ashore and spells of foreign service lasted up to three years. Wives were seldom able to follow their husbands abroad. Admiral Sir Arthur Duff, both of whose sons became naval officers, did not serve ashore from the time he qualified in gunnery as a young lieutenant until his last appointment as a flag officer, and his was no exceptional case.

There was a widespread belief that in order to prepare boys for such a life it was necessary to catch them young. Fisher was an extreme exponent of this policy, though his views were not universally shared. Admiral of the Fleet Lord Cork wrote that '. . . the old idea that it was necessary to send a boy to sea young so as to inure him to a sea life is quite obsolete'. In every other way a sturdy supporter of the 'establishment', he believed that boys should not join until their general education was finished on leaving school at the age of seventeen or eighteen.[48]

There can be no doubt that early entry did instil a pattern of thought among the majority who were able to accept naval life, and produced exceptionally high standards of devotion to duty, a readiness to accept any challenge and to believe that the impossible could be achieved. But it also produced a conservative and rather rigid outlook which discouraged new ideas or critical thought.

Young officers were taught that they belonged to the finest service in the world, which set itself the highest standards. That these standards often related to seamanship, smartness and cleanliness and by-passed fighting efficiency was the result of one hundred years of comparative peace. These years of peace had, as we have already seen, built up the cult of the admiral as an all-seeing, all-knowing autocrat who could do no wrong.

By 1911 the new naval colleges at Osborne and Dartmouth,

which covered the first four years of cadets' training, were in full operation, though the majority of the executive officers had been trained in the floating hulks which made up the *Britannia*. Cadets joined at twelve and a half, and their training was a mixture of the theoretical and the practical, the professional and the general, which they continued at sea as subordinate officers. The young man started as a cadet in the training cruiser and then went to a midshipman's billet in the gunroom of a battleship or cruiser.

There was much to commend in a midshipman's training, particularly if it was carried out in a good ship with an enthusiastic captain. Midshipmen belonged neither to the wardroom nor to the lower deck, but shared the confidence and friendship of both. In his long spells in charge of ships' boats, whether under oars, sail or power, the young officer got to know the sailor, to respect him and usually to gain his respect. On the bridge, in the gun-turret and wherever he worked, the midshipman had the opportunity to make the mistakes necessary to get a deep and thorough knowledge of his profession without losing face or confidence.

But in the years before the First World War, there were some dark aspects of the midshipman's life. Some captains took little interest in his training, and the monthly signature of his 'journal' represented the extent of their effort. Instruction was often unimaginative and haphazard and was constantly interrupted by the demands of boat-running and other ship's duties.

Another sombre side of the midshipman's life was the bullying which went on in some gunrooms. Each gunroom had its rigid hierarchy of rank—usually there were the juniors or 'warts', the middle layer, and the Senior Midshipmen, while the whole was presided over by the Sub-Lieutenant. A tradition that the 'warts' must be toughened by harsh treatment had grown up, and in many gunrooms the juniors lived in a state of fearful anticipation of the evolutions which were part of guest-night dinners. These harsh and ignominious affairs are vividly described in Charles Morgan's *The Gunroom*, and accounts of similar practices in many biographies and stories of the time confirm that he was not exaggerating to any great extent. There is a particularly poignant picture of the young hero of the book, John Lynwood, fresh from the training cruiser, joining his first ship. He is leaving a cab, the driver of which is an old naval man. 'Good luck to 'ee, Sir,' says the old sailor, and as he turns away he adds under his breath, 'And Gawd 'elp 'ee.' And later on in the book, when Lynwood is a Senior Midshipman and no longer subject to bullying, he is given some words of wisdom by an elderly Warrant Engineer Officer who has been promoted from the lower deck: 'I knows how it is with Midshipmen. The lower deck sees a lot that the lower deck doesn't care to see. And it ain't against Midshipmen. Them that suffer ain't against them that suffer. And don't forget that when you get to the Wardroom. It's the men who don't forget that the hands'll run for.'

Morgan was a very sensitive character with highly developed artistic leanings, who was unsuited to the life of a naval officer. He paints too dark a picture, and he compresses into one novel the faults of numerous ships.

Gunroom bullying was not universal, but it was not exceptional, and such conditions did not bring out the qualities of leadership which were needed.

It is clear that some officers did not know of or did not care about the evils of bullying, and when, in 1904, there was a 'ragging' scandal which reached the newspapers, the captain of the ship concerned, a distinguished officer of a humane and kindly character who later reached the highest ranks of the Navy, knew nothing of what went on in his gunroom.

Reflecting on a society in which such situations were tolerated, one comes to the conclusion that the age was much harder than the present, and that the treatment of fellow humans was harsher. Certainly only the tough, mentally and physically, survived. But it was a wasteful and inhuman method of selection of the fittest, and it ruined some young naval lives and left scars on the minds of others.

The exceptional emphasis on seniority, too, helped to pinion thought. In the Naval Colleges, a cadet was not allowed to talk to another in the term above—a boy only three months older; in the gunroom, the gap between senior and junior was immense. Thus an outlook of exaggerated regard for rank and seniority was engendered, which was responsible for much of the rigidity of thought and reluctance to criticize characteristic of the average naval officer.

The long years of peace had not only solidified tactical thought but had built up a somewhat stultifying routine, especially when ships were in harbour. Captain Lionel Dawson, later a well-known destroyer officer, served a rather unhappy spell in Lord Charles Beresford's flagship in the Channel Fleet, and remembers the ship as 'flag-happy' and dominated by pomp and ceremonial.[49] 'Follow the Admiral's motions' had become a fetish.

Instruction of junior officers and training of the men was carried out spasmodically—Lord Cork records that: 'The Commander in Chief had a passion for making all the boats of the ships race round the fleet. At all times of the day it was necessary to keep a look out for the signal "away all boats, pull round the fleet" and off they would go, eighty to a hundred of them, upsetting many carefully thought out programmes for training and instruction.'[50]

The attitude to higher education in the Navy was unfavourable. It was realized that the technological revolution required some education for the specialist officer in his chosen field—gunnery, torpedo or communications; but, as for tactics and strategy, a general belief prevailed that so long as an officer was a competent seaman and spent most of his service afloat he would absorb instinctively the principles of these arts.

Admiral Godfrey, in an interesting analysis of training in 1910, says that the yardstick of comparison between ships (other than in 'housekeeping') was in coaling, evolutions, gunnery practices, regattas and games, and little account was taken of the ship's efforts to train officers and men or to develop ideas and original thought.

One discovers many differing opinions on the attitude to games and sport in the Navy. Some writers complain of the advantages gained by officers who played polo and hunted, and certainly in Malta there was much polo and racing in the years before the war. Yet Lionel Dawson, an Anglo-Irishman who was seldom voluntarily separated from a horse, writes that: 'Hunting was disapproved of in the service and only cricket, rugger and hockey were respectable. David Beatty, Cradock and Charles Beresford were exceptional.'[51] So it is hard to get the picture right.

But, in general, it may be said that naval officers were serious, professionally competent in seamanship and the operation of their weapons, but unimaginative, conformist and uncritical. They were devoted to the service and endured long and arduous commissions cheerfully, but they lacked outside interests and were inclined to intolerance. Behind everything was a sense of superiority, verging on complacency, based on past history and present excellence in seagoing. However, their standards were high and their morale unequalled.

The Fisher-Beresford feud

No account of the Navy in the first years of the century is complete without reference to the Fisher–Beresford feud, to which attention has already been drawn in these pages. Until about 1905 Fisher and Beresford saw eye to eye on most matters, and there are many examples of letters from Beresford expressing agreement with the need for change in the Navy. But things went wrong later; during Fisher's period as First Sea Lord the breach between them became a scandal, and Beresford automatically opposed everything that Fisher did.

Fisher was trying to reform in five years the mental sloth of one hundred, and drastic methods were needed. He did not hesitate to use them, but the end, surely, justified the means. The tragedy is that a service which had been so well knit should have become so divided, and, although Fisher's methods must take some of the blame, if Lord Charles had been the great man he claimed to be he would have never allowed such a situation to occur.

Opinions are unanimous in the records I have read that Beresford was a born leader, a man of great charm and a competent seaman, but that he was less than well equipped intellectually and lacked the power of concentration. By 1911 he was on the retired list, and though he remained vocal in the House of Commons the wounds in the Navy were beginning to heal.

The Selborne–Fisher reforms

The best known of the changes brought about when Fisher became Second Sea Lord in 1902 concerned the entry and training of officers.

There were three main objects. The first was to provide a wider and more democratic field of selection for officers. Hitherto entry had been confined to the comparatively well-to-do, but Fisher insisted that: 'Brains, character and manners are not the exclusive endowment of those whose parents can afford to spend one thousand pounds on their education. . . . Let every fit boy have his chance, irrespective of the depth of his parents' purse.'[52] He wanted to see all fees abolished at the Naval Colleges, so that all classes in the community could afford to send their children into the Navy as officers. But, as in so many other things, Fisher was ahead of his time, and so, in 1911, little had been done.

Next, he wanted officers to become a genuine band of brothers by abolishing the artificial distinctions between the Executive, Engineer, Paymaster and Instructor branches, which were based mainly on snobbery* and were divisive of wardroom unity. Thirdly, he wanted to give all officers a modern education and training suited to the technological age.

He hoped to achieve these last two objects by a system of common entry of Executive, Engineer and Marine Officers. (He hoped at one time to include the Paymasters, but this plan fell by the wayside.) After common training, which was to include a thorough course in practical and theoretical engineering, an officer would volunteer to join the Executive branch (and possibly sub-specialize further in gunnery, torpedo, and so on) or to become an Engineer or a Royal Marine. On reaching the rank of Commander, each officer would drop his speciality and revert to the Executive branch, except for a few of the most talented Engineers or Marines who would fill the higher posts in the Admiralty and dockyards and in the Marine Corps. The aim was that every officer would be capable of keeping watch both on the bridge and in the engine-room,

---

* A snobbery which was general in British society at the time.

and that the partitions between branches would be torn down and all would be 'of one company'.

There was much opposition to the changes. Beresford had agreed that officers should be given better technical training, but fought Fisher's scheme. Common entry and training were opposed by Dewar on the grounds that 'it was not possible to learn both the Seaman's and the Engineer's trade, particularly when such advances have been made in both'.[53] (And this criticism was advanced by a rebel who normally supported change.) Certainly there was force in his argument, and the situation today, which follows closely most of Fisher's other ideas, reflects Dewar's criticism.

Only a few Royal Marines were brought into the scheme, which mainly concerned the Executives and Engineers; but the common-entry system was introduced in 1904 and was going strong in 1911. A common list of officers was formed with no distinction of title or uniform, and the distinctive purple cloth between the gold stripes of the Engineer was abolished for the new class of officer. Fisher had had to use very strong pressure indeed to push through his schemes; unfortunately, owing mainly to the war and to the upset of training which came with it, the full programme was never implemented; but today, fifty years later, the General List would I am sure have gained Fisher's full support.*

The reader will probably be surprised to see so far no mention of naval ratings becoming naval officers—the 'tarpaulins' of Marryat's tales. Warrant officers, such as the Gunner, the Boatswain and, later, the Warrant Engineer, were well-established figures, but they lived a separate life in separate messes and their status was far below that of the wardroom officer. Admiral Godfrey describes how, in a minute gunboat of only a few hundred tons, there were three officers' messes, the Captain's, the wardroom of two officers and the warrant officers' mess of two. Social

---

* One or two common-entry Engineer specialists commanded ships and subsequently reverted to engineering only. In the 1920s, the Engineers left the common list and re-shipped their purple stripe, which was only removed again in 1956.

conditions of the day were such that they could not all live together.

In the past, promotion from the lower deck had been possible, and several admirals had started their careers as seamen, but in 1911 there was no way by which a naval rating could reach the wardroom, though some of the warrant officers were given commissions after many years of service. This state of affairs was deeply resented.

Conditions on the lower deck

When Fisher became Second Sea Lord in 1902, the Navy was manned by volunteer long-service men, but the outlook of the officer towards the man had hardly changed from that of the days when ships' companies were mostly composed of pressed men and some of the sweepings of the gaols. Discipline was still harsh, being based on capital and corporal punishment, and had become unsuited to the new type of educated mechanic-cum-sailor needed in greater and greater numbers to man the new ships. Punishments were awarded for trivial offences. Lionel Yexley, editor of *The Fleet*, a magazine of the lower deck, wrote in his book *Our Fighting Seamen** in 1911 that '. . . [the Navy] had a century of peace to develop a pseudo-discipline that expects an intelligent man to study wireless telegraphy or some other scientific subject all day, and then contentedly stand in a dark corner for two hours each night because the "S" in *Sovereign* on his cap ribbon was not over the nose'. Yexley, who had served for many years on the lower deck, expressed the general feeling of grievance. In addition to an archaic and inhuman system of punishment, pay was poor, food deplorable and the conditions under which it was eaten primitive. Sanitary arrangements were bad and there was a shortage of bathrooms, laundries and other facilities which produced a large sick list. Libraries and recreation rooms were unknown.

Relations between officers and men were cool in the big ships, though cameraderie could be achieved between the midshipmen of boats and their crews and between officers of turrets

* Stanley Paul.

and their men. Few officers played soccer and still fewer sailors played cricket or rugger. Hockey was then an officers' game entirely. In any case, few sailors had the inclination to play games and there was little opportunity to take part in them.

Routine, especially for seamen on the upper deck, was a constant succession of parades and musters, for there was apparently no confidence that men would get on with their work. The day started when hands fell in to be told off for scrubbing decks. After breakfast came stations for cleaning guns, followed by Divisions, a formal parade which included an inspection and prayers. After Divisions the seamen fell in again to be told off for work for the forenoon, a process which was repeated after dinner. At four o'clock came Evening Quarters, when the hands were inspected and mustered again. That ended the day for all except for the duty watchmen who were mustered before carrying out the many domestic duties required by a man-of-war outside working hours.

The atmosphere in small ships—the destroyers and submarines, for example—was quite different, and the relations between officers and men, based on proximity and on community of interests, were excellent. There was plenty to do on board and no need to invent ways of passing the time.

Lionel Dawson relates some good examples of the trust and support of the lower deck for some of the remarkable characters who commanded destroyers in the early days. The Captain of the *Swale*, for instance, when lying at Portland, went off to play golf at St Andrew's without taking the precaution of asking for leave, leaving a new and inexperienced sub in charge of the ship. The local senior officer unexpectedly decreed general drill in the absence of the Captain, but the ship's company rallied round, did well in the evolutions, and the Captain's golf was never revealed.

These unconventional characters managed to endear themselves to their ships' companies, and Lionel Dawson records that the subject of this yarn did well in the Grand Fleet destroyers in 1914–18. But in the large ships there was no doubt that many officers were not in close touch with their men.

This picture of the lower deck must not be read too darkly. The British sailor was a sturdy character who endured hardship and discomfort for small reward, and, when called upon for special effort, never failed. But there was a deep sense of grievance, of which Fisher was well aware and which he was determined to banish. He did much to improve living conditions, but he had no time to tackle pay, discipline and such matters. A general 'wish' of the Admiralty was, however, sent to flag and commanding officers in 1907 that the severity of punishments should be relaxed, and this had a satisfactory effect, for offences decreased in number, contrary to the expectations of the older officers.[54]

By 1911, therefore, the situation of the sailor had improved, some grievances had been rectified, but much remained to be done. Yexley wrote at the time that: 'The idea of perfect discipline—starve and drive—is dying a hard death. To give the men pleasant and satisfying meals as an aid to discipline is still looked upon as heresy.'[55]

Material matters

In its peacetime functions—suppressing native rising, rescuing slaves and ships in distress, exterminating pirates, trapping smugglers, aiding the victims of earthquakes and other disasters, charting the seas and 'showing the flag'—the Navy was efficient. What was so desperately wrong was that it had its priorities so upside down. Spit and polish and seamanship were more important than preparation for war. Beresford could well complain [in a letter to Balfour, 8/4/1900] that 'the Fleet is not ready to fight, or nearly ready to fight . . . our want of preparation in many ways is WORSE than the Army before South Africa exposed necessities which were wanting'.[56]

This quotation from Marder is based on carefully sifted evidence and gives, I believe, a true picture. As confirmation, it is interesting to read what Admiral Sir William James says when discussing the senior officers at the turn of the century:

Until the advent of Lord Fisher and Captain Percy Scott, all their thoughts and energies had been on the smartness of their ships and ships' companies and maintaining a high standard of seamanship. Gunnery and torpedo practices were a perfunctory business to be completed with the least possible trouble and it was not uncommon for the gun mounted on the quarterdeck to remain unfired all the Commission so that the enamel paint, paid for by the Commander, would not be cracked.

When this way of life was abruptly terminated by a surge of enthusiasm to improve the performance of the guns now attainable with Percy Scott's inventions, Senior officers who had hitherto taken little interest in gunnery and technical devices found themselves in a new world—a world in which so much they cherished would be sacrificed to the new God of Gunnery.[57]

When Fisher became First Sea Lord in 1904 he immediately instituted a series of reforms which had been carefully prepared beforehand by a committee of officers at Portsmouth when he had been Commander-in-Chief. First he tackled the ships. The Dreadnought, an 'all big-gunned', turbined battleship made existing capital ships obsolete. He also scrapped a large number of ancient and useless warships which were achieving little but using badly needed men and much money. He saw that Germany was the probable enemy in war and so he recalled many ships from foreign parts and concentrated the most powerful fleet in Home waters. These reforms can be set down in a few words, but they quickly brought a genuine revolution to the Navy. Each one was fought bitterly: the Dreadnought because it was claimed that the great British superiority in capital ships had been swept away and all nations started equal; the scrapping policy because valuable ships might be unavailable in an emergency; and the concentration in Home waters most bitterly of all, especially by the Foreign Office, which thought that there were 'important British interests in distant seas where the opportune presence of a British ship of war may avert disaster which can only be remedied later at much inconvenience and considerable sacrifice'.

But by the exercise of potent persuasion, and because of the essential validity of his policies, Fisher succeeded in achieving the great majority of his aims—indeed, he was much more successful in the technical field than in that of personnel.

Gunnery

In the period between 1902 and 1911, the Navy emerged from 'stone-age gunnery' (to quote Admiral Usborne) to a

F

high degree of proficiency at ranges of up to 10,000 yards. Target practice, which used to be carried out at stationary targets at 2,000 yards, was replaced by firing at towed targets at long range, and the percentage of hits had increased greatly despite the added difficulty of the conditions. Admiral Sir Percy Scott, supported by Fisher, was mainly responsible for this change, in which the Royal Navy led the world.

Torpedo

This weapon, whether fired from a surface ship or from a submarine, had greatly improved its performance over the initial prototype by 1911. Its diameter had grown from fourteen to twenty-one inches and its range had increased to 10,000 yards at thirty-five knots. Many claimed that the torpedo had made the battleship obsolete, and a fleet in harbour was adjudged to be especially vulnerable. However, in the Russo-Japanese War the torpedo had not achieved the results expected—the Japanese had fired 370 torpedoes and scored only 17 hits—and its importance was disputed.

Anti-submarine

Little progress had been made in anti-submarine warfare, and there was no means of detecting a submerged boat, nor any weapon except the ram. This state of affairs was in large part due to the tragic accidents which had marred the first trials of ways of defending the Fleet against submarine attack in the early years of the century. There had been talk of developing a bomb with a delayed-action fuse, but nothing had been done.

Mines

The Royal Navy had looked upon the mine as the weapon of the weaker power and had made little progress in this field, which was left to the Russians and Germans. The Russo-Japanese War showed how dangerous the mine could be, and some interest was aroused, but the gun was the dominant weapon in the Navy and the mine remained a poor relation.

Communications

By 1911 wireless sets had been fitted in all ships, but ranges were short and reception was unreliable. A few able officers, led by Henry Jackson, later to be First Sea Lord, had pioneered these new methods, in which the Navy led the world. But for tactical purposes, flags and light-flashing were still supreme and radio looked upon with suspicion.

Naval aviation

Progress in aviation in Britain had been slow, and lagged behind America and France. The Navy had been no exception. By October 1911 two aeroplanes were owned by the Admiralty, four officers had learnt to fly officially and some others privately, and there was a small band of enthusiastic supporters of the new art. The only lighter-than-air machine, the airship *Mayfly*, had been a disastrous failure, breaking up at her moorings before ever taking flight.

General

By 1911 a technical revolution had swept the service. In fifty years a mast-and-sails navy had been converted into one of turbines, high-velocity guns, torpedoes and submarines. These great changes had brought an accent on material matters, and indeed this was essential if efficiency was to be attained. But the pendulum had swung too far; technical efficiency and material progress had been allowed to crowd out strategical and tactical problems. The Navy was being prepared materially but not mentally for war.

Conclusion

Marder writes about the moment in January 1911 when Lord Fisher was relieved by Sir Arthur Wilson:

It was just as well that Fisher left Whitehall when he did. In the Navy he had by now as many enemies as he had friends. More serious, the spirit of unity, which had long been one of the most marked characteristics of the service, had been shattered. This was not entirely Fisher's fault, yet because of his methods he must bear a portion of the blame for weakening the old band-of-brothers feeling, which had been Nelson's principal legacy to the Navy. The Navy needed a period of rest, a surcease from recrimination and bickering.[58]

Nine months later, when Churchill took over from McKenna,

the period of rest had borne some fruit, the spirit of unity was being restored and the factions gradually forgotten.

But Fisher's successor, although he contributed much to the restoration of unity, was not otherwise a successful First Sea Lord. He was incapable of any delegation of authority, and he refused to confide, even to his trusted friends, his views, motives or intentions. The Second Sea Lord, Sir Francis Bridgeman, said of him that '. . . there is no joy to be found in serving either with him or under him. Deadly dull and uncompromising as you know. He will never consult anyone and is impatient in argument even to being impossible.'

Moreover, he was, as we have already seen, firmly opposed to the creation of a naval war staff and believed that its work could and should be done by the First Sea Lord himself, helped by an assistant.

But there were great assets on which to draw. The tremendous ship-building programme in progress produced an unequalled sense of purpose: the standing of the Fleet in the country was undiminished. The Navy, despite some faults, was guided by the maxim that every decision made, every action taken, must be for 'the good of the service', and personal considerations must never affect the issue, whatever the sacrifice. There was something in this spirit of service which inspired both officers and men and which impressed every outsider who encountered it. As McKenna's biographer says: 'Mysteriously and perhaps mystically, the navy had to him become something more than a service, the Admiralty more than a department; they fired the imagination of a man who seemed in general to despise rhetoric and to distrust romance.'

There was much the young First Lord had to do, and many obstructions to be cleared away: but the foundations of the service were sound.

4

FIRST LORD—HIS RECEPTION AND HIS AIMS

*A survey of Mr Winston Churchill's utterances on the subject
of the Navy suggests that he has sometimes sought to 'tickle
the ears of the groundlings' with his references to reduced
expenditure, as when at Manchester on 24th May, 1909, he
ridiculed a 'braggart and sensational policy of expenditure on
armaments' and when on 18th October, in the same year at
Dundee, he said they were not going to be driven into a 'showy,
sensational and Jingo policy'. His sneer at the 'blue water, or
to express it more accurately the blue funk school' (Dundee
6th Jan., 1910) is well remembered. He has spoken with a
greater sense of responsibility on some other occasions.*[59]

THE NAVY

*I laboured continually to check and correct the opinions with
which I had arrived at the Admiralty by the expert information
which on every subject was now at my disposal.*[60]

WSC

THIS sentence, from the opening chapter of Churchill's
description in *The World Crisis* of his time as First Lord,
echoes the buzz of activity in those early days. Not only
did the First Lord call on the Admiralty for facts and opinions,
but he neglected no other available source. He called back
Jackie Fisher. 'He was abroad in sunshine. We had not seen
each other since the dispute about the naval estimates of 1909.
He conceived himself bound in loyalty to Mr. McKenna, but
as soon as he learned that I had nothing to do with the
decisions which had led to our changing offices, he hastened
home. We passed three days together in the comfort of
Reigate Priory.'[61]

Incidentally, McKenna showed great generosity of spirit by
begging Fisher to give Churchill the benefit of his knowledge
and experience. But the latter does not mention that he also
sent for Lord Charles Beresford, who, on 28 October 1911,
wrote to his old Chief of Staff, Sturdee, that he had been
invited to the Admiralty by Churchill 'as he was sure that I
could help him in his new difficult duties, etc.'.[62] Beresford

wrote that, after consultation with the Conservative party leaders, he had decided to accept the invitation, but that 'he would answer questions but not provide a policy for him'. I can find no record of the meeting—which is not surprising, as Winston was well aware of Beresford's deficiencies as a thinker and the whole affair was probably aimed at satisfying the opposition that the new First Lord's mind was not closed to any opinion other than Fisher's and that he was ready to listen to technical advice from any quarter.

Haldane was also an early visitor, as we shall see later. And Churchill was not content with seeing senior officers and statesmen: he also interrogated junior officers whenever he had an opportunity. Oswald Frewen, his cousin, records in his diary that when he visited Winston at the Admiralty on 31 October 1911 he was subjected to a very close questioning about his ship, the minelayer *Intrepid*.

Winston was very nice but thirsting for knowledge, and cross-examined me mercilessly on minelayers, mines, their capability and behaviour, as a stern Captain on a seamanship board. Elucidated the information that he is very pleased to be where he is and has been wanting to get there 'ever since he realized how vitally important it was'. Winston is a great man, greater than I thought.[63]

Winston was certainly thoroughly content. Lady Violet Bonham Carter writes about the day he was offered the Admiralty by her father:

He was tasting fulfilment. Never . . . have I seen him more completely and profoundly happy. The tide of happiness and realization was too deep even for exuberance, though at one moment, in the middle of a purple passage about the scope and range of his new powers, he interjected: 'Look at the people I have had to deal with so far—judges and convicts! This is a big thing—the biggest thing that has ever come my way—the chance I should have chosen before all others. I shall pour into it everything I've got.'[64]

He poured everything into the job from the moment he arrived at the Admiralty. He was obsessed with the mystique of the Navy and he lost no time in acquiring a deep knowledge of the ways, customs and technicalities of the service. He immersed himself completely in his work. As Lady Violet says: 'His work was his life. Leisure or relaxation would have been punishment.'

When he was not in his office in Whitehall, he was in his mobile office in the Admiralty yacht *Enchantress*, in which he spent 182 days of his first eighteen months as First Lord. These periods in the *Enchantress* were spent in a series of inspections of ships, fleets, naval dockyards, bases, schools and training establishments, during which he bombarded all whom he met, whether senior or junior, with questions.

Eddie Marsh wrote at the end of the first month: 'We have made a new Commandment—the seventh day is the Sabbath of the First Lord, on it thou shalt do all manner of work.' Oswald Frewen records a dinner party in the *Enchantress* at Chatham in January 1912, at which the principal guests were the first naval aviators, Samson, Longmore and Gerrard, who were relentlessly questioned about the progress of the flying training at Eastchurch. After the aviators had left, the remaining guests, among them the Civil Lord, Sir Francis Hopwood, the Naval Secretary, by then Admiral Beatty, and Eddie Marsh 'discussed naval topics exclusively. . . . Then Beatty engaged Winston in a diagrammatic PZ [tactical] exercise and not unnaturally tonked him. Winston who started with the tactics of a cavalry officer realized by one a.m. that it was no use trusting to the élan of battleships.' Again we find these military images distorting the First Lord's ideas on naval operations.

When writing in *The World Crisis* about the Royal Review in the spring of 1912 at Portland, Winston gives a magnificent picture of his delight and pride in the job.

These were great days. From dawn to midnight, day after day, one's whole mind was absorbed by the fascination and the novelty of the problems which came crowding forward. And all the time there was a sense of power to act, to form, to organize: all the ablest officers in the Navy standing ready, loyal and eager, with argument, guidance, information: everyone feeling a sense that a great danger had passed very near us; that there was a breathing space before it would return, and that we must be better prepared next time. Saturdays, Sundays and any other spare days I spent always with the fleets at Portsmouth or at Portland or Devonport, or with the flotillas at Harwich. Officers of every rank came on board to lunch or dine and discussion proceeded without ceasing on every aspect of naval war and administration.

And after picturing the Fleet itself and its ships, he ended: 'Guard them well, Admirals and Captains, hardy tars and tall marines; guard them well and guard them true.'[65]

And now it is time to examine Winston's reception—to see if his delight was shared by others.

The Press was, on the whole, ready to give him a chance. Even the professional publications like the *Navy Annual* (Brassey), the *Navy League Annual* and the *Navy*, the journal of the Navy League, were prepared to forget the battles over the building programmes and to judge by results. In these circles, his reception was not so cold as would have been expected.

The Editor of the *Navy League Annual* wrote in October 1912, in a smug and unctuous review of the past twelve months:

The past year has been a remarkable one in the history of British naval administration. In November [*sic*], Mr. Churchill and Mr. McKenna exchanged offices—and it cannot be said that the change was regarded with much public favour, but the inherent instinct for fair play which is ever present in the British race, expressed through the Press of all parties a desire to belie his former tendencies towards the suicidal economy of the little navy group.

The *Navy*, too, gave him a cool reception. It could not:

. . . feel much satisfaction at the change which has taken place in the personality of the First Lord of the Admiralty. Mr. McKenna, whatever his original views may have been, was brought to realize the vital responsibilities which lay upon him and was moulded by strong hands into a big navy man. . . . It is a Minister who has been credited with a leaning to dangerous retrenchment who is now First Lord of the Admiralty. It would be unwarrantable and unfair to question the patriotism of the new First Lord or to prejudge his actions. . . . He has now at any rate an unrivalled opportunity of vindicating his capacity as a statesman.[66]

One may wonder what McKenna thought of his 'moulding by strong hands'. Anyhow, Winston had soon 'vindicated his capacity', for in March 1912, before the Naval Estimates debate, the same editor hailed him as the 'man of the hour', saying that when he had expressed his views on naval policy in a speech at Glasgow, 'We could not wish to have that policy defined in more forceful, definite or patriotic terms. . . . It is, therefore, with confidence and hope that the Navy League welcomes the statesmanlike words of the First Lord . . .'[67]

It was an altogether complete reversal of opinion on a man who had been received with such deep suspicion.

In the Navy itself—and we must be careful to differentiate between opinion in the service and the views of a civilian organization run, with the highest motives, for propaganda purposes—the atmosphere was not much different. Suspicion was tinged with admiration and mingled with political prejudice. The prejudice was soon swept away by Winston's whole-hearted enthusiasm for his task. But the suspicion took longer to eradicate and in many minds remained fast. In particular, one aspect of his methods irritated many officers: his insistence on mastering (his enemies would say 'interfering with') every detail.

Admiral Sir William James recounts that in 1912:

> His curiosity about the service for which he was responsible seemed to many of the older officers almost indecent. They had no intention of putting themselves out when he came on board.
>
> After the night firing was completed, I invited our visitor to the wardroom. It was now past midnight and we found only a sprinkling of officers who had been concerned with the night firing. We sat down by the fire and Churchill began to pepper me with questions about our system of control and what steps we were taking to improve the performance of the guns and searchlights. The wardroom gradually filled, and soon a large circle of officers was listening intently to the discussion, into which Churchill drew many of those who had hitherto avoided him.[68]

His readiness to sound out every quarter was also criticized and he was accused of currying favour with the lower deck by his tough public probing of officers' knowledge and capabilities.

One admiral, then the First Lieutenant of a cruiser, remembers returning to the wardroom after a long inspection during which the First Lord had insisted on entering the punishment cells. 'Why didn't you lock him up?' his mess-mates shouted.

Even the German Naval Attaché reported that:

> The sea-officers of the British Navy are often enraged against Mr. Churchill in spite of their unlimited appreciation of his merits in Navy politics, for the youthful civilian Churchill, on his frequent visits to the fleet and dockyards, puts on the air of a military superior. Through his curt behaviour he offends the older officers in their feeling of rank and personal pride.[69]

Asquith took an affectionate if cynical view of his youthful colleague, and when he went to sea with him to watch some gunnery firings and saw him 'dancing behind the guns, elevating, depressing, and sighting', remarked, 'My young friend yonder thinks himself Othello, and blacks himself all over to play the part!'[70]

At another time, during the *Enchantress*'s Mediterranean cruise, Lady Violet Bonham Carter tells how Winston had to be dragged away from the boiler-room where he was giving a hand. Her comment—'*What* fun for the stokers!'—seems optimistic.[71]

Frewen's Diaries also give a useful line on the Navy's reception of the First Lord. On 28 October, he records: 'The skipper is almost bitter and said that Winston had the Admiralty because the Home Office were tired of him,' and adds, 'I am interested in this opinion—all I have gathered so far is that they think he will fight Tug Wilson. Personally, I don't. He's no fool, is Winston.'

Oswald Frewen was right. Winston did not fight Wilson. He sacked him, politely but firmly, and with no ill feeling, and Wilson's dignified departure is typical of the man.*

---

* Wilson was a most modest and selfless man. The King had to use much persuasion to get him to agree to relieve Fisher, and recounts that at the interview Wilson said to him: 'Only once, Sir, have I ever asked a favour of anyone since I entered the Navy and that was of Sir John Fisher. When he was about to lay down the appointment of Controller of the Navy, Fisher had already arranged for his successor, but he cancelled the arrangement and secured the appointment for me. I assure you, Sir, that I was absolutely the worst Controller the Navy has ever had and if I am to succeed Fisher again I may probably become the worst First Sea Lord in the annals of the Navy.[72]

Eddie Marsh, in a letter in 1911, wrote: 'The sailors seem to like him very well and he has completely changed his character in some ways to come out with a brand new set of perfect manners and a high standard of punctuality. Everyone seems anxious to give him a chance and the service takes a real pleasure in having such a fighting man as First Lord.'

His aims

In *The World Crisis* Churchill gives a list of the important points to which he proposes to give priority. It seems convenient to list and then discuss them—not necessarily in the same order—so that the success achieved in fulfilling his aims may be assessed.

1. Improve the War Plans of the Fleet.
2. Reorganize the Fleet so as to increase the immediate strength for war.
3. Establish measures against surprise attack.
4. Set up a naval war staff.
5. Initiate co-ordination between the Admiralty and the War Office.
6. Improve the gunpower of ships.
7. Make changes in the high command, both at sea and ashore.

In addition, two other important fields of activity commended themselves to a man intensely interested in technical invention and yet deeply devoted to the improvement of the lot of his fellow human beings. One was naval aviation and the other the conditions of service on the lower deck. These will be discussed in later chapters.

He realized from the first that to succeed in improving the organization and planning departments, ashore and afloat, there was one essential prerequisite—the formation of a war staff—and this therefore was the first job to be tackled.

Soon after the turn-over from McKenna had been completed, Haldane was invited to come over to help with plans for the naval staff. Prince Louis, then commanding the 3rd and 4th Divisions of the Home Fleet, took a prominent part in the discussions, and Winston also had the benefit of a memorandum from General Douglas Haig, then commanding at Aldershot.

In a letter from his flagship on 22 October 1911, Prince Louis gave a clear picture of a Chief of Staff who was to be advised by the heads of three divisions of the staff, concerned with Intelligence, Operations and Mobilization,* and who in turn would be responsible directly to the First Sea Lord. He described the logical procedure to be adopted by a 'new nation with a seaboard' and provided a classical picture of what naval staffs have been struggling to achieve ever since.

1. A study of the international situation which would be the outcome of this new prospective Navy.
2. The determination of which of other existing fleets—single or in combination—might be arrayed against it.
3. A study of the strength and composition of such possible hostile fleet or fleets, that is, of the several types of fighting vessels to be found there, and also of the dockyards and naval bases at their disposal.
4. A determination of the strength required to fight these hostile fleets with a reasonable chance of success.
5. In further detail it would now be necessary to decide upon the numbers and particulars of the different types of vessels to be built—working upon some plan spread over several years ahead.
6. Officers and men must be provided to work these. Their entry and training to be considered, and in view of their slow, automatic growth, by comparison with the possible rate of shipbuilding, this requires looking ahead for several years.
7. Dockyards and naval bases must be created, at points where they would be most useful.
8. The defence of these must be provided for in consultation with the War Office.

---

* 'Intelligence' is self-evident, but the other two terms are deceptive to a modern reader. 'Operations' really meant 'war plans', and 'Mobilization' meant 'war arrangements'. Today, it is Plans Division which makes war plans and Operations Division which looks after war arrangements. This change was made during the First World War.

9. The ships and vessels of all kinds being duly built and manned, must be organized in fleets, squadrons, and flotillas, and given a geographical peace position, from where they can most readily take up their initial war station, in accordance with the carefully thought out plan of campaign.

10. This grouping and stationing of ships must be continuously revised to meet changing conditions in the political situation.

11. The Admirals in command must be given frequent opportunities of exercising their command tactically and strategically.

12. The reports of these must be critically examined by experts at the Admiralty, the mistakes communicated to those who made them, and fresh exercises arranged for by the light of the experience gained.

13. The War College, which will by now have been established, will assist in the study and elucidation of these many problems, whilst imparting instruction in the art of naval warfare to selected officers.[73]

A draft scheme was produced, based largely on Prince Louis's proposals and Haldane's experience at the War Office. Haldane says: 'Churchill wanted it [the Staff] to be put directly under himself as First Lord. To this I objected stoutly, saying that it would be inert unless it were under the First Sea Lord. Prince Louis of Battenberg, a well trained expert, agreed with me and the staff was placed directly under the First Sea Lord.'[74]

There is, however, no mention of this in *The World Crisis*. Certainly it was essential that the staff should work under the professional head of the service, who must give it impetus, or even, as the *Navy* put it, '. . . if ever he should prove less vigorous than some First Sea Lords we are acquainted with, [the staff] will think for him.'[75]

A long memorandum on a Naval War Staff and its training was issued as early as 28 October 1911; its language is Churchillian and he and his advisers must have worked late to produce the paper so promptly. Its arguments are convincing, and though it is too long to reproduce in full, some of the more striking passages deserve mention.

The First Lord starts, after an explanation of why a staff is needed in modern war, by saying: 'This is recognized in the organization of all the more important combat services in the world except the British Navy,' and continues:

> The small number of officers employed upon war plans at the British Admiralty have received no systematic training whatever in the broad strategic principles which all historians agree in emphasizing as permanent in their application, or in the general tendency of the foreign politics of the day, or in the substance of the Treaties and Agreements with other Powers which affect or limit our freedom of action as a belligerent, or our rights as a neutral.

Discussing the chaotic state of war planning, he says:

> The contents of the Admiralty Record Office show how the views of one First Sea Lord may be utterly at variance with those of another. Each naturally recommends what he thinks best, but it is evident from a perusal of their minutes and their actions that many reached office without any previous study of the history of war. The result has been an entire absence of continuity in Admiralty policy, with consequent financial waste. A certain First Sea Lord must have been responsible for the concurrence of the Admiralty in the futile strategic theories which prompted the building of the Palmerston Forts with money which should have gone to the Navy. Another was responsible for the introduction of coast defence ships into a service whose whole policy in three hundred years of successful war was to assume the offensive and fight out of sight of our coast altogether. And at least one of his successors must have agreed. . . . It would have been quite impossible for an officer of ordinary ability with a proper historical training to have committed any of these blunders, and there is no reason to suppose that ability was lacking.

The situation was that: 'A competent strategist *might* occupy the position of First Sea Lord in the event of war no doubt, but not at all necessarily.'

He went on to discuss the training necessary to fit officers for a war staff (and for high command) and suggested that a twelve-month course would be enough, of which two months might be spent at the Foreign Office, together with a short course at the shipping department of the Board of Trade and 'attendance at Lloyds'. He thought that selection should be by an examination which tested power of reasoning rather than memory, and he finally insisted on the need for the service to recognize the staff officer as a specialist equal in prestige to the other specialist branches. One shrewd remark shows his appreciation of the naval attitude to 'desk work': 'One of the reasons for the indifference of the junior ranks of the Navy to appointments to the Admiralty is a conviction that service at Whitehall is regarded by the Board as the performance of duties of an inferior description, because in the matter of all advantages it compares unfavourably with service at sea while imposing harder work.'[76]

Altogether, this is a most impressive document, which stands up admirably to the judgements of events. In a reasoned comment, made in the mid-twenties in the 'History of the Naval Staff' on the first organization of the war staff, the staff is viewed officially as a body composed of three main branches: 'a branch to acquire information on which action may be taken; a branch to deliberate on the facts so obtained in relation to the policy of the State and to report thereon; and thirdly a branch to enable the final decision of superior authority to be put into effect'.

After pointing out that the functions of the war staff were to be advisory, it sums up the organization as a new Charter for the Staff. It goes on:

> Much was achieved but there was a reverse side to the picture. The idea of a staff was by many still regarded with indifference, if not with distrust. The Navy had no use for the word 'Staff' in the Army sense, in which the staff was regarded as a system of machinery indispensable to the conduct of operations of war. . . . Mr. Haldane was supported by the best minds in the Army. Mr. Churchill had not the whole body of Naval opinion behind him. The Chief of Staff was merely a responsible adviser to the First Sea Lord. He did not sit on the Board and the new staff hardly constituted a staff system in the army sense of the word.

In retrospect it is easy to see that the weak point of the scheme was the position of the Chief of Staff, but this was difficult to foresee at the time. Later on, during the course of the war, the First Sea Lord assumed the Chief of Staff's duties, and a deputy took the burden of detail off his shoulders. Today the First Sea Lord is still Chief of the Staff, and the Vice-Chief, who is a member of the Board, looks after the detail.

The Staff History sums up as follows: 'The war staff had been working barely two years when war broke out. As the war dragged on, it proved unable to cope with its tremendous task, and in May 1917 it was re-organised by Admiral Sir John Jellicoe, and the office of Chief of Naval Staff was merged in the older office of First Sea Lord.'[77]

But there is no doubt that the main features of the original scheme were sound, and they remain essentially unchanged today. Admiral Wilson, however, was unalterably opposed to any form of a naval staff, and the remaining Sea Lords seemed to share his views.

The salient points of the memorandum which Admiral Wilson sent to the First Lord in early November 1911 are admirably summarized in the Staff History. 'He was not in favour of any position such as that of Chief of the Staff. The preparation of War Plans he regarded as a matter to be dealt with by the First Sea Lord himself. He preferred to trust to men rather than to an organisation.'

The Memo itself is a long one, but some extracts will give more evidence of the immobility of the thinking behind it.

The Navy has learned by long experience thoroughly to distrust all paper schemes and theories that have not been submitted to the supreme test of trial under practical conditions by the Fleet at sea. . . . The preparation of war plans is a matter that must be dealt with by the First Sea Lord himself, but he has to assist him, besides his naval assistant, the Director of Naval Intelligence and the Director of Naval Mobilisation. . . . It is often suggested by advocates for a War Staff that special officers should be selected and trained for duty on the Staffs of the Admiralty and Admirals at sea. . . . The service would have the most supreme contempt for any body of officers who professed to be specially trained to think. There is no service where there is more thinking done, but officers are judged by what they can do when they are afloat.

And:

> ... another reason why a War Staff which is a necessary feature in army organisation is unsuitable for the Navy is that it is impossible to produce conditions really resembling war in peace manœuvres ashore, Army policy must be framed principally from the records of past wars and the opinion of officers who have taken part in them, while naval policy is based almost entirely on experiment and the result of actual practice at sea.[78]

Faced with this determined obstruction, Churchill decided on a clean sweep of the Board. In a letter to Asquith on 5 November 1911, in which he enclosed Admiral Wilson's paper on the War Staff, he proposed that Wilson should be relieved in January, two months ahead of time, so that his successor could examine and accept responsibility for the Naval Estimates which were in course of preparation, and that the Second Sea Lord should be relieved by Prince Louis of Battenberg as soon as possible. A further letter dealt with the question of a new Fourth Sea Lord—Captain Pakenham was selected—so that only the Controller, who had not been long in the post, remained of the old Board.[79]

The changes were carried out quietly, smoothly and in a spirit of loyal acceptance by those involved. In the country as a whole the reaction was surprisingly calm and the 'naval' Press caused no trouble. Bridgeman, the new First Sea Lord, had a reputation as a sound seaman, and Battenberg as a brilliant officer of considerable talents. Simultaneously, the First Lord took advantage of the general post by appointing Callaghan and Jellicoe to the key commands in the Home Fleet, and also securing David Beatty as his Naval Secretary.

There was a minor difficulty over obtaining the consent of the king, who was *en route* to the Delhi Durbar in the liner *Medina*. The request for approval had to be sent in a long cypher signal which needed many repetitions owing to difficulty in decoding, and Winston was told by the Monarch to keep his signals shorter. He had first said that he could wait till the New Year for a new Board but:

> He now feels it will not be possible to delay them so long. The interests of the State and of the Service ask whether a new Board

at the Admiralty should be appointed forthwith and that important questions of policy which have to be dealt with at this season of the year should be decided by those who will be effectively responsible both to your Majesty and to Parliament for the consequences of their decisions and not by a moribund administration. . . . Although no differences of any kind have yet been disclosed within the present board, he humbly submits . . . the following proposals . . .[80]

The proposals received the immediate assent of the King. Admiral Wilson was offered a peerage, which he refused, and the Second Sea Lord was sent as Commander-in-Chief, Portsmouth. The first essential moves had been made and the First Lord had secured some ready helpers for the reforms required.

Admiral Beatty attracted Churchill. He had many of the qualities which the latter most admired: poise, dash and a reputation for physical courage. In addition, he had a wide experience of action outside normal naval routine, both in the Sudan and in China. But one may be allowed to believe that some of the qualities which attracted the First Lord were dangerous and did harm in the end. 'It became increasingly clear to me that he viewed questions of naval strategy and tactics in a different light from the average naval officer: he approached them, as it seemed to me, *much more as a soldier would*.'[81] Here again, I sense a clue to some of Churchill's later mistakes in the handling of naval operations. Indeed, I am firmly convinced, as will be seen, that they were caused by his inability to address himself to naval problems other than with a soldier's mind.

He saw other qualities in Beatty. 'He did not think of *matériel* as an end in itself but only as a means. He thought of war problems in their unity by land, sea and air.' These were admirable qualities, and must have contributed largely to Beatty's later great distinction, but it is clear that it was the freshness of approach which appealed especially to the First Lord. Beatty was not good on paper and this was a serious handicap, since he did much of the First Lord's staff work for him in the early days. His biographer, when discussing the papers which Beatty had produced for the First Lord, writes: 'Most are sound in principle if not too well expressed. Beatty must have burnt much midnight oil over them, and Churchill probably tore his hair reading them. Both must therefore have welcomed the day when the First Lord's efforts to introduce a war staff at the Admiralty at last bore fruit.'[82]

Once the new Board had been settled, the Naval War Staff was formed remarkably quickly and a paper was published in January 1912. The First Lord was careful to defer to those who feared the build-up of a powerful staff corps of chairborne officers, as will be seen from this short extract from a long memorandum.

The art of handling a great fleet on important occasions with deft and sure judgement is the supreme gift of the Admiral, and practical seamanship must never be displaced from its position as the first qualification of every sailor. The formation of a war staff does not mean the setting up of new standards of professional merit or the opening of a road to advancement to a different class of officers. It is to be the means of training of those officers who arrive or are likely to arrive by the excellence of their sea service at stations of high responsibility. . . .[83]

On the whole he was successful in allaying the worst fears of the sceptics and the transition was a smooth one. But as he wrote later in *The World Crisis*:

It takes a generation to form a general staff. No wave of the wand can create those habits of mind in seniors on which the efficiency and even the reality of a staff depends. Young officers can be trained, but thereafter they have to rise step by step in the passage of time to positions of authority in the service. The dead weight of professional opinion in the service was against it. They had got on well enough without it before. They did not want a special class of officer professing to be more brainy than the rest. Seatime should be the main qualification and after that technical aptitudes. . . .

The 'silent service' was not mute because it was absorbed in thought and study, but because it was weighted down by its daily routine and by its ever-complicating and diversifying routine. We had competent administrators, brilliant experts of every description, unequalled navigators, good disciplinarians, fine sea officers, brave and devoted hearts: but at the outset of the conflict we had more captains of ships than captains of war.

At least fifteen years were required. . . . Fifteen years! And we were only to have thirty months![84]

As there were no trained officers in the Navy, it was necessary to start a staff course, and this was done at the War College at Portsmouth. The course closed down at the start of the war and did not reopen until June 1919, this time at Greenwich. It was not very successful at first and its graduates were looked upon with suspicion. But a start was made; and Churchill, and Churchill alone, was responsible.

If I may be allowed a postscript, it is to say that 'fifteen years' was certainly not an exaggeration. More than a generation had to pass away before suspicion of staff officers had been banished. In the twenties an appointment to the Naval Staff College was regarded as a mixed blessing—a risk which might hinder a career. By the thirties the attitude had changed, and the Second World War was to establish the trained staff officer in his rightful position.

In every way the First Lord encouraged officers to read, to study history and to think about strategy and tactics and other non-technical problems. He was a strong supporter of the project of starting the *Naval Review*, which had been born at a meeting at Captain Richmond's house on 27 October 1912. This privately circulated journal, which still prospers today, has always encouraged independent thought by officers of all ranks and might well have been throttled at birth by the objections of the bureaucrats, but for the determination of the First Lord.

Battles with the King and with the admirals

To a generation impressed by the deep devotion of Prime Minister Churchill to the Monarch, whether King George VI or Queen Elizabeth II, it comes as a surprise to read of the First Lord's struggles with King George V about the naming of ships.

It was a question on which both felt strongly. The King, because he had been a serving sailor, knew the officers and men and was determined that they should serve in ships with acceptable names; the First Lord, because of his intense interest in history and, I suspect, because he was determined to leave his mark on the Navy in many ways.

The trouble started early. In November 1911 the First Lord cabled a request for approval of a number of new battleships' names, among them *Liberty*, *Assiduous* and *Oliver Cromwell*. The King replied promptly that he could not agree to these three names and suggested instead *Delhi*, *Marlborough* and *Wellington*. This change was accepted, though in the event the ships became *Emperor of India*, *Marlborough* and *Iron Duke*.

But the following year, when the next building programme was considered, the First Lord produced *Oliver Cromwell* again. This was too much for the King, who disliked his battleships' being called after regicides, and ordered his Private Secretary to return the submission 'as he [the King] feels sure there must be some mistake in the name of *Oliver Cromwell* being suggested for one of the new Battleships. For that name was proposed for one of the ships of last year's programme; His Majesty was unable to agree to it and on his return from India personally explained to you the reasons for his objection.'[85]

The First Lord was not to be deflected. He wrote again—to be sharply rebuffed—and then again, this time quoting extracts from eminent historians' eulogies of Cromwell's services to the Royal Navy. He ended his argument with a characteristic flourish: 'It certainly seems right that we should give to a battleship a name that never failed to make the enemies of England tremble.'[86] Hardly a tactful remark to an English monarch, one of whose predecessors had been beheaded by this same man. The King was as firm as a rock and another sharp reply was sent which produced capitulation. 'I bow to the King's wish about the battleship's name and will submit the name of *Valiant* as a substitute.'[87]

One would have thought that twice was more than enough, but a year later the battle started again with a proposal to call two of the next class of battleships *Pitt* and *Ark Royal*.

The King disliked both names: *Ark Royal* for reasons which do not now seem convincing—and this was the only example out of five names when his judgement does not seem absolutely right—and *Pitt* because 'His Majesty is inclined to think that the name *Pitt* is neither euphonious nor dignified. . . . There is also the danger of the men giving the ship nicknames of ill-conditioned words rhyming with it.' Here speaks the sailor

King in words well drafted by a skilled courtier,* and it would have been expected that the First Lord would bow again. But no. He returned several times to the charge, despite the entreaties of the First Sea Lord, Battenberg, and of the Naval Secretary, de Chair. He even went so far as to inquire whether the King would prefer not to be consulted about the names of ships, which infuriated the Monarch, and then suggested that the procedure of submitting names to the King for approval was a modern practice, based on no good authority.

This claim produced a reasoned rebuttal from Stamfordham, in which, after observing that the last two *Pitts* in the Navy had been coal depots, he pointed out that the practice of consulting the Monarch was hallowed by tradition and that:

> The King quite recognises the interest and trouble which you have taken in this matter, and indeed in everything connected with the great Service over which you preside. But at the same time His Majesty yields to no one in his concern for all that affects the daily life of the Sailor, with which the name of the Ship, wherein he lives, and wherein he may have to fight, must always be closely associated.
>
> Under these circumstances the King hopes that you will see your way to carry out his wishes and submit two other names, which, together with the three already agreed upon, would meet with His Majesty's approval.
>
> Would it not avoid difficulties if in the future you were to ask to see the King and talk over such matters with His Majesty before sending in the formal submission? As you know, the King is only too glad to receive you at any time.[88]

This at last was enough. The First Lord discussed the matter with the King. Stamfordham reported the result as satisfactory. And the ships emerged as the famous *Royal Sovereign* class. But the affair shows a strange lack of comprehension of the feelings of others by the young statesman, and Lord Esher had the last word when he commented on the story: 'For so clever a man, he [Churchill] is sometimes exceedingly foolish.'[89]

---

* De Chair, who had discussed the question with the King at the request of the First Lord, reported H.M.'s reactions to Churchill, who replied, 'I think that unworthy of the royal mind.'

On another matter connected with the King, which might have proved very difficult, the First Lord was more successful. He was anxious to make economies to compensate for the new pay scales and the rising costs everywhere, and one of his targets was the Royal Yacht, which was given an expensive annual refit.

He wrote a tactful letter to Stamfordham[90] in which he said that he was 'sure the King would be surprised to see the enormous charges [which] are made for quite small things. I know His Majesty would disapprove anything in the nature of wasteful or extravagant expenditure.' He added that he was sending Hopwood to Portsmouth to investigate.

After some further exchanges in which Stamfordham said that H.M. was against extravagance but pointed out 'that the Dockyards authorities are quite inclined to include under the head of "Royal Yacht" sums which are required to meet other charges'—a practice which undoubtedly existed—the matter was satisfactorily settled.[91] Hopwood saw the King and discussed estimates with him, and the Commodore Royal Yachts was told to cut his expenditure by a half.

But another example of lack of tact and sensitivity is illustrated by what came to be known as the 'Poore Case'.

The best way of describing it is to quote the contents of a letter from Sir Francis Hopwood to Lord Stamfordham in November 1913. But before doing so, it is interesting to consider this unusual character whose letters to the Palace were so frequent and so full of information.

Winston Churchill brought Hopwood into the Admiralty as 'Additional Civil Lord' in January 1912, when the new War Staff was being formed.* The object was to provide an expert administrator to deal with the complicated contractual questions arising out of the ship-building programme, and so allow the Controller to concentrate his energies on the broad technical problems of his job. Hopwood had been a distinguished Civil Servant and he came to the Admiralty as a 'non-political' Lord—a status which no longer exists, though

---

* Hopwood had been Permanent Secretary at the Colonial Office with Churchill.

there is a near parallel in recent appointments of academic figures to various Ministries in London. He was a member of the Board.

Despite the fact that Churchill had appointed him and that he was a friend, he seems to have set himself up as the King's personal spy on Churchill, and he wrote a series of letters, almost all critical of his colleague's work. He emerges from this correspondence as a sinister and somewhat unlikeable figure.*

On 9 November 1913, he wrote to Stamfordham:

There is a fierce quarrel raging between Churchill and his Naval Lords.—C. very foolishly travels round the coasts holding reviews and inspections and so forth without reference to Naval opinion and regulation.—He is also much addicted to sending for junior officers and discussing with them the proceedings of their superiors; this naturally enrages the latter and is very mischievous to the former.—It is on this score of breaches of discipline that the present trouble has been founded. The facts as described to me are as follows: Churchill interviewed a Lieutenant of the *Vernon* and encouraged him to put forward some scheme or other about torpedo working. The Captain of the *Vernon* refused to forward it to the Commander-in-Chief at the Nore en route to the Admiralty, whereupon the Lieutenant said 'Then I shall send it direct to Mr. Churchill who invited (or ordered) me to do so . . .' Then the row began. The Captain of the *Vernon* wrote in strong terms of complaint to the Commander-in-Chief who wrote on in equally strong terms to Jellicoe criticising the First Lord's method. Now somehow Churchill had heard that this correspondence had begun.—Perhaps the Lieutenant at the *Vernon* had written him to say he had got into trouble. But anyhow Churchill sent his Private Secretary to Jellicoe to say that if any despatch came from the C-in-C at the Nore on the subject he (Churchill) desired to see it immediately. It did come and Jellicoe finding it couched in strong terms determined, in order to keep the peace, to send it back for some amendment. Jellicoe accordingly returned the despatch with a private letter of his own enclosed. When a few hours later C. found the despatch had been sent back he went dancing mad and on his own sent a telegram to the General Post Office asking that the letter should be found and returned at once to *him*. He also telegraphed the C-in-C Nore to

---

* See also Chapter 7.

Asquith in 1908

Sir Edward Grey in 1911

Churchill in 1916

Admiral Sir John Fisher
on board HMS *Renown*,
1897

Admiral Sir David Beatty

HMS *Lion*

First Lord and First Sea Lord, 1914

return the letter to him at the Admiralty unopened. He got it back from the GPO and so came into possession of the correspondence and also Jellicoe's private letter with comments! To get out of the difficulty of the latter he professes not to have read it! Jellicoe has of course intimated that he will resign. Churchill has now announced that he will get rid of both the C-in-C Nore and the Captain of the *Vernon*. On that issue Moore and Pakenham both want to go. Prince Louis felt that way at first but Jellicoe tells me that Churchill has talked the First Sea Lord over. Churchill is reported to have told the 4 Naval Lords that if any one of them desired to criticise his methods he should expect him to resign as they could not work together.

C. has not mentioned the subject to me, all this comes from the Admirals. Of course it is very private but The King may be interested in the facts as unless differences are composed there may be a resignation and some publicity at any moment. It is deplorable.[92]

As so often in his correspondence, Hopwood had not got his facts right, but the essentials are correct though the minor matters are exaggerated. The incident complained of occurred at Sheerness, where the *Enchantress* was on a visit connected with the Royal Naval Air Service. The ship concerned was not the *Vernon*, but the *Hermes*, the parent ship of the air service, and the subject discussed was aviation rather than torpedoes. This explains why Jellicoe was the recipient of the letter from the C-in-C, Poore, for he was then, as Second Sea Lord, superintending the newly formed naval air service, and, in fact, Poore had sent him the letter for vetting so that it could be changed if necessary before delivery.

On 10 November, Hopwood wrote:

There are evidences of saner mind. I think there will be a climb down *if* a way can be found. Perhaps it would be well to keep my letter back until tomorrow as one does not want to worry HM if the crisis is going to pass. If it blows over he can read what has happened with an equable mind.

The real difficulty will be to find a way of sufficiently scolding the C-in-C to satisfy Churchill without really affecting that officer unduly.[93]

And again on 13 November:

The crisis is over, no thanks to the First Lord. We got as far as all four Naval Lords signing their resignation. But we induced Poore to withdraw his letter and express regret and under vast pressure he agreed not to resign. Winston would not be flattered if he knew the arguments used by the Naval Lords to keep the Commander-in-Chief from going. They were in short that he (Churchill) was so much off his head over the whole business that Poore need take no notice of it![94]

Jellicoe had been much upset by the affair and, as a result, resigned his responsibilities as superintending Lord of the Naval Air Service,[95] a step which can only diminish his stature in the light of history as he had recorded his interest and belief in this rising arm of the Navy.

As to the First Lord, there can be little doubt that the incident restrained his less wise activities,[96] and so the story has a comparatively happy ending.

The Bridgeman case

There was one other controversy in which Churchill found himself in trouble—over the supersession of Sir Francis Bridgeman as First Sea Lord by Prince Louis of Battenberg in December 1912. The affair caused a major storm in Parliament and the Leader of the Opposition, Bonar Law, advised by Lord Charles Beresford, made a bitter attack on the conduct of the First Lord.

But here it is difficult to see how he could have avoided trouble, for his handling of a delicate problem, that of getting rid of an officer with whom he had no specific quarrel but whom he believed was unfit for his high office, seems to be hard to fault.

Sir Francis Bridgeman was chosen to succeed Sir Arthur Wilson in December 1911, after much discussion of a rather small field of choice. He was a fine seaman and had the confidence of the service, but it had already been noted that '. . . he had not developed the particular qualities required in the office [First Sea Lord]—especially, holding his own in committee [CID] against practised debaters and insistent soldiers'.[97] Marder describes him as phlegmatic and colourless and believes that he would have made a reasonably good First

Sea Lord had he served under anyone but Churchill. But in the event he did not prove phlegmatic enough and could not conceal his repeated resentment of Churchill's interest and interference in everything.[98]

During his first year of office, Bridgeman's health had been poor, and at the end of November 1912 he wrote to both Prince Louis and Beatty saying that he was worried by his condition and had considered resignation.[99]

The First Lord seized what must have seemed a heaven-sent opportunity and wrote a tactful letter to Bridgeman in which he said that he had been anxious about the First Sea Lord's health, and suggested that he might retire for 'if, by any misadventure, we were to be involved in war, I feel that the burden might be more than you could sustain'.[100] And in his letter to the King seeking approval for the appointment of Prince Louis of Battenberg to relieve Bridgeman (and of Jellicoe to relieve Battenberg) the First Lord stressed his concern over health, saying that he 'can no longer feel satisfied that this officer would be capable of bearing the immense responsibility and strain which would be cast upon him if by any misfortune we were involved in a great naval war'.[101]

The King approved the changes—he did not agree to the suggestion that Bridgeman be made an additional Admiral of the Fleet as a recompense, but this is irrelevant to the main issue—and it seems probable that Bridgeman would have accepted his fate despite an improvement in health in early December.

Indeed after one letter in which he said that he thought he would be able to continue in office, he answered a further firm request from the First Lord with: 'I now realize that you expect me to resign and I am happy to be able to meet your wishes.'

But then he came to London from his Yorkshire home and mentioned the matter to friends in the Opposition, who saw an opportunity to get at Churchill, and, supported by Lord Charles Beresford, encouraged him to resist supersession. A most disagreeable and bitter exchange of letters then took place between Bridgeman and the First Lord.[102] The exchange included letters to the newspapers and culminated in a full-dress debate in the House of Commons on 20 December. And, as seems inevitable, Hopwood was busy in the background stirring up trouble for his chief and encouraging Bridgeman in his agitation.[103]

In the end, with the help of the King, who sympathized with Bridgeman but approved the change, the matter was allowed to drop, and Bridgeman withdrew his demand for publication of the correspondence. After reading all these letters,[104] one can only agree with Churchill, who, in a letter to the King just before Bridgeman was received in audience on giving up office, wrote:

> Mr. Churchill has no reason to object so far as he is concerned, to the full publication which is now proposed by Sir Francis; but he thinks that it would be deeply injurious to Sir Francis Bridgeman . . . who has clearly allowed his mind to be poisoned by persons who wish to make party attacks in Parliament. . . . Your Majesty may desire to warn him of the deplorable folly of persisting further in disclosures damaging only to himself.[105]

The King declined to offer any advice, but immediately after the audience Bridgeman wrote to the First Lord withdrawing his request for publication. He also assured Stamfordham that he would do his best to stop further publicity, but he added: '. . . I hear rumours of a deep-laid agitation against Churchill; I am using every bit of influence I possess to arrest it and have asked Balcarres [Opposition Chief Whip] to do the same. I am afraid Beresford is difficult to hold and I unfortunately can do nothing with him.'[106]

One final affray with flag officers must be mentioned. In 1913 Admiral Limpus, writing from Turkey, where he had been carrying out some difficult but successful negotiations about the construction of warships for the Turkish Navy, sent a long report on his activities to the Admiralty.

The First Lord, in his reply, congratulated him rather coolly on his success and then went on to criticize his use of English at great length.

> I have received your letter of the 3rd instant, and I am glad to hear from you and from other quarters of the agreement which has been reached between the Turkish Government and Messrs Vickers. I recognize that you have played a useful and effective part in the negotiations, and I congratulate you upon the result.

I find it necessary to criticise the general style and presentment of your letters. A flag officer writing to a member of the Board of Admiralty on service matters ought to observe a proper seriousness and formality. The letters should be well written or typed on good paper; the sentences should be complete and follow the regular English form. Mere jottings of passing impressions hurriedly put together without sequence, and very often with marked confusion, are calculated to give an impression the reverse of that which is desirable. You do not do yourself justice in these matters. No one can be so busy as not to be able to cast a letter to a superior in a proper form. You should make up your mind beforehand exactly what you mean to say, and study to say it in the clearest and shortest way, if necessary re-drafting your letter. In your latest communication three letters appear to be mixed up without beginning or end. Knowing the good work which you did in South Africa and your zeal in your Turkish mission, I am able to dispel from my mind the impression which the chaotic character of your correspondence would otherwise convey.[107]

Such letters did not endear the young First Lord to the senior officers of the Navy, and, I believe, accounted for much of the dislike which the First Lord aroused among officers as a whole. This seems hard on one who did so much for the Navy, but equally one must understand the feelings of admirals who resented being treated like schoolboys.

5

PERSONNEL REFORMS

*But the important element of British sea-power is not the
ships, essential though they are, but the officers and men.
Whatever mistakes in naval policy Mr. Churchill may or
may not have committed, the nation owes to him a debt of
gratitude for the persistence with which during his period of
office at the Admiralty he demanded from Parliament repeated
increases of the personnel, while at the same time making more
adequate provision in respect of pay and laying on a surer
foundation the system of promotion from the lower deck to
commissioned rank.*[108]

NAVY LEAGUE ANNUAL

Officers

THE reader will remember from the third chapter that
the general state of personnel in the Navy in the first
decade of the century was not satisfactory. Fisher had
steamrollered through the obstruction of the traditionalists
to introduce his wide-ranging reforms of the methods of entry
and training of officers, and had initiated changes in the
structure of the officers' corps.

When Churchill took over from McKenna, therefore, there
was not much to do in this field except to ensure that the
momentum of change was maintained and to see that Fisher's
reforms were not reversed. But some adjustment was necessary; the age of entry of officers being an example. Fisher had
an excessive enthusiasm for 'catching them young', and his
entry age of twelve and a half did not fit the educational
pattern of the social classes from which officers were then
drawn. Boys had to leave their preparatory schools early,
which was unpopular. Moreover, in an increasingly democratic
society, dressing up young boys in uniform and calling them
officers was becoming an anachronism, and the sailor resented
taking orders from children. Churchill quickly raised the age
of entry to thirteen and a half, which was the usual age at
which boys left their preparatory schools, and the course of
training at Osborne—Dartmouth became the equivalent of

the public school. This reform remained unchanged for forty years.

Early in his time in office, he instituted an inquiry under Admiral Custance into the education and training of midshipmen and cadets. A report was issued in 1913 and the proposals were quickly put into force. They were not revolutionary. Churchill, in announcing the decisions in Parliament, said that 'we have been struck by the age and the size of the senior midshipmen', and went on to announce that the time spent at sea as a midshipman would be reduced by eight months, that the annual examination for midshipmen would be abolished and that the number of examinations for acting sub-lieutenants would be reduced. In this way, young officers reached commissioned rank earlier.

The expansion of the Navy in 1912 and 1913 brought serious shortages of officers in the Fleet. Churchill, against much opposition, sponsored the 'public-school' entry, by which young men were recruited for the Navy at the age of eighteen and, after special training ashore and in a training cruiser, were joined up with the Dartmouth-trained officers as midshipmen. Traditionalists feared that the 'special entry', as it was called, would not mould boys into the type of naval officer required, and to calm their fears the announcement of the new scheme stressed that it was a temporary measure due to the expansion of the Fleet. But it was continued, and many distinguished officers entered in this way. The evidence is now clear that there was little if anything to choose between the products of the two methods; indeed, the normal age of entry is today eighteen.

The lower deck

Fisher had not had time to tackle the reforms needed on the lower deck, and in this field there was much to do. Every aspect of the sailor's life demanded attention, but pay was probably the most pressing.

The memorandum which the First Lord submitted to his colleagues in the Cabinet on 17 October 1912 bears all the marks of his personal interest (and also of his rolling prose). It showed that the years of duty at the Board of Trade and the

Home Office had given him a real appreciation of the problems of the poorly paid workers, of the difficulties of wage differentials and of the influence of the trade unions on the wage structure. It was clear, too, that in one year the First Lord had gained a good knowledge of the sailor's daily life, conditions of service and domestic problems.

The memo speaks for itself and I do not apologize for quoting large extracts.

For the last sixty years no increase has been made in the substantive pay of the British sailor. His food has been improved, and the number of specialist ratings to which it is open to him to rise have been multiplied by the ever-growing complexity of naval science. [The substantive, or basic, pay of Able Seamen and Stokers 1st Class, who formed the majority of the Lower Deck, was 1s. 8d. per day; that of Leading Seamen 1s. 10d.; Petty Officers 2s. 8d.; and Chief Petty Officers 3s. 4d.]

Meanwhile, outside the naval service everything has advanced, and the relative position of the bluejacket compared to the soldier, the policeman, the postman, the fireman, the railway man, the dockyard labourer—in fact, to everyone with whom he comes in contact at the great ports, has markedly declined. This comparison would prove more invidious if extended to skilled artisans, such as those engaged in the ship-building industry, or in dangerous trades like coal-mining. The concentration of the Fleet in Home Waters has diminished the sailor's opportunities of saving money, and led him into constant expenditure. It has induced a greater proportion of marriages. The serious rise in prices of the last twelve years, amounting to 15 per cent, has increased the stringency of life in the dockyard towns. Owing to the movements of the Fleet, a large amount of railway travelling is necessary for the men to get to their families, and this alone is a new and heavy drain upon their resources. On the other hand, the service becomes more strenuous every year; the number of practices and exercises of all kind continually increases, and the standards are raised. A large proportion of the men are very highly educated and extremely intelligent. On leaving the service, they have no difficulty in finding good employment at high wages. They know themselves to be remunerated far below their true economic rate. The comparatively frequent opportunities of leave which Home service affords bring them in contact with Trade Unionist relations and friends. They are fully aware that, but for the fact that they were caught as boys and bound to a fifteen years' engagement before they knew anything about the service, far greater inducements must have been offered them by the State; and, secondly, that there is nothing between them and the improved conditions which their comrades in civil life have won but their respect for naval discipline.

The sailor's life is one of exceptional hardship. Service in a ship of war is not only more strenuous, but more uncomfortable than twelve or fourteen years ago. Instead of seeing something of the world, the young sailor knows nothing but the North Sea and a few war anchorages round the coast. The construction of the modern warship renders it extremely uncomfortable and even unhealthy as a living place. Nothing is possible in the nature of a recreation room on board, nor are there facilities for any kind of rest, privacy, or amusement. A man has only the mess deck to go to, where he is herded with several hundred others in messes of about sixteen. If he wants to read or write in quiet there is no place for him. Now that the armour has been carried to the upper deck, he has to subsist on artificial light and ventilation. If he wants to smoke or see the daylight he has to go on deck, where there is scarcely any shelter. When the majority of ships were abroad in good climates this would not have mattered so much; but the life of the bluejacket and stoker in our finest ships of war around the British coasts and in the North Sea is one of pitiable discomfort, which cannot, while the present competition in armaments continues and the present types of warship construction prevail, be effectually alleviated.

As regards leave, the sailor is at a great disadvantage compared with the soldier. In a ship all leave has to be taken by watches, i.e. in two halves. It is often impossible for the ships to be sent round to the three Home Ports, where the majority of the men have their homes. As a rule, half the Fleet have to lie at Portland or Harwich, and the men have to travel to their homes at their own expense. As regards short leave, when the ships in the course of cruising visit frequented ports, there are nearly always great difficulties in getting the men to and from the shore. The distance at which ships lie from the shore makes a frequent boat service impracticable. A man cannot just step ashore for a few hours, and come comfortably back on board when he wants to. The liberty boats are slow and crowded, as well as few and far between. There are long delays, which take away a lot of the pleasure of going on leave; and when a man does get on shore in a strange port in Home Waters, there is hardly anything for him to do except loaf about and spend his money, and take care, under severe penalties, that he does not miss the return boat. For long periods at a time the ships are at sea or off unfrequented places carrying out gunnery practices or manœuvres, and then the sailors, when their work is done, have nothing to do in their leisure but potter about the crowded decks under constant supervision.

If these conditions be compared with life in the Army in time of peace, the contrast is very great. A soldier has a comfortable barrack room and recreation room and ground; he can smoke, read, or play billiards in comfort while off duty. In the ordinary routine he has practically all his afternoons free. He can make his home near his place of duty with certainty that he will not be ordered away to the other end of the kingdom at a moment's notice. Service ashore in the naval barracks is looked upon as the greatest luxury in a sailor's life: it is the ordinary experience and routine of the soldier. The growth of German armaments is compelling us every year to maintain a larger number of ships in full commission, and consequently the disproportion of service afloat to service ashore, with consequent separation from wives and families, is continually aggravated. It has always been recognised that the conditions of a sailor's life afloat are much harder than those of the soldier in time of peace. It must now be recognised that those conditions are increasing in severity, and the proportion of time afloat constantly growing.

The 1s. a day pay of the infantry soldier received its first addition in 1876, when he was given deferred pay of 2d. a day, paid out in a lump sum on his discharge. In 1898 the grant of deferred pay ceased, and he was given a messing allowance of 3d. per diem at a net extra cost to the nation of £200,000. In the year 1902, during the South African War, Parliament decided to increase the pay of the soldier, and a net addition of 7d. a day, or 50 per cent, was made to the pay of soldiers of over 2 years' service if 20 years of age. In all a fresh sum of £1,520,000 a year was distributed among the 210,000 soldiers serving in Great Britain and £786,000 per annum among those serving in India. The subsequent modifications of Lord Haldane by making part of the extra pay depend on musketry proficiency have to some extent reduced the total cost, but the great increase that remains has produced most beneficial effects in the class, character, conduct, and contentment of the Regular Army.

No corresponding increase was, however, made in the pay of the Navy, and in consequence their position in relation to the soldier has been substantially impaired, and all pecuniary recognition of the extra hardships of the sailor's life has been swept away. This deterioration of the sailor's relative position has synchronised with the increased severity and discomfort of the naval service afloat and the rise in the cost of living ashore. Moreover, the sailor in the mercantile marine has only recently been given a rise in wages of 2s. 6d. a week, equivalent to a 12 per cent to 16 per cent increase on his previous wages.

In consequence of the facts briefly referred to above, there is a deep and widespread sense of injustice and discontent throughout all ranks and ratings of the Navy. This discontent and the grievances which produce it are fanned and advertised in Parliament and the press. It is rendered more dangerous by every successful strike for higher wages which takes place on shore. It is rendered more legitimate by the social legislation upon which Parliament is engaged, and by measures like the Minimum Wage Bill which secure to the coal-miner minimum rates of wages which, though spoken of in terms of biting contempt by the miners, are nearly double what the sailor can hope to obtain. A boy getting the minimum wage receives more money wages for 8 hours' work from bank to bank than a 1st Class Stoker in the Navy for 8 solid hours of the hardest work I have ever seen done. The boy lives with his parents; the stoker has to keep a home without enjoying any of its economies.

The sailors have hitherto been restrained by their sense of discipline and loyalty, but we have no right to trade on this indefinitely. Although it is still possible to get boys who know nothing about the Navy, and who are put in by their parents on a 15 years' engagement before they can exercise any conscious choice, in sufficient numbers to man the Fleet, practically all who are not promoted to be petty officers leave the moment their engagement is up; and all our efforts this year to induce a proportion of them to re-engage or to return have been absolutely futile. It is just this seaman class which was caught and bound to such a long contract so young, who cannot escape from it without severe punishment, and who are the best educated, among whom a serious explosion might occur. The reports of the German agents dwell continually upon the discontent of the sailors with the conditions of their pay, and there is no doubt that the German opinion on this point is as well founded as it is widespread. We have had great mutinies in the past in the British Navy, and we ought not to continue to bear the responsibility of refusing all redress to grievances so obvious and so harsh.[109]

The proposals fell under three broad headings: the pay of Able Seamen and Stokers 1st Class; the pay of leading rates, Petty Officers and Chief Petty Officers; and lastly marriage allowances.

It was proposed that any increase in the pay of junior ratings should not be spread evenly over all, but concentrated 'so as to give improvements substantial to fully grown and fully trained men of twenty-two and twenty-three arriving at marriageable age'. The basis of the scheme was, rather than to give an all-round increase of twopence a day, to give a four-penny increase to the 'Able Bodied Seamen and 1st Class Stokers who are properly qualified and who have four to five years man's service, apart from boy's service, to their credit'. (This would affect about half the men in these ranks.) Churchill added: 'The others are under twenty-two and twenty-three, who, for the most part, have no dependants and who ought to be taught to put off marrying till they get their rise of pay.' For the higher ranks and ratings, an increase of sixpence a day was proposed. The total cost of these improvements was estimated to be about £552,000 per year.

The First Lord went on to say that there was no marriage- or separation-allowance in the Navy, whereas in the Army and Royal Marines considerable numbers of men were able to use married quarters or draw lodging- or separation-allowance. He asked that these privileges be extended to the Navy, at an estimated cost of £634,000 per year.

The memo ended with a request for a small increase— amounting to £35,000—in officers' pay, which was to be devoted to abolishing inequities and to improving the scale of half-pay which caused hardship to some officers.

There was a long and bitter fight with the Treasury, led by Lloyd George, over the pay increases, and eventually, after some very acrimonious exchanges, the Board had to accept a considerable reduction of their proposals. Despite the views of *The Navy*, expressed in December 1912, that the Fleet was in 'a state of deep discontent',[110] the fourpence-a-day increase for junior ratings was reduced to threepence, and the rise of six-pence for senior ratings to fourpence. No marriage- or separa-tion-allowance was granted, though a small sum, amounting to some £8,500 a year, was put aside for the provision of free kit on entry, the lack of which had been a real grievance. The officers' pay increase was granted in full, but instead of the £1,186,000 asked for (£552,000 for pay and £634,000 for marriage-allowance), the total grant was only £366,000.

The parsimonious award was surprisingly well received, both in the Fleet and by the public, though Churchill was bitterly disappointed. *The Navy* commented in January 1913:

> The increase of pay in the Navy probably represents the best that could be done with the money made available by the Treasury. But it can only be regarded as an instalment towards the settle-ment of the long standing claims. . . . The Admiralty are entitled to the thanks of the country for the carefully considered adjust-ment of the increases, and for having done very well with the comparatively small amount of money that the Treasury have made available.[111]

Oswald Frewen recorded in his diary that one of his sailors had said, on hearing of the pay award, 'Old Winston's got a nice old mug, like his Ma.'

But in a letter to the King, the First Lord wrote: 'Mr. Churchill hopes that Your Majesty is pleased with the new scheme of pay. He confesses that it is not all that he could have wished for. . . .'[112]

He ended with the good news that: 'The increases in pay have been made to date from the 1st of December in order that the men may have a month of the increased rate available for their Christmas leave. . . .'

Promotion

The First Lord was keen, from the start, to open the prospect of an officer's career to the best men on the lower deck. Helped by Lord Fisher, he quickly commissioned a scheme for selecting and training young Warrant Officers (and Petty Officers who had passed for Warrant Officer) for early promotion to ward-room rank. In a speech on 18 March 1912, he said that the

Navy was short of officers and that he required an immediate increase in the Lieutenants' list. He went on:

> Everyone acquainted with the Navy must have been struck by the extraordinarily high qualities of discipline and intelligence which are displayed by the best class of Warrant Officer. These are the days when the Navy which is the great national service should be opened more broadly to the nation as a whole. . . . We propose, therefore, to select a considerable number of the younger Warrant Officers by yearly instalments of twenty-five to thirty up to a total of one hundred, possibly more, for promotion to the rank of 'Mate', which is equivalent to that of Sub-Lieutenant. . . . They will of course be eligible for promotion, strictly on their merits, to the higher ranks. As, however, they will start as commissioned officers some years later than those who enter the Navy through the naval colleges, it is probable that the bulk of them will retire content with a career which will have carried them from bluejacket to commander.

At the same time he announced that, to help those not selected for the new Mate scheme, Warrant Officers would in future be promoted to commissioned rank after fifteen years' service as such instead of twenty—'a change which they have so long desired'.

The new scheme was widely welcomed, especially on the lower deck, whose members now felt that merit could at last be fittingly rewarded. Although Lord Fisher later complained that the Mates were not given their full opportunities, a number reached the rank of Commander and a few Captain and Admiral. The scheme was a success and was progressively improved over the years—it was quickly extended to the engine-room branch, for example. It is paradoxical that today there is little need for such a system of promotion, for it now only provides for late developers. Any promising boy, whatever his wealth or background, can enter the Navy as a cadet if he has the right qualifications.

Discipline

In his first Estimates speech, on 18 March 1912, the First Lord told the House that he was setting up three inquiries— the first into the gunnery efficiency of the Fleet, the second, which has already been mentioned, on the entry and training of young officers and:

> ... thirdly, the time has come when there must be a full inquiry into the system of summary punishments,* which are now in force including their consequential effects as regards pay, position, badges and pension. It is of high importance to the interests of the Navy that the system of punishments should be physically and morally beneficial as well as corrective, and that it should be so devised in regard to offences where no dishonour is involved as not to wound the self respect of fighting men.

It will be remembered that there was discontent in the Fleet in 1911 which was freely expressed in books, in naval periodicals and in the proceedings of the various benevolent societies which many branches of the service had formed.

The inquiry referred to was undertaken by the Brock Committee, instituted in February 1912 with wide terms of reference. Admiral F. E. Brock was Chairman and the other members were Captain Pratt and Mr Evans, an Admiralty Civil Servant. Paymaster Butcher served as secretary.

The committee heard much verbal evidence and received many letters and memoranda from officers and ratings.[113] It is clear that, while some of the senior officers agreed with Captain Fremantle of the *Dreadnought*, who wrote, 'I do not think that much is wrong with the discipline of the Navy at the present day,' a very large number of others, both senior and junior, were unhappy with the situation. Indeed, Fremantle wrote that: 'Administration has tended to become unsympathetic,' and wanted to abolish some forms of punishment.

Commander Dewar wrote:

> Although ships differ widely, the discipline is not good in the Navy at the present time, by which I mean that the administration does not get as willing and cheerful work out of the men as it should. The large number of punishments also suggests that something is wrong.
>
> I suggest that it is no one's job to take an interest and know the men for their own sakes, and no one is responsible that a

---

* Summary punishments are those awarded by the Captain of the ship, as compared with those by courts martial.

particular set of men conform to the discipline of the ship except the Commander (executive officer).

He went on to advocate decentralization to the Lieutenants and an improvement in the divisional system.

A separate witness, Lieutenant E. A. Nicholson, thought: 'My first point is that the officers are very much out of touch with the men, and if there were sympathy between them, among many other advantages, the personal influence of the officers would tend to reduce the number of small breaches of discipline which are unfortunately so numerous.'

Lieutenant Pilcher drew an unfavourable comparison between the discipline in the Navy and that of a regiment, and wanted a better divisional system. Another officer wanted a scale of punishments drawn up for the guidance of Captains, affirming that: 'There is a tremendous disparity between different Captains' views on leave-breaking and resultant injustice.'

Probably the most general criticism was that of over-centralization on the Commander, though a remarkable feature was the unanimous dislike of the ship's police who were often described as *agents provocateurs*.

There is one interesting letter from Captain S. S. Hall of the cruiser *Diana*, in the Mediterranean, who had formed a committee of officers and men to produce ideas for Admiral Brock. I think that its recommendations give a good indication of the main complaints of the sailor.

1. Improvement in the design of the accommodation of ships.
2. Less time to be spent on cleaning ship and more on useful instruction.
3. Men never to clean or polish in their best clothes.
4. No Sunday parades of any kind and Sunday Church service to be made voluntary.
5. The abolition of some of the older forms, ceremonies and customs in order to simplify the day's work.

Finally, the Judge Advocate of the Fleet, a practising barrister who acted as the Admiralty legal adviser, provided a paper which drew attention to two points which he thought needed change. The first was a technical point about the procedure for awarding detention as a summary punishment; the other was of much substance, and recommended that Petty Officers should be given the right to choose to be tried by court martial rather than be disrated summarily by the Captain.

The committee reported on 8 July 1912,* and the First Lord announced in the House on 25 July that 'action was being taken to improve the system of punishments which is in force and also to regulate the position of Petty Officers in disciplinary matters'.

A comparison between the written evidence sent to the committee, the committee's report itself and the Admiralty letter announcing the changes which would be made as a result of the report shows quite remarkable agreement. The committee accepted most of the suggestions made by the witnesses and in turn the Admiralty agreed almost exactly with the committee.

The Brock Report is a cautious document. It finds nothing seriously wrong, but there are hints of past weaknesses and abuses—for example, 'It appears that the abuse of authority which some years ago was rampant among the ships' police is practically non-existent or very rare now.' There is one classic statement about social conditions which will, I suppose, be found in any report on discipline, wherever or whenever written. 'Unfortunately, in the present day discipline in all grades of life has diminished, and the ideas of obedience have given way to that of questioning authority on every possible occasion. . . .' And there is another dictum which will find an echo, I fancy, today and at any time: 'The young officers of the present day are not brought up to look after the interests of the men serving under them with the same care as used to be the case.'

But the report sharply attacks the rigid routine followed in

---

* The Admiralty docket containing the Brock Report, and, worse still, the Board comments on its recommendations, have been pulped by some stupid official, so that much of what follows is logical guesswork. The report itself may be found in the Admiralty Library.

the main fleets and the interference to training caused by surprise drills.

> The routine and work of the ship must be closely connected with discipline. The committee are of the opinion that, if Captains were given a freer hand in arranging the routine of ships, a more efficient and up-to-date scheme might be evolved. Unnecessary work should be eliminated, so that to the man who uses his brains there should always be a substantial reason for the work on which he is employed. That there must be a fleet routine is obvious, but this should be for fleet work, and unless there is some express purpose to the contrary, general drills should be carried out at certain specified times; there should be less watching the flagship and following her motions in harbour, with consequent loss of time. . . . Uncertainty of what is going to happen is the greatest evil that any organisation has to contend with, and constant upsetting of a day's work once started is unsatisfactory. . . .

These were brave words; but they were heard. The results were immediate and sweeping. In September, a stream of circular letters started to flow to the Fleet repeating almost word for word not only the conclusions of the report but often the reasoning leading to them as well. Improvements in the relationships between officers and men, development of the divisional system, reform of fleet routine—all were included.

The Admiralty also agreed, with one exception, with the recommendations on punishments. Scales of punishment for leave-breaking were standardized, injustices in the classification of men for leave abolished, and the hated 'Ten A', which involved standing on deck under a sentry's care, was replaced by a more suitable and productive punishment.

The right of appeal against unjust or severe sentence was reaffirmed, and a more easily understood and straightforward procedure for stating complaints was instituted.

Reflecting on this feature of the report, one is struck by the beneficent power of the Press in matters of discipline and service conditions. In the 'bad old days', when some Captains behaved like tyrants, when conditions in ships were abominable and punishments often cruel, there was little a man could do legally to seek redress. But the growth of literacy and with it the spread of the popular Press brought a change. A seaman who had been treated unfairly could and did write to one of the popular papers, and the knowledge that this might happen checked, I am sure, some excesses and abuses, and produced a happier and more humane service. The appeals procedure introduced in 1912 by Churchill made recourse to the Press unnecessary (though I do not suppose that the Editor of the *Daily Mirror* will agree with me).

On one question the Admiralty went further than the com-mittee—that of the right of Petty Officers to demand trial by court martial for offences which might lead to disrating. The committee did not want to alter the prevailing system, by which the Captain could disrate a Petty Officer summarily, merely recommending that a summary of evidence should be taken and that the Senior Officer's approval should first be obtained. But the Admiralty introduced the right to opt for a court martial, a privilege which in practice was seldom used, but which raised the Petty Officer's status to that of NCOs of the Army and Royal Marines.

The system of summary punishments introduced in 1912 by the First Lord lasted, with only minor changes, until 1950, when appeals against courts martial were instituted and the procedure for investigating summary offences improved. And it is a great tribute that the Pilcher Committee of 1950 found so little to criticize.

It might well be thought, from this account of the great personnel reforms, that Churchill, encouraged and advised from backstage by Lord Fisher, was alone responsible for the changes. This is not so, of course, and the Sea Lords, particu-larly Battenberg, provided very powerful support. But, because of the destruction of the Admiralty files, it is difficult to judge the contribution of the admirals, whereas the First Lord wrote most of the papers himself and bore, ultimately, the responsibility.

Increases in personnel

Lastly, Churchill's success in procuring the increase in the numbers available to man the Fleet must be recorded.

Many new ships were being built, some additional to the

strength, others to replace old ships, but in every case more men were required. Moreover, the complexity of the new equipment demanded higher skills. The new sailors had to be better educated, better trained and more intelligent than their predecessors if they were to maintain the weapons and operate the machinery.

The figures tell their own story. In 1911, there were 134,000 officers and men. In 1912, 137,000. In 1913, the total had risen to 141,000, and in 1914, before war came, to 146,000.

This expansion required great efforts from the recruiters and from the officers and men of the training service, but with the encouragement and support of the Admiralty and the imagination and enthusiasm of the First Lord every demand was met, and the war at sea was never hindered by lack of officers or men.

6

TECHNICAL IMPROVEMENTS AND NAVAL AVIATION

To change the foundation of the Navy from British coal to foreign oil was a formidable decision. As Churchill recognized, 'To commit the Navy irrevocably to oil' was indeed 'to take arms against a sea of troubles'. He thought the gains worth the difficulties and risks, and so did Fisher, who plumped for oil like mad. It was the most vital decision Churchill ever made....[114]

A. J. MARDER

Winston was a constant visitor to our station ... and it was not long before I had taken him up in the Borel. *.... Winston was anxious to know what we young enthusiasts thought about the development of naval flying as it would affect naval warfare.*[115]

AIR CHIEF MARSHAL SIR ARTHUR LONGMORE

Churchill made us young submarine or flying people feel we were useful sailors—not just children playing with toys, as some big-ship people seemed to think us.[116]

COMMANDER J. H. OWEN, RN

....

IT will be remembered that one of the tasks which the First Lord set himself was 'to increase the gun-power of ships'. But this is too narrow a compass for the range of technical advance which his nimble and acute brain encouraged and I will cover other technical matters as well.

From a survey of *The World Crisis*, it is evident that it was the production of the fifteen-inch gun and the construction of the fast division of five *Queen-Elizabeth*-class battleships to carry it of which Churchill was most proud. Certainly the devastating fire of the 5th Battle Squadron, composed of four of these ships, at Jutland, the moral effect of the *Queen Elizabeth* at the Dardanelles, and the capacity to take punishment shown by the *Warspite* provide ample proof of their excellence. And this is not all. In the Second World War, all

111

five ships were to give yeoman service, in particular the *Warspite*—probably the most active big ship of the war—the *Valiant* and the *Queen Elizabeth*, all three of which were given a major modernization between the wars.

The story as Churchill recounts it in *The World Crisis* is fascinating.

Until I got to the Admiralty I had never properly appreciated the service which Mr. McKenna and Lord Fisher had rendered to the Fleet in 1909 by their great leap forward from the 12″ to the 13·5″ gun. . . . The increase in calibre of the gun was enough to raise the shell from 850 pounds to 1,400 pounds. No fewer than twelve ships were actually building on the slips for the Royal Navy armed with these splendid weapons, quite unsurpassed at that time in the world. . . . I immediately sought to go one better. I mentioned this to Lord Fisher at Reigate and he hurled himself into its advocacy with tremendous passion. Nothing less than the fifteen-inch gun could be looked at for all the battleships and battle-cruisers of the new programme. To achieve the supply of this gun was the equivalent of a great victory at sea; to shrink from the endeavour was treason to the Empire.

He goes on:

The Ordnance Board were set to work and they rapidly produced a design. Armstrongs were consulted in deadly secrecy and they undertook to execute it. I had anxious conferences with these experts, with whose science I was of course wholly unacquainted, to see what sort of men they were, and how they really felt about it. They were all for it. . . . But there could not be any absolute certainty. All sorts of stresses might develop in the 15″ model. If only we could make a trial gun and test it thoroughly before giving the orders for all the guns of the five ships. . . . But then we should lose an entire year and five great vessels would go into the line of battle with an inferior weapon to that which we had in our power to give them. Several there were of the responsible authorities who thought it would be more prudent to lose the year. I hardly remember ever to have had more anxiety about an administrative decision than this.

Lord Fisher was consulted again and was 'steadfast and even violent'. 'So I hardened my heart and took the plunge. . . . But everything turned out all right. British gunnery science proved exact and true, and British workmanship as sound as a bell and punctual to the day. When I saw the gun fired for the first time a year later and knew all was well, I felt as if I had been delivered from a great peril.'

To give these ships the speed required, oil fuel was necessary. Encouraged by Fisher, the First Lord was pressing his colleagues for twenty-five knots, four knots faster than any other battleship. Thus was consolidated the vast naval revolution of the change from coal to oil which the First Lord quickly pushed through. By appointing Fisher as the Chairman of the Royal Commission on Oil Supplies he made certain that the urgency of the problem was understood. The resulting arrangements with the Anglo-Persian Oil Company speedily provided the oil needed, and moreover proved an extremely profitable investment for Britain. There were many tributes paid to the First Lord's skill and persistence in piloting the intricate measures required through the House of Commons.*

Oil was also adopted as the fuel for all future destroyers, for although one class had been fitted to burn it in 1908, the next two years' ships had reverted to coal. The First Lord also insisted on high speed without a reduction of gun or torpedo armament, and this policy was approved by the Board without difficulty.†

In 1911 there were nine different classes of cruiser, ranging from the big armoured *Minotaur*s to the small unarmoured *Boadicea*s. It was decided to reclassify these ships into 'heavy cruisers' (there were thirty-five of them afloat) and 'light

---

* It is right to note that Lord Jellicoe strongly disputes Churchill's statements in *The World Crisis* that the provision of war reserves of oil fuel for the Fleet stood the test of war. During the discussion in committee, Jellicoe had insisted on six months' estimated consumption being held in reserve. For reasons of economy, this was reduced, and he says in his book that as First Sea Lord in 1917 he had to restrict movement of ships because of shortage of fuel.

† However Richmond, then in the Operations Division of the Admiralty, criticized the balance between guns and torpedoes, asserting that the first task of destroyers was to sink enemy battleships and that defence against enemy torpedo craft came second. He would have had more torpedoes and fewer guns.

cruisers', whose task was mainly to screen and provide information for the Battle Fleet. No more heavy cruisers were to be built.

The design of the new light cruiser required much controversy and discussion. The First Lord called for two designs, one a 'super-destroyer' of high speed and no protection, armed with four-inch guns, and the other a larger ship, slower, but with light protection and armed with a combination of four- and six-inch guns. Both would carry torpedoes. After a conference with the cruiser admirals, it was agreed that the latter design was right (Fisher disagreed violently—high speed was all that mattered to him), and the *Arethusa* class was the result.

The First Lord, who had personally fought for the six-inch guns, presented the design to Parliament in these words.

> They are described as Light Armoured Cruisers, and they will be in fact the smallest, cheapest, fastest vessels protected by vertical armour ever projected for the Royal Navy. They are designed for attendance on the Battle Fleet. They are designed to be its eyes and ears by night and day; to watch over it in movement and at rest. They will be strong enough and fast enough to overhaul and cut down [here speaks the cavalryman] any torpedo-boat or destroyer afloat, and generally they will be available for the purposes of observation and reconnaissance.

This class was most successful, and developed into the 'C' and 'D' classes which were built during the First World War and continued to give useful service right through the Second. Except for the first twelve, these ships were built with a uniform armament of six-inch guns, and here again the First Lord was proved right by events.

The more one reads, the more one is struck by his urge for technical advance and by the extraordinary correctness of most of his views. In 1913 the War Staff produced a plan for the extensive use of mines—offensively in the Heligoland Bight, defensively in the Strait of Dover. This first stirring of British interest in a weapon already developed by Russia and Germany was opposed by the Board, with the exception of the First Lord, who alone showed interest. But even he jibbed when he learnt the cost.

Similarly, when the War Staff made an evaluation of the 1912 North Sea manœuvres, they drew attention to the danger to the Fleet from German submarines, which had up to then been considered as useful only for coast defence. Of the Board, only Churchill and Battenberg paid any attention; the remainder considered the danger non-existent, an attitude which led directly to the disastrous losses of the *Hogue, Cressy* and *Aboukir* in 1914.

The First Lord was a consistent supporter of the submarine service and did a great deal to increase its stature in the Navy. There were still some senior officers who looked upon submariners as pirates for whom no fate was too bad. The results of exercises in which submarines had done well were minimized. Umpires were usually unfriendly, and any mistakes and failures were well publicized. As with the aviators, the First Lord instinctively sided with submarine officers in their struggle with prejudice, and he saw to it that their voices were listened to in high places. On one question only did he seem to have a blind spot—on the danger of submarine attack on British commerce. He was not alone in this. Lord Fisher and Sir Percy Scott believed that the Germans would be forced to use U-boats to attack merchant shipping without warning, but they were unique. The Board of Admiralty and the Cabinet, both advised by eminent lawyers, declared that no nation could descend to such uncivilized breaches of international law. Certainly the Germans had no such plans before the war.

In a secret memorandum circulated to, among others, the Prime Minister early in 1914, Fisher gave a carefully reasoned exposition of the potential of the submarine, for attacks both on surface warships and on merchant shipping. He believed that German submarines would attack merchant ships without warning and without a care for the safety of their crews. He looked upon this as a grave threat to our food supplies and asked for special measures to protect shipping and hamper submarine operations, among them the blocking of the Straits of Dover by mines. Fisher had no doubt that the Germans would ignore international law, saying, 'the essence of war is violence; moderation in war is imbecility,' and his main thesis was 'it is not invasion we have to fear, but starvation'.

But he spoilt his argument by his last conclusion: 'On the whole, therefore, it is clear that while the development of submarine warfare will render us absolutely safe from overseas attack, it cannot possibly cripple our trade to anything like the same extent to which it can be made to cripple that of our enemy.'[117] This was really irrelevant, as German seaborne trade was a luxury, while Britain's was a necessity.

While Fisher was bombarding his colleagues in the CID, Sir Percy Scott was writing letters to *The Times*, warning of the dangers ahead. However, Scott was so busy attacking battle-ships that his warnings on the submarine threat to commerce fell on unsympathetic ears.

Nothing was done to prepare for U-boat attack against merchant shipping, and I think that this is the only serious failure of which Churchill can be accused in his judgement of the shape of warfare ahead.* But this was an era when the sanctity of treaties was still observed, when the contemptuous phrase 'scraps of paper' had not been invented, when war between fully mobilized nation states was still to come.

The introduction of director-firing into the Navy was bitterly opposed by many officers. By this method, all the guns were controlled and fired by one man from a position aloft. The advantages were many. The director was clear of spray and of cordite smoke from the guns, individual errors were eliminated and concentration of fire on the correct target was made much easier. Time has shown the importance of director-firing, and its principal proponent, Sir Percy Scott, has been proved right in every claim he made for the new system. But the first tests were not, for various reasons, conclusive, and it seemed that inertia and resistance to change might delay or even prevent the introduction of the new method of firing.

Encouraged by Jelicoe's strong support, Scott, who was then on half-pay after his battles with Lord Charles Beresford, tackled the First Lord. With the aid of an ingenious model and

---

* However, the proceedings of the CID during 1914 show the great care taken by the First Lord to help introduce the War Risks Insurance scheme. This scheme was brought into force soon after the war started and without it no ship would have dared leave harbour.[118]

his convincing logic, he persuaded him of the merits of the system, and new tests were at once ordered which led to the decision to fit the equipment generally in the Fleet.

On the question of the position and design of the masts on which the director tower was carried, Scott was less successful. He managed to convince the First Lord that the mast should be moved from its initial position abaft the foremost funnel, where the director was often blinded by funnel smoke. But the constructors provided only a single mast, which vibrated so much that the director-layer had difficulty in keeping his telescope on the target. Scott was right, but even Churchill failed to move the Board. When Prince Louis became First Sea Lord, the decision was correctly taken to fit tripod masts, but much time and money had been wasted.

The road of an innovator like Scott is a hard one, but Scott rejected tact and persuasion and instead used abuse and assertion. Even then, Churchill supported him to the end, and, it will be seen later, recalled him when the war started.

In matters of technical advance, the First Lord was always in the van, always supporting the pioneers, always sweeping aside the obstruction of the unimaginative. It is frightening to picture the plight of the Navy in 1914 if his drive and enthusiasm had not invariably supported progress.

Lord Jellicoe, in the heat of post-war resentment of Churchill's criticism, may have written, 'Mr. Churchill was very apt to express strong opinions on purely technical matters . . . but his fatal error was his inability to realise his limitations as a civilian quite ignorant of naval affairs.'[119] But Sir Roger Keyes, who had appreciated the First Lord's support of the submarine service when he had been Inspecting Captain and later Commodore (S), disagreed. He wrote: 'Churchill's quick brain and vivid imagination were invaluable and, in the majority of cases, his intervention was in the best interests of the service.'[120] I believe that history supports Keyes.

Naval aviation

As Home Secretary, Churchill had attended several of the CID meetings concerned with the development of 'aerial navigation', as flying was then described in Whitehall documents. His fertile mind and vivid imagination quickly seized upon the possibilities of this new dimension in warfare, and he became fascinated by it during his time at the Admiralty.

The *Enchantress*'s visits to Chatham and Sheerness, from where the First Lord could inspect Eastchurch aerodrome and discuss progress with the naval air pioneers, were frequent. He was also an *ex officio* member of the Aviation sub-committee of the CID and he took a prominent part in its work. A stream of memoranda and minutes flowed from his office, all devoted to the aim of encouraging flying in the Navy, both by improving the conditions of the officers and men concerned and by concentrating technical talent on aviation problems.

In a minute to the Second Sea Lord in December 1911 about the proposed new flying corps, he said:

[2.] Terms and conditions must be devised to make aviation for war purposes the most honourable, as it is the most dangerous* profession a young Englishman can adopt.
[3.] No regard to military or naval seniority should prevent the really young and capable men, who have already done so much for the new arm, from being placed effectively at the head of the corps of airmen.[121]

And, in keeping with his character, he did not confine himself to exhortation from behind a desk. He took to the air as often as possible, and endeared himself to his instructors by his zeal and unexpected humility as a pupil.

But the instructors were 'frightened stiff of having a smashed First Lord on our hands', and he was passed on from one to another because no one was prepared to take the responsibility of sending him up solo. Although he did many hours of dual instruction and flew over 140 times, he was unable to take his certificate before family pressure forced him to give up this dangerous pursuit.

Brassey's *Naval Annual*, never an uncritical judge of Churchill, said in 1914: 'The First Lord showed particular

---

* There is no doubt as to the danger. Statistics speak for themselves. The number of flights for every death in aviation was 500 in 1910, and 1,500 in 1911. In 1912 it had risen to 5,000.[122]

interest in all matters relating to the Naval Air Service and made many flights in aeroplanes and seaplanes. No occupant of this high office of state has made corresponding effort to acquire a practical knowledge of the work of the Navy. . . .'[123]

It was unfortunate that the difficult decision on the future of airships came early in his reign. The report of the Court of Inquiry into the failure of the *Mayfly*, presided over by Admiral Sturdee, had been most unfavourable.* No blame was attributed to the officers and men of the airship, but the fact that the failure was due to insufficient strength in the keel member, caused by miscalculations which had been pointed out to the designer, was either ignored or not understood. Nor does the success of the Zeppelins across the North Sea, both for passenger-carrying and reconnaissance, seem to have been taken fully into account. The enthusiasm of the 'heavier-than-air' men also must have influenced the argument. Finally, there can be no doubt that the First Sea Lord, Sir Arthur Wilson, had a fixation against airships and used his powerful influence freely. Anyhow, it was firmly decided at a meeting in the First Lord's room on 25 January 1912 to give up development of airships and the officers and men of the section were forthwith returned to general service. And although Admiral Sueter later claimed that the aviators did not support the proposal to do away with airships,[125] a report of the CID technical committee on 29 February recommended that '. . . the prospects of the successful employment of the rigid type airships are not sufficiently favourable to justify the great cost, and that naval experiment should be confined to aeroplanes and hydroplanes. . . .'[126]

Sueter gave evidence to the committee, but Samson and Gregory, the two naval members, were both 'heavier-than-air' pilots and this may have been crucial.

A series of events followed which quickly caused the decision to be reviewed. Jellicoe was much impressed by a flight in a

---

* One commentator has suggested that Sturdee, who was a Beresford man, rejected the airship because it had been sponsored by Fisher and Bacon. He suggests that Sturdee, who labelled the *Mayfly* as the work of a lunatic, was opposed to it not for logical reasons but because of its origin.[124] I believe that this is far fetched and extremely improbable.

Zeppelin, and a Continental tour by Mr O'Gorman* and Captain Sueter,† together with eulogistic reports from our attachés in Germany, brought much information about progress abroad. On 25 April 1912, at the 116th meeting of the CID, Churchill raised the airship question again, and it was agreed to ask the technical committee to review the matter. Considerable controversy followed. The CID considered the question several times[127] and listened to attacks on airships by Wilson and to support by Seely, Churchill and others.

As the Prime Minister with his usual clarity observed at one meeting, the report of the technical committee had clouded the issue. The report praised airships, stressed the threat which they posed to this country, and then went on to ask for some to be built. But there were two problems: firstly how to defend ourselves from aerial attack (and this could come from aeroplanes and guns, not airships); and secondly, whether we needed airships ourselves. Two separate problems had become mixed. Decision was deferred several times, but finally, at the 122nd meeting, on 6 February 1913, it was agreed that the Navy should take over the development of airships and that an airship section should be formed with the help of the Army experts. In July the First Lord ordered two rigid and six non-rigid airships to reinforce the few small craft taken over from the Army. But it was too late, and the Navy started the war with no airship capable of operating with the Fleet in a reconnaissance role.

It is interesting to speculate on what would have happened if Winston Churchill had over-ridden his advisers in January 1912, as one suspects that he would have liked to have done. After the war, Churchill claimed that he thought little of the airship and 'did everything in my power to restrict expenditure on airships and concentrate our narrow and strained resources on aeroplanes'. But the evidence of the CID meetings does not confirm this, and I think that he was being wise after the event. The truth is that he encouraged anything to do with aviation, whether heavier or lighter than air, and rightly.

* Superintendent of the Royal Aircraft Factory, Farnborough.
† On half-pay after his post as Inspecting Captain of Airships had been abolished.

Perhaps airships would have worked with the Fleet at Jutland and other battles, and given better information than the seaplanes which were present in 1916. Certainly, German airship-surfaceship co-operation had some disappointing results, and on one occasion in August 1916 the reports of Zeppelin *L13* seriously misled the Commander-in-Chief, Scheer. But Admiral Sueter quotes several examples of successful work, notably on the morning after the Battle of Jutland, in the raid on Yarmouth, and in the sinking of the *Nottingham* and *Falmouth* in August 1916.[128]

There seems to be no reason why British air-sea co-operation would not have been better than the German, and I find it hard to dissent from the judgement given in Brassey 1913 after the *Mayfly* decision:

> There is no doubt that if the ship had been reconstructed or another built immediately, the lesson learnt would have been of the greatest value and well worth the cost involved. This accident is really a more serious matter for the Empire than appears at first sight, as it put back the building of our aerial battle fleet for several years and gave to other Powers a lead. . . .

The airship controversy was accompanied by a long wrangle between Sir Arthur Wilson (then retired, but on the CID) and the First Lord and his advisers. In January 1913 Wilson sent to the First Lord a memorandum attacking airships, using arguments which were hotly disputed by the experts, and many of which today appear nonsense. An extract shows the fallacy of his arguments: 'Airships when out of sight of land very soon lose their reckoning; in the North Sea it is doubtful if a more extended view would often be obtained from an airship than a cruiser, as the atmosphere is rarely sufficiently clear and the use of a telescope from an airship would be more difficult.'[129] They were easily refuted in Churchill's reply.

But the interesting part of the correspondence is Wilson's suggestion that a *Dido*-class cruiser should be converted to carry aeroplanes. The mainmast was to be removed and the after funnel hinged to allow a length of flight deck on which the aircraft would land and derricks fitted to transfer the aircraft from aft to the forecastle for flying off.

A month earlier, in December 1912, Beardmores, the Clyde shipbuilders, in consultation with Captain Sueter, had submitted a design for an aircraft-carrier.[130] Admiralty officers and departments were enthusiastic, and a joint meeting of naval officers and technical experts was suggested in order to discuss some modifications which were clearly needed.

The First Lord had shown an interest in both proposals for a carrier, as indeed he had in an earlier idea put forward by Lieutenant Williamson,* but, for some reason which I cannot fathom, no meeting was held. So nothing was done beyond the provision of seaplane-carriers which had to stop both to hoist out their seaplanes and to recover them. The *Argus*, in 1918, was the first ship to be used regularly for landing on aeroplanes, and thus four years were lost.[131] It is difficult now to appreciate the reasons for this delay.

After this diversion to airships, it is necessary to return to flying in general in the autumn of 1911. There was much activity, civilian, military and naval, but it was uncoordinated. The 'Air Battalion' was flying airships and some aeroplanes on Salisbury Plain. The naval pioneers were very busy at Eastchurch, and in December 1911 Commander Samson flew off the battleship *Africa* lying at a buoy at Sheerness. Seaplanes were also being tested with the help of the Short brothers.

In December Captain Sueter, the Inspecting Captain of Airships, sent a long report to the First Lord, which he had framed with Samson's help and which suggested the formation of a naval air service. In Whitehall, the Aviation subcommittee of the CID under Haldane was discussing the formation of a national Corps of Airmen in very general terms, and had delegated to its technical subcommittee, under Seely, the task of working out the details.

The report, issued on 29 February 1912, expressed concern 'at the backward state of aerial navigation in this country when contrasted with the progress made by other great naval and military powers'. It proposed that 'all the country's resources should be absorbed and utilised in one organisation', which

---

* See p. 126.

would be the Flying Corps. 'The Flying Corps should supply the necessary personnel for a Naval and a Military Wing, to be maintained at the expense of and to be administered by the Admiralty and the War Office respectively. The Corps should also provide the necessary personnel for a Central Flying School, and a reserve on as large a scale as may be found possible.'

The subcommittee based its proposal on its conviction that:

While it is admitted that the needs of the Army and the Navy differ, and that each requires technical development peculiar to sea and land warfare respectively, the foundation of the requirements of each service is identical, viz. an adequate number of efficient flying men. Hence though each service requires an establishment suitable to its own special needs, the aerial branch of one service should be regarded as a reserve to the aerial branch of the other. Thus in a purely naval war, the whole of the Flying Corps should be available for the Navy, and in a purely land war the whole Corps should be available for the Army.

After this rather idealistic attitude, for independent wars of the type visualized are rare, the report made practical proposals.

A Central Flying School should be established for the training of flying men on Salisbury Plain, to be maintained at the joint expense of the Admiralty and War Office and to be administered by the War Office. After graduating at the Flying School, flying men should become members of the Flying Corps, and should then be detailed to join either the Naval Flying School at Eastchurch for a special course of naval aviation, or one of the Military Aeroplane squadrons for a special course of military aviation, or to pass into the reserve of the Flying Corps.

The Naval Wing of the Flying Corps, entry to which should ultimately only be obtainable by qualifying at the Central Flying School, should for the present have its headquarters at the Naval Flying School at Eastchurch. It is impossible to forecast what its ultimate organisation will be, as this depends to a great extent on the results of experiments, which are about to be commenced, with hydro-aeroplanes.

The Military Wing of the Flying Corps should consist at first of eight squadrons (seven for aeroplanes, one for airships and kites), entry to which should ultimately be confined to those who have qualified at the Central Flying School. The whole of these squadrons are required for use in connection with the Expeditionary Force. Expansion of the Military Wing will be necessary.[132]

The report was generally accepted, the Prime Minister provisionally approved it, and the Royal Flying Corps was formed on 13 April 1912, before the CID had formally considered the matter. The first Commandant of the CFS was Captain Godfrey Paine, RN, who had already taken great interest in flying at Eastchurch, and his appointment was delayed until he had obtained his Pilot's Certificate.

The scheme was well intentioned, and it was obviously sensible to concentrate primary training and many technical matters. But in an environment dominated by the strongly individualistic characters who were the pioneers of aviation, it never really worked. Many naval aviators continued to get primary training at Eastchurch,[133] which gradually became more the headquarters of a naval air service than of a naval wing. The split widened. There were many reasons. Plain inter-service rivalry was one. Naval interest in seaplanes, which were of no concern to the Army, was another. And while the naval aviators complained of the attitude of many admirals the generals were even more reluctant to accept the aircraft as a weapon of war, and the sailors therefore wanted to keep clear of War Office control. There is a revealing correspondence[134] between the War Secretary and the First Lord in which Colonel Seely tried to enlist the help of Churchill in his efforts to improve the conditions of army aviators. Seely ended, rather pathetically: 'Fortunately, your sailors [aviators] have none of these troubles.'

Prince Louis, both as Second Sea Lord in 1912 and as First Sea Lord in 1913 and 1914, showed great interest in aviation and encouraged the pioneers by his visits to Eastchurch, where, Sir Arthur Longmore recalls, the Prince's son, 'Dickie', was given his first flight at the age of about twelve. One of the admirals in the Nore Command, Lambert, also took a personal interest in flying.

Fundamentally, the weakness of the system was that money was provided separately and independently by the Admiralty and the War Office respectively, and the co-ordinating committees could only advise. They had no real power.

The First Lord gradually came round to the view that some divergence was desirable, and he voiced this opinion officially in January 1913 at a meeting of the CID to consider the composition and function of the Air Committee, which was to take over the task of co-ordinating the work of the two wings.[135] There was a sharp clash with Haldane and Colonel Seely when Churchill explained that, while he had been originally in favour of a joint military-naval air service, he had changed his mind.

As one historian of the Fleet Air Arm puts it: 'Thus naval ties with the Royal Flying Corps never got beyond the paper stage. The term "Royal Naval Air Service" soon came into use and the "R.F.C. Naval Wing" was sunk without trace, though it was not until July, 1914, that the separate entity of the R.N.A.S. was officially recognised.'[136] Or, as the more sedate official history records: 'That was the plan. So far as the Military Wing was concerned, it was punctually carried out. In the Naval Wing a certain centrifugal tendency very early made itself felt. . . .'[137]

It was a gradual process, which was then accompanied by some ill-feeling and which has since resulted in much re-crimination; but it seems to have been inevitable if the personalities of those chiefly concerned are considered.

Naval aviation made early progress, particularly with sea-planes. The alliance with the Short brothers, who set up a factory near Eastchurch, flourished and produced some excellent machines. Mr Sopwith's help was also enlisted and he designed some good aeroplanes and seaplanes. Avros also built successful aircraft for the Navy. As the official historian says:

> . . . the Naval Wing paid more attention than was paid by the Military Wing to the use of the aeroplane as a fighting machine. . . . The Military Wing, small as it was, knew that it would be entrusted with the immense task of scouting for the expeditionary force, and that its business would be rather to avoid than to seek battle in the air. The Naval Wing, being entrusted first of all with

the defence of the coast, aimed at something more than observing the movements of an attacking enemy. Thus in bomb dropping and machine gunnery the Naval Wing was more advanced. . . .[138]

One commentator, when comparing service attitudes to the procurement of aircraft, writes:

During November (1912) a scheme was projected with regard to the manufacture of aircraft for the Military Wing by private firms, and it was decided that no general specification of the details of an aeroplane for purposes of tendering should be issued to such firms. In particular cases, where it might be found necessary to give orders to private firms, it advised that those selected should be furnished with an exact specification, and, in such cases, all persons concerned, both in the manufacture and trials of the machine, should be bound to observe the provisions of the Official Secrets Act. The Admiralty policy, on the other hand, was more liberal, in that it encouraged private manufacturers, while making clear that it had no intention of relying on any particular firm for its aircraft needs. This policy proved to be a wise one, and one result was that at all times (until the pooling of manufacturers' productions when the Royal Air Force came into being) the machines belonging to naval units were superior to those belonging to the Army.[139]

Naval experiment covered every aspect of sea/air warfare.[140] Trials were carried out in early 1912 to discover whether submarines could be detected and attacked from the air. The officer concerned, a submariner-turned-aviator called Williamson, also put up a design for a ship to carry aircraft which would land on wires stretched along the deck.

The use of W/T in aircraft received much attention. Bomb-dropping was practised, and a few machine-guns and cannon were fitted in aircraft. In 1914 the first torpedo was dropped from a British aircraft by Lieutenant Longmore. The protection of ships and dockyards was seen as a naval responsibility and many experiments were made in the attack on airships from aircraft, using bombs, grenades and machine-guns. Night flying was exercised for the first time.

The *Hermes*, an elderly cruiser, was converted to carry seaplanes, and in the North Sea manœuvres of 1913 seaplanes from the *Hermes* aided one side and seaplanes and aeroplanes from shore stations the other, with considerable success; in 1912 an amphibian had been flown off the *Hermes* when the ship was entering Cromarty Firth.

Air Chief Marshal Sir Arthur Longmore, one of the four naval pioneers, is of the opinion that it was in 1913 that aviation 'caught on' in the Fleet by demonstrating its practical capabilities. He quotes the sighting of a periscope from the air, during exercises in the Moray Firth, as an occasion which impressed many senior officers.[141]

By the summer of 1914 relations with the Military Wing had further deteriorated, and there is an interesting letter about aviation from the First Lord to Asquith, acting Secretary of State for War in place of Seely, who had resigned after the Curragh incident.

The First Lord made four main points:

1. That it was ridiculous to move the Airship section to a new site at Wolverhampton from Farnborough, with all the expense involved, just because the Navy had taken over airships. 'No one would think of moving them if the Navy and Army were managed as one service.'

2. That 'we have reason to complain of the treatment we have received from the Royal Aircraft Factory', and he quoted examples of the delays and of the increases in costs of aircraft produced there.

3. That there was not a full interchange of information with the Military Wing. He quoted correspondence with the War Office about the RE aircraft and he believed that 'we should receive more considerate treatment from the French or even possibly the Russian Governments'.

4. That the Central Flying School was too expensive and that the Navy could train its own pilots at one-third the cost. His recommendations, which were overtaken by war, included one that Eastchurch should take on the training of all naval pilots, aircrew and mechanics, a suggestion which reflects the frustration which gripped the RNAS and its wish to escape from military shackles.[142]

At the outbreak of the war, the Royal Naval Air Service was flourishing. There were 39 aeroplanes, 52 seaplanes, a few small airships and about 120 pilots. Moreover, the machines were good, the pilots well trained and morale unequalled.

When reviewing the early days of aviation it is easy to criticize the reluctance of some officers to accept the aeroplane. But after reading much current literature on the subject one is struck by the monstrous exaggeration of some of the enthusiasts. One article in Brassey of 1914, for instance, suggested that the seaplane was the right machine for the Navy because if its fuel ran out, or if it met too strong a head wind, it could alight on the water and return to harbour by using the wind on its propellor to turn a screw in the water. Nonsense like this must have shaken the confidence of those who had to make judgements on the new arm in the validity of more serious aeronautical claims, and can have done the cause nothing but harm.

Nevertheless, as will be seen, the Royal Naval Air Service, when it was absorbed into the Royal Air Force in 1918, was the largest and most efficient air force in the world. By his active encouragement and forthright methods Churchill cut red tape, dispelled mistrust and helped to produce miracles.* He must be credited with a considerable share in a remarkable achievement.

As Air Commodore Samson wrote, prophetically, in 1928: 'Without his [Churchill's] help and driving power, the Royal Naval Air Service would not have reached the state of advancement it had done in 1914. One of these days, the nation will understand what a great administrator he is.'[143]

---

* For instance, he deftly parried some awkward Parliamentary Questions about aviators taking their lady relations and friends for flights. After horrifying the bureaucrats by saying, 'My policy is to encourage these young officers to fly as much as possible,' he made mollifying noises by adding that he thought that the regulations should be revised.

Admiral de Chair writes in *The Sea is Strong*: 'Churchill was equally keen [on aviation at sea] and while he was at the Admiralty helped to press the scheme forward. We owe a good deal to him for this, for he fought the Treasury when they tried to block progress.'

Admiral Bell Davies recounts in *Sailor in the Air* that Churchill also invented the term 'seaplane' to replace the ugly 'hydro-aeroplane'.

7

RIVALRY WITH GERMANY: THE APPROACH TO WAR

Today we are lucky in having Mr Churchill at the helm. . . .
Mr Churchill was strong enough to either convert or crush the
economist element in the House, and managed to instil into his
colleagues the fact that the recommendations of the Sea Lords
could not be consistently curtailed with advantage. . . .
According to Mr Arnold White, the Fleet was fully mobilised
this summer on Mr Churchill's own initiative, and that he
threatened to resign unless his wishes came into effect.[144]

THE NAVY

War plans

IT will have been noted, from the description in Chapter 3 of the meeting of the CID during the Agadir Crisis, that Churchill disagreed fundamentally with the plans of the Admiralty as expressed by Sir Arthur Wilson. He quickly made it clear that the Admiralty must work closely with the War Office in the dispatching of the Expeditionary Force to France at the start of a war, and arrangements were put in hand. There was disagreement with the War Office, however, on the proportion of the Regular Army which should be sent over. The War Office argued that all six divisions should go; the First Lord thought that four only should be sent at once and the remaining two be held to repel German raids which might be slipped across the North Sea. He said: '. . . the presence of these two divisions and the Territorial Force would make it not worth while for the Germans to invade except with an army large enough to be certainly caught in transit by the fleet. . . . You will not expect the Navy to play international football without a goalkeeper.'

The argument continued until the war began, when both sides reversed their policies sharply. In Churchill's words: 'Lord Kitchener decided to send only four divisions to France, while I, on behalf of the Admiralty, announced at the great War Council on 4th August that as we were fully mobilized and had every ship at its war station, we would take the responsibility of guarding the island in the absence of all six divisions.'[145]

And, as a further postscript, it is clear from historical records that the Germans never seriously considered an invasion of Great Britain. Tirpitz had been telling the truth when he said to the Naval Attaché in Berlin in 1908 that '. . . it was impossible . . . to embark such numbers as say 100,000 men and . . . quite impossible that they should be disembarked on the other side. . . .' 'Even if the troops landed,' Marder observes, 'the Germans would not be able to keep open the lines of communication.'[146]

As has happened so often in our history, we had overestimated the enemy capabilities and intentions—it was in the interest of the 'bolt-from-the-blue' school to do so in order to support the campaign for conscription. Intelligence estimates are only valid if prepared by men with no vested interests in one service or weapon, and these men are hard to find.

As to the close blockade advocated by Wilson, the new First Lord had little difficulty in gaining agreement to its replacement by the distant blockade. The fortification of Heligoland and other islands which the Admiralty had planned to seize on the one hand, and the increasing menace of the submarine on the other, made clear the folly of the old policy. But Churchill made the change reluctantly, for he feared that the offensive would be lost, and he kept searching for new ideas to 'so conduct ourselves that the sea is full of nameless terrors for the enemy—instead of for us. This means an offensive at the outset. . . .'

The Fleet dispositions were accordingly changed so as to block the exits of the North Sea—by a cordon of destroyers backed up by old battleships in the Dover Straits, and by the stationing of the Grand Fleet at Scapa Flow. By this means it was hoped to seal off Germany from the oceans and to force her Fleet to come out to fight in the open sea rather than in her defended waters.

Such a policy required the development of defences for Scapa, as well as for Cromarty and Rosyth, where parts of the Fleet would be based. Here the First Lord encountered much obstruction, for the defence of ports was a War Office responsibility and the soldiers did not want to spend money on naval projects. The Chancellor, Lloyd George, was also singularly unhelpful, and so nothing was done. In despair, Battenberg and Churchill improvised defences at Cromarty with naval guns manned by Royal Marines—'the only new work completed before the war broke out'.[147] The CID discussed this question frequently but with no avail, and the minutes make sombre reading.

Discussions about the possibility of invasion were resumed in 1913, and the Invasion Subcommittee of the CID met many times. The First Lord describes how he took part in strategic games at the Naval War College, in which he often took the German side—games designed to stimulate thought in the Admiralty War Staff and to expose weak points in our arrangements.[148] He prepared many papers on the invasion problem, on the possibility of raids and two 'imaginative exercises couched in half-serious vein'. One of the latter, called the 'Timetable of a Nightmare', forecast a situation in which the Germans attacked when most of the Fleet was west of Ireland exercising, and involved the capture of Harwich, a landing in the Shetlands and a raid on Newcastle. The paper received much criticism, but it had the merit of making people think. Perhaps its main object was to show the folly of denuding the country of all regular troops at the start of a war.

Surprise attack and readiness for war

In 1908, the CID had ruled that 'if it made the difference between victory and defeat, Germany would not stop short of an attack on the Fleet in full peace without warning or pretext',[149] and another of the new First Lord's early actions was to take measures likely to discourage surprise attack. Firstly, he laid a new psychological foundation of preparation by organizing duty officers at weekends at the Admiralty and by keeping a chart in his office which was daily marked with the position of the High Seas Fleet. In the field of fleet movements, plans were made to 'avoid the possibility of the British fleet being surprised or caught dispersed and divided by a serious German force of surface vessels', and, as an example, 'our fleet did not go on its cruises to the coast of Spain until we heard that the German High Seas Fleet was having its winter refits'.[150]

New Fleet dispositions

In the broad field of Fleet dispositions, an amendment to the German Navy Law, which followed the failure of the Haldane mission to Berlin in February 1912, gave an excuse for changes which improved the readiness of the Fleet for a war with Germany by increasing the number of battleships in Home Waters.

As soon as the German *Novelle* had been translated and fully understood, the First Lord sent a note to the War Staff giving his views on the situation and calling for proposals for increasing the strength of the Fleet in Home Waters at the expense of the Mediterranean. As usual he was quick to initiate action.

A new Home Command was formed in March 1912, to consist of: a 1st Fleet of four fully manned Battle Squadrons and a fleet flagship—twenty-nine ships in all, rising to thirty-three when the fourth Battle Squadron reached its full strength of eight; a 2nd Fleet of two Battle Squadrons of four ships each with nucleus crews which could be brought to full strength without mobilization; and a 3rd Fleet of two Battle Squadrons with care and maintenance parties only. Thus by 1913 forty-one fully manned battleships could be ready in Home Waters to face a High Seas Fleet of an estimated twenty-five ships.

This reorganization was to be achieved by bringing the Atlantic Fleet home from Gibraltar and renaming it the 3rd Battle Squadron, and by transferring four of the pre-Dreadnought battleships of the Mediterranean Fleet from Malta to Gibraltar, where they would form the new 4th Battle Squadron which was planned to be brought up to a strength of eight ships as new construction joined the Fleet.

At the end of May the Prime Minister and the First Lord, who were cruising in the Mediterranean in the Admiralty yacht, met Lord Kitchener, who came from Egypt, in Malta to discuss the new Fleet dispositions.[151]

Kitchener was strongly opposed to any diversion of the Fleet from the Mediterranean, and the meeting was not very successful, though relations between the First Lord and the Field Marshal were better than when they had last met in the Sudan many years earlier. Some sort of draft agreement was reached that: (a), agreement should be sought with France that, in return for British protection of her northern coast, the French Mediterranean Fleet should be maintained at a strength great enough to take on both the Austrian and Italian Fleets; (b), the 4th B.S. at Gibraltar should cruise in the Mediterranean, though available for service elsewhere in the event of war with Germany; (c), a squadron of two or three battle-cruisers should be kept permanently in the Mediterranean, based on Malta; (d), submarine defences should be maintained at Malta and Alexandria.

But the implementation of this provisional agreement was to await the meeting of the CID. A brisk political controversy was caused by the new planned dispositions. The British position was clearly much weakened. Italy and Austria—both members of the potentially hostile Triple Alliance—were building Dreadnoughts. Although apparently on the same side, they were building ships against each other, but the mutual hostility could not be guaranteed. It was not popular to rely on the French for support. A memorandum by Lord Esher on 17 June 1912 puts the critics' case with clarity.

The effect of Winston Churchill's proposals for the redistribution of the Fleet denudes the Mediterranean of Battleships; deprives Malta of Floating Batteries for purposes of defence; and leaves unguarded our Black Sea trade during the early stages of a war with the Triple Alliance; closes our military and trade route to India and the Far East; renders reinforcement for Egypt impracticable; and Malta and Gibraltar insecure.

In Peace it lowers the prestige of Great Britain in India, in the Crown Colonies, and in the eyes of all the Nations of the World; it weakens the value to Japan of the British Alliance; and lessens to France and Russia the value of the British Entente; its reflex action upon the minds of the manifold dark races under British Dominion cannot fail to be harmful; it renders the adherence of Italy to the Triple Alliance inevitable; and tries very high the patience of Spain, which might not inconceivably be driven into the arms of Germany, by considerations of prudence, and by a natural desire to obtain possession of Gibraltar as the outcome of a successful war.

No juggling with the number or quality of a limited cruiser squadron for the Mediterranean; no partial rearmament of Maltese fixed defences; and no transference of a few military units from South Africa to Egypt can be an adequate substitute for a Battle Fleet in the Middle Sea.

It is equally certain that neither in War nor in Peace can an Alliance or a Convention with France serve the double purpose of Great Britain, that is (1) to maintain such Mediterranean Sea-command as will in Peace give assurance of support to distant parts of the Empire, and (2) in War to keep open the military route to India and safeguard our principal avenues of seaborne trade.

The strategic intention of Winston Churchill's Naval Policy is perfectly sound; that is to say the concentration against the most probable enemy of an overwhelming naval force at the crucial point of contact. That is not in dispute.

What is in dispute is whether the Naval power of Great Britain should not provide both (a) for reasonable security in the North Sea, and (b) for the maintenance of those interests in the Mediterranean, inclusive of the safety of Malta and of the waterway to India, which have cost this country so much blood and treasure during the past hundred years.[152]

Churchill was not impressed by Esher's views. He believed that the First Lord, in close touch with the Prime Minister, must be the final arbiter of Fleet dispositions, though he was glad to seek the support of the CID.

At the 117th Meeting of the CID, on 4 July 1912, the subject was very fully discussed, together with the general naval position vis-à-vis Germany. It was an important meeting, attended by, among others, the Prime Minister, the Foreign Secretary (Grey), the Chancellor (Lloyd George) and the Lord Chancellor (Haldane), as well as the Admiralty and War Office Chiefs, political and professional. Lord Esher, Lord Fisher and Sir Arthur Wilson also attended in their positions as consultants, but Balfour could not be present.

The meeting opened with the consideration of a table of relative naval strengths prepared by the Admiralty, in which the US Navy had been included. The Committee did not agree that the USA should be taken into consideration as 'one of the powers against which we have to build', and Churchill said that he would have another table prepared, showing a comparison between the standard of sixty-per-cent superiority over Germany on the one hand and a two-power standard over 'any reasonably probable combination of powers' on the other. It was also agreed that France should be taken as friendly for the purposes of the discussion.

Next an Admiralty paper was discussed which McKenna criticized as requiring a sixty-per-cent superiority over Germany and practical equality with Austria and Italy in the Mediterranean. Even Churchill agreed that such a policy was neither possible nor desirable, though the Prime Minister said that it was useful to know what figures of ships would be required. Then, after listening to further criticism of the move of the battleships from Malta to Gibraltar, Churchill said that 'by reason of the building of the Austrian and Italian Dreadnoughts, the sea command of the Mediterranean had in fact passed from us', and argued that to leave battleships at Malta was 'a useless and expensive symbol of power'. The only way to regain command would be to replace these ships by a squadron of modern Dreadnoughts, but these were all needed for the North Sea. This was the nub of the argument, and a long discussion followed about the strength needed in the North Sea, in which McKenna attacked both the new dispositions and the idea of an alliance with France. The possibility of the United Kingdom being attacked simultaneously by Germany, Austria and Italy was also questioned.*

The Colonial Secretary, Harcourt, suggested that if war occurred Malta might be lost, but Churchill thought that it should hold out for four months. (Shades of the Second World War!) A long discussion of the defences of Malta and of Egypt followed, in which the War Office representatives declared that

---

* The existence of a secret annexe to the Triple Alliance, in which Italy excluded the possibility of war with the United Kingdom, was, of course, not then known, though suspected.

they could not provide the defences necessary against the scale of attack thought possible—an estimate which in the light of events seems more groundless than is usual even in the most pessimistic intelligence circles.

Perhaps the most effective intervention was by Lord Fisher, who disagreed strongly with Arthur Wilson's proposal to build more ships to keep the Mediterranean open. He supported the First Lord's contention that 'the first necessity was the certainty of victory in the North Sea', and he believed that the fourth Battle Squadron based on Gibraltar, together with the battle-cruisers also planned to be stationed at Malta, was enough, and that an adequate force of destroyers and submarines would look after the enemy battleships in the Mediterranean. He did not think that this sea would be open to trade during war.

The Foreign Secretary had the last word. To back up diplomacy he wanted a fleet of 'one-power standard' available for the Mediterranean—it would be best at Malta, but this was not essential. McKenna argued that it must be based permanently at Malta, but the Prime Minister ruled against him and a conclusion was reached which appeared to confirm the Admiralty proposals. 'There must always be provided a reasonable margin of superior strength ready and available in Home waters. This is the first requirement. Subject to this we ought to maintain, available for Mediterranean purposes and based on a Mediterranean Port, a battlefleet equal to a one-power Mediterranean standard, excluding France.'

There was much argument later about the interpretation of the conclusions of the meeting, for it was thought by many that the phrase 'based on a Mediterranean Port' would allow the 4th Battle Squadron at Gibraltar to qualify for this duty. Eventually, it seems to have been agreed that a separate battle squadron should be formed for the Mediterranean by about 1915, when most of the Italian and Austrian Dreadnoughts would be at sea. But the immediate result was that all the battleships were withdrawn from the Mediterranean in the summer of 1912, being replaced by three battle-cruisers.

This disposition remained unchanged until the outbreak of

war, and the decision stood the test of events. The battle-cruisers were enough for the *Goeben* and *Breslau*, though they should have sunk them; the Austrian Fleet never offered a serious threat and Italy did not join Britain's enemies.

Churchill was often accused of inconsistency in changing his policy when he became First Lord and giving in to the 'big-navy' party. But his Mediterranean policy was certainly consistent, for only fifteen months earlier, in one of his regular onslaughts on McKenna, he had begged the then First Lord to reduce the Mediterranean Fleet to one cruiser squadron, in order to concentrate British strength in Home Waters. He argued that so long as Gibraltar was secure the Mediterranean could be re-entered at will, for sea-power was flexible. This note is of great interest because, in addition, it stated that 'it is no longer possible to force the Dardanelles, and nobody would expose a modern fleet to such perils'. A remark which he must have later regretted. The note also suggested that the Mediterranean 'could never be a true war route' and that 'Aden and the Cape are the main naval points for maintaining the road to India and the East'.[153]

Canadian ships

Shortly after its discussion of the Mediterranean problem, the CID held another important meeting about naval policy, this time with the Canadian Prime Minister and four of his colleagues.[154] As has already been shown, the United Kingdom was anxious that the dominions should contribute more to Imperial defence; Australia and New Zealand had each ordered a battle-cruiser, and it was hoped that Canada would help too.* The Admiralty had suggested that this contribution should take the form of three battleships which, it was argued, would by 1915 provide the three extra capital ships needed to form a battle squadron in the Mediterranean.

Grey started with a survey of the political situation in Europe, which concluded: 'The object of my remarks has been

---

* In the spring of 1912, his friend Max Aitken had proposed that the First Lord should go to Canada to enlist the help of the Government and people. Churchill was keen to go, but could not find time.

to show how closely foreign policy and naval policy are connected, and as you go into the question of naval policy more
closely and more from the technical point of view than I can,
so you will realise how much foreign policy depends on naval
power. . . .'

With this encouraging lead, the First Lord continued with a
long and eloquent survey of the whole naval position, one in
which there were several pauses to allow the Canadian
Ministers to question him in order to elucidate points. He
ended thus:

> It comes to this, that we really ought to lay down three more
> ships over and above the four we are building. . . . But it is a
> difficult thing for us to lay down three new ships now . . . because
> here are our numbers four, five, four, four, four, which we have
> collated, and which we have made correspond to the German
> construction. If we come forward now all of a sudden and add three
> new ships, that may have the effect of stimulating naval competi-
> tion once more and they would ask us what new factor had
> occurred which justified or which required this increase in building
> on our part. If we could say that the new fact was that Canada
> had decided to take part in the defence of the British Empire,
> that could be an answer which would involve no invidious com-
> parisons, and which would absolve us from going into detailed
> calculations as to the number of German and Austrian vessels
> available at any particular moment. It would be an answer
> absolutely inoffensive to any of the great powers of Europe, and
> no answer could possibly contribute more effectively to the
> prestige and security of the British Empire. The need as I say is a
> serious one and it is an immediate need.

After the CID meeting the Canadian Ministers met the First
Lord and his Admiralty colleagues several times. There was
much discussion, most of it rather rushed, and Borden thought
it best to take home a full appreciation of the naval situation.
He and his colleagues had evidently been very impressed by
the Admiralty case, which had been put eloquently and con-
vincingly by Churchill. Borden asked for two papers—one for
his Cabinet and officials, which gave the full picture, the other
in a form suitable for publication without giving away secrets
to the Germans.

After several drafts and re-drafts,* a 'Memorandum on the General Naval Situation' was produced and sent off on 26 August 1912, together with a slightly shorter paper for publication. The Memo, which is a very long one, gives a comprehensive history of the Anglo-German naval rivalry from 1898 when the Naval Law was passed. As a picture of the struggle whose results were to have such a dominating effect on the destinies of mankind in 1914–18, it cannot be bettered. It considers the problem from three points of view: those of the Conservative Opposition, the Liberals and the Germans; and, not surprisingly, it shows that the British Government had done everything possible to reduce tension, to gain German confidence and to make a pause in the building race. The expected balance of naval power in 1915 is fully described, and it is clear that according to the planned programmes of all the nations concerned there would be strength for marginal safety in Home Waters, but unacceptable weakness in the Mediterranean.

The concluding paragraphs are strong in tone; perhaps they might have been better expressed:

We have before now successfully made head alone and unaided against the most formidable combinations and the greatest military powers: and we do not at all despair, even if left wholly unsupported by our kith and kin, of being able by a wise policy and strenuous exertions to watch over and preserve the vital interests of the Empire. The Admiralty will not hesitate if necessary to ask next year for a further substantial increase beyond anything that has at present been announced, with consequent additions to the burden of the British taxpayer. But the aid which Canada could give at the present time is not to be measured only in ships or money. It will have a moral value out of all proportion to the material assistance afforded.

The memo ends with: 'On these grounds, not less from purely naval reasons, it is desirable that any aid given by Canada at

---

* The First Lord complained in one letter to the Prime Minister that he had spent three whole days of his holiday on the Canadian papers. There is also evidence that his first drafts did not meet with the approval of his colleagues.

this time should include the provision of a certain number of the largest and strongest ships of war which science can build or money supply.'[155]

Borden was convinced. Much correspondence flowed on the details of the aid to be provided.[156] The most important decisions were whether the ships should be built in Canada or the United Kingdom, and whether they should be manned and controlled by Canadians or by the Royal Navy. The Admiralty argued that Canadian shipyards would take too long to produce these modern warships, and the cost, too, was estimated to be much higher. The need for a centralized control of all warships was also stressed. Finally, after a long exchange, Borden introduced his 'Naval Aid' Bill on 5 December 1912. It authorized funds for three battleships, which were to be built in the United Kingdom and maintained and controlled by the Royal Navy. These last provisions were, it is clear in retrospect, the fatal bars to the Bill. The Opposition, led by Sir Wilfred Laurier, argued that Canada must have a Fleet built in Canadian yards, manned by Canadians and controlled by the Canadian Government. Although the House of Commons passed the Bill in February 1913, it was rejected by the Senate in May, and the project was dead for ever. Laurier also suggested that there was no urgency in the situation, an argument which received support from some of Churchill's Cabinet colleagues. And although a start was made on a Royal Canadian Navy, it was slow and halting, and the impetus had gone out of naval expansion in Canada.

The outcome of the long negotiations was a great disappointment to the First Lord, who had become so closely involved. He took quick action to accelerate the building of three ships of the next year's programme,* but though assailed by the Opposition and the Navy League he did not increase the programme as a whole.

Looking back on the correspondence, one cannot but be struck by the patronizing tone adopted. It was in tune with the times, I suppose, in an age of paternalism. But it would have been wiser, perhaps, to have agreed to the ships being built in

---

* See p. 149.

Canada and manned and controlled by the RCN, and to have accepted the delay in their production as well as the help in personnel and material know-how which would have been needed.

In the event, Canada made a tremendous war effort, mainly on land. A fully prepared and trained naval contribution would have been invaluable in the middle of the war, and it might also have led to the retention of a Navy worthy of the name in 1919. As it was, a force which in the thirties consisted of a few hundred men expanded in the forties to one of hundreds of thousands, and the experience was a severe strain.

But it is easy to be critical after the event, and one must remember the sense of impending conflict which, rightly, pervaded the Admiralty in 1912, and which gave such a sense of urgency to its policy.

The French Navy

Co-operation with the French Navy was also a question which received attention, particularly after the decision to weaken the British Fleet in the Mediterranean. The First Lord had two conflicting aims. He wished for closer ties with France, but he did not want an unquestioning support of French policy. In 1912 he wrote that 'we have the obligations of an alliance without its advantages', and he was worried, rightly, that the French naval concentration in the Mediterranean would provide a moral obligation which would force us to intervene to protect the French northern coasts in time of war, whatever the causes of the conflict. He wished to leave an element of doubt about our intentions which would allow the British Government to exercise some restraining influence on French policy in a crisis.

In August 1912 the Cabinet authorized Anglo-French naval staff talks, and an agreement was signed in February 1913. There was no question of automatic involvement, and the arrangements made were contingent on the free decision of the British Government to join France in a war. Signal-books were produced, exchanges of intelligence made, and proposals for co-operation in Home Waters, in the Mediterranean and in the Far East agreed.

Unfortunately, this process did not go far enough, for the failure to bring the *Goeben* and *Breslau* to action in the first days of war was in great measure due to the Commander-in-Chief's ignorance of the French intentions.

It was a very difficult problem. To have carried co-ordination very close might have encouraged the French to reckless adventures; but the certainty that if France was attacked we would have to go to her aid made lack of co-operation stupid. The Admiralty tried to steer a course between these two extremes, and inevitably it led to shoals. There is a paradoxical reflection of this dilemma today. De Gaulle leaves the NATO organization, but not the Alliance, because he fears that if he becomes too closely integrated with NATO plans he will be committed to reckless American adventures.

The ship-building programme

Soon after taking over office, the First Lord determined to find out if there was any chance of getting agreement with the German Government on a reduction in ship construction. Lloyd George was anxious that an understanding should be gained, and Churchill agreed; both had preached that there were no real obstructions to friendship, and now was a chance to put theory into practice.

Accordingly, a mission to Berlin, arranged through Sir Ernest Cassel, approved by the Cabinet and undertaken by Lord Haldane, set off in early February 1912. Haldane, with his experience of Germany and friendship with many Germans, was the obvious choice, and he and the First Lord worked hard together to prepare for the task. Haldane's reception was encouraging, and he had some friendly and businesslike conversations with the Kaiser, the Chancellor (Bethmann Hollweg), the Secretary of State (Kiderlen) and Tirpitz.

But despite frankness on both sides, and despite the promising gesture when the Germans handed over the unpublished text of the *Novelle* announcing changes in the Navy Law, no progress in reaching agreement was made. The reports of the conversations make sad reading.[157] Both sides seem entrapped in a circle from which there was no escape, and there was

142

always Tirpitz in the background to paper over any cracks which threatened to appear.*

The issues on which the talks broke down were simple and of long standing. The Germans would not alter their naval expansion plans without a political agreement; the British would not make a political agreement until they saw concrete evidence of good will in the shape of a reduction in the tempo of expansion. In addition, Germany demanded a guarantee of British neutrality in *any* war in which she was involved; the British would only guarantee neutrality in a war in which Germany was not the aggressor, and made it clear that their agreements with France and Russia must stand. There was deadlock. The Germans refused to change the *Novelle*: the Government then had to implement their policy of keeping a sixty-per-cent superiority in capital ships.

Churchill was accused of having caused the failure of the negotiations by the famous '*Luxus Flotte*' speech at Glasgow on 9 February. It had been suddenly conceived when reading a newspaper report of a speech in which the Emperor had boasted of 'the German people which had no lack of young men fit to bear arms', and in it the First Lord had said that, while the Navy was a necessity to Britain, it was a luxury to a large continental power like Germany. When Haldane returned from Berlin, however, he said that the speech had been a help to him, as it had reinforced his arguments, and the Cabinet critics, at least, were appeased.

The implications of the *Novelle* were alarming. The more the Admiralty studied them, the less it liked them. They are well described in the First Lord's speech at a meeting of the CID at which Mr Borden and other Canadian ministers were present.

---

* Grey's comment on the 'remarkable interview between Lord Haldane and Count Metternich after the mission' was: 'It would seem from what was then said that the German Chancellor had (for the moment) got the better of Admiral Tirpitz and that the German Government are prepared, if we can offer them an acceptable formula, not to press the provocative points of the proposed Navy Law.' This, I think, admirably describes the power struggle in Berlin.

Until we saw the new Navy Law, we thought that its intention
would be to develop building on a large scale, but when we got it
and began to study it, we saw that it was not so much the building on a large scale which was its feature, although there was
considerable building, but that it was the development of immediate striking power which they were aiming at. The effect of
the law is to put slightly less than four-fifths of their fleet permanently into full commission, that is to say, in the category of
ships instantly ready for action, with no reserves needed, no
mobilization required, nothing lacking. A great development of
personnel is also a characteristic of the new law.[158]

The new law, and the widening of the Kiel Canal to allow the
largest German ships to pass through, had changed the whole
character of the threat posed by the German Fleet.

Negotiations continued, but without result. Metternich, the
Ambassador in London, was desperately anxious to gain
agreement, and did his best to produce an acceptable formula,
but his only reward was his recall on 9 May 1912. He had been
too friendly to England.

A report by Captain Watson, who had been Naval Attaché
in Berlin for three years, made it very clear that neither the
Emperor nor Tirpitz really wanted agreement.

I consider that the time has come to place on record that though
when I was first appointed naval attaché I endeavoured to think
otherwise, I am now forced to the opinion that there is no way of
stopping the naval expansion of Germany unless the impossibility
of continuing it is driven home to the German people by effective
answering of increases on the part of England. Further . . . the
conviction is forced on me that the naval policy of Germany
though apparently perfectly honest and straightforward, and
though by pointing to the fleet law, the Minister of Marine can
say that the policy of Germany is open to the whole world, it is
really by no means so honest as is claimed and is conducted on a
basis of always trying to make it appear that the action of
England is provocative and so to twist and turn announcements
as to lay the blame on England, and in this the naval authorities
do not scruple to use the press and other methods.

Just a year ago statements were circulated in a certain set in
Berlin that the present fleet law represented the limit of German
naval ambitions. Regret was expressed to me and to others that

England did not trust Admiral Tirpitz in this matter. I have before reported on this, and that the scepticism and lack of keenness for the negotiations for the interchange of information both on the part of his majesty the Emperor and his Minister of Marine was really due to a disinclination to be burdened with an inconvenient measure than to a doubt of its efficacy.

Captain Watson was by no means anti-German—indeed the reverse was the case, as he made clear.

I would in no way take anything back from my strong opinion that German naval officers as a whole deeply deplore the bad feeling between Germany and England, and would be the first to welcome an improvement in the relations between the countries and the navies. But it is impossible to blame them if they, led on by clever heads, see their chances of rivalling the British fleet growing as it appears to them at present, and chances of additional employment becoming open to them.[159]

His conviction, reluctantly reached, that Germany was determined on her programme of naval expansion, and that no agreement would be allowed to interfere, makes convincing reading and evidently impressed both the Foreign Office and the Admiralty.

The Naval Estimates were therefore presented to Parliament in the knowledge of the contents of the new *Novelle*, though this could not be made public. The First Lord's speech made a great impression. For the first time the irrelevance of the two-power standard was acknowledged, and the new policy of a sixty-per-cent superiority in Dreadnoughts over Germany's present programme together with two keels for every one laid down additionally was announced.

This was brutally frank language. It saddened the radicals. But it cleared the air. Strange to say, it improved relations with Germany—a country which has always understood strong language and firm policies.

The First Lord called for a 'naval holiday' in which no new ships would be laid down for one year, but the reception was cool at home and abroad. The closing paragraphs of his speech must be given.

The spectacle which the naval armaments of Christendom afford at the present time will no doubt excite the curiosity and wonder

145

of future generations. Here are seen all the polite people of the
world as if moved by spontaneous impulse, devoting every year
an enormous and ever-growing proportion of their manhood,
their wealth, their scientific knowledge to the construction of
gigantic military machinery which is obsolescent as soon as it is
created; which falls to pieces almost as soon as it is put together;
which has to be extensively renewed and replenished on a large
scale; which drains the coffers of every government; which
denies and stints the needs of every people and which is intended
as a means of protection against dangers which have perhaps their
only origin in the mutual fears and suspicions of men.

The most helpful interpretation which can be placed upon this
phenomenon is that naval and military rivalries are the modern
substitute for what in earlier times would be actual wars and just
as credit transactions have in the present day largely superseded
cash payments, so the jealousies and disputes of nations are more
and more decided by the mere presence of war power without the
necessity for its actual employment.

If that were true, the grand folly of the twentieth century might
be found to wear a more amiable aspect. Still we cannot conceal
from ourselves that we live in an age of incipient violence, and
strong and deep-seated unrest. The utility of wars even to the
victor may be in most cases an illusion. Certainly all wars of any
kind will be destitute of any advantage to the British Empire.
But war itself, if it comes, will not be an illusion—even a single
bullet will be found real enough.

The Admiralty must leave to others the task of mending the
times in which we all live, and confine themselves to the more
limited and more simple duty of making sure that whatever the
times may be our island and its people will come safely through
them. (*26 March 1912.*)

These sentiments are relevant today, with the 'nuclear-
deterrence' strategy substituted for Churchill's 'naval and
military rivalries'. One can only hope and pray that modern
deterrence will be more successful.

The estimates were well received, except by the radical wing
of the Liberals, and even the 'Naval' Press welcomed the statement, though regretting a small reduction in the total estimates
compared with 1911–12. The main feature, of course, was
the firm decision to embark on a programme of capital-ship
construction which was deliberately designed to match the

146

German programme ship-for-ship. The details, which were delayed until July so that they could officially take into account the current *Novelle*, gave a tempo of 4,5,4,4,4 ships per year, and the first year's batch was quickly raised to five by the gift of the *Malaya* from the Federated Malay States.

In July 1912 the new Fleet dispositions were also announced —both matters forming the meat of the Supplementary Estimates then introduced, amounting to just under a million pounds. Again the First Lord's speech was well received, and the Tory Press and the navalist papers congratulated him on his powers of persuasion over his Cabinet colleagues.

In between these two estimates, there was much to be done to prevent the delays which were holding up the construction of new ships, and to improve the system of contracting and ordering. The First Lord and his colleagues, especially the Civil Lords, were very active, and there was a round of meetings, visits to firms and exhortations. Good results were shown, and despite the great increase in the complication of the 'super-Dreadnoughts' the time from laying-down to completion reverted to two years.

Then came the preparation of the 1913–14 estimates. Five battleships were due to be laid down; eight cruisers, sixteen destroyers and some submarines were added. This represented an increase of over a million pounds over the last year's estimates. The atmosphere was confused by a statement by Tirpitz in February 1913 that Germany would accept the 16-to-10 standard (or sixty-per-cent superiority) announced by Churchill. Reception in Britain was mixed and predictable. The verdict of history is that:

Tirpitz's suggestion, so far from being a friendly acceptance of a British proposal, was an attempt, very cleverly made, to persuade Britain to lower the margin which the Admiralty had announced as necessary for British security. . . . The proposal was made at a time when the German Admiralty realised that the plans for increasing the army would block any naval increase for that year.[160]

Grey must have been of the same opinion, as no reply was made to Tirpitz's speech.

147   L

The estimates for 1913–14 were introduced in speeches on 26 and 31 March 1913. The First Lord started with an eloquent description of the pitiful folly of the armaments race and suggested an 'almost instantaneous mitigation to the nations of the world from the thraldom in which they are involving themselves'. This was another proposal for a naval holiday.

The first speech was long and detailed, and received praise for its comprehensive nature. Much space in it was devoted to justifying the capital-ship-building programme and the question of contributions by the dominions and colonies also received attention. The debate raged widely and fiercely, and Lord Charles Beresford delivered a sharp attack on the First Lord which was answered in the winding-up speech with pulverizing power. The design of the fast division of battle-ships—the *Queen Elizabeths*—was announced with the remark that 'we have effected a far-reaching change of principle in the design of what are called battle-cruisers'. The design of a new small cruiser was also mentioned.

As usual, the reactions were predictable. The Tories approved grudgingly, and said that not enough was being done. In particular they called for six instead of five battle-ships. The Liberals approved reluctantly, for many of them feared that too much was being done. The Navy League wanted more ships and more money and demanded 'six large armoured ships and nothing less than six', and also pointed out that large sums had remained unspent from the last Estimates, calling for better administration and more drive in the Admiralty. They were warm in praise of the large increases in personnel planned, and in general: 'The Admiralty is to be congratulated that they have done so well to face the future though they might indeed have done much better.'[161]

But by July 1913, when the ship-building vote was discussed in the House of Commons, the First Lord's stock had taken a deep dive in Navy League circles. While praised for the clarity and forcefulness of his exposition of the oil-fuel policy, which had formed much of the July speech, he was severely criticized for not building more capital ships. 'No Minister of the Crown has ever made a braver show in words, none has been a more hopeless failure in faculty of performance.'[162] The failure of Canada to provide the three Dreadnoughts expected (the Senate had rejected the Bill in May 1913) demanded, they said, a Supplementary Estimate. They did not get one. Instead the Admiralty announced the acceleration of three of the contract-built ships of the 1913–14 programme (*Ramillies, Resolution* and *Revenge*), explaining that they still hoped that Canada would provide the three ships. Attacked by the navalists on the one hand, the First Lord was getting into severe difficulties with his Cabinet colleagues on the other. The preparation of the Estimates for 1914–15 was to cause a genuine crisis.

On 18 October 1913, at Maidstone, Churchill warned of the need for increased expenditure on the Navy unless a measure of agreement on disarmament was reached. Simultaneously, he made another appeal for a naval holiday in the most explicit terms, saying that if Germany would delay for twelve months the laying-down of the two Dreadnoughts planned for the coming year, Britain would in return put off the start on the four ships due to be laid down in the comparable period. Reaction abroad was again cold, and he was criticized at home for pandering to the Radical wing of the party. In the next speech, made at the Guildhall on 10 November, the First Lord firmly flung the cat among the radical pigeons by warning the nation that 'the next Estimates would show a large increase because of the large ship-building programmes of foreign powers'.

In the Cabinet, McKenna, Harcourt, Samuel and Runciman were, according to Hopwood in a letter to Stamfordham,[163] encouraging Lloyd George to resist any increases. Certainly the Chancellor seemed to need little encouragement. His first comment on the speech was 'a piece of madness' and on New Year's Day 1914 he published his views on the situation in the *Daily Chronicle*. Today it seems to us unusual for a Cabinet Minister to publish details of his disputes with his colleagues, but Churchill had done the same in August 1909, though, on that occasion, he and Lloyd George had been on the same side.

Lloyd George based his demands for reduction on three

grounds, none of which looks very convincing in retrospect, especially the belief that 'now was the most favourable moment of the last twenty years for a reduction'. He also taunted Winston by referring to Lord Randolph's resignation because of 'bloated' expenditure. The public controversy between the two caused much discussion. In the many Cabinet meetings on the subject, the First Lord was accused by some of his colleagues of extravagance in administration, and Lloyd George said that, if the Estimates of £50,500,000, which was an increase of £3,000,000 over the previous year, were pressed, more taxation would be necessary in an election year. So the First Lord was directed by the Cabinet (17 December 1913) to submit reduced Estimates, which he did by taking about £500,000 off the bill for the air service and for the oil reserve. But ship-building was unchanged.

The radicals—and Churchill said at one stage in the argument that he was in a minority of one—insisted on a reduction from four to two in capital ships. The issue was complicated by the official request which had been made to Canada in the autumn of 1912 for three Dreadnoughts which, it had been stated, were needed to balance the 'emergency German ship-building'. If Britain reduced the 1914–15 programme from four to two ships, it would make nonsense of the statement to the Canadian Government and make certain that Canada would not provide the ships.

So the First Lord would not agree to a reduction and deadlock was reached. It seemed as if he must resign; but the Prime Minister, who, while appearing impartial, had been convinced by the Admiralty case, adjourned the discussion till mid-January: a characteristic and successful Asquithian tactic.

During the respite more facts, figures and arguments were marshalled by both sides. Hopwood, the additional Civil Lord, was apparently trying to persuade the Sea Lords not to follow Churchill if he had to resign but to reserve this weapon for the next occupant of the post, who might be less strong in support of the Admiralty.[164] Hopwood himself certainly had no intention of resigning, and saw the whole affair as one designed to force Churchill out of the Cabinet by his colleagues, a prospect which Hopwood evidently relished.* But the Sea Lords were determined to resign if the capital ships were reduced from four, and Lambert and MacNamara, the Civil Lord and Financial Secretary, both radicals by persuasion but both convinced by logical argument, would have followed them.

The First Lord, while on holiday in the South of France, had produced a memorandum which ably set out the Admiralty case. One paragraph stands out.

> Besides the Great Powers, there are many small states who are buying or building great ships of war and whose vessels may by purchase, by some diplomatic combination, or by duress, be brought into the line against us. None of these powers need, like us, navies to defend their actual safety or independence. They build them so as to play a part in world affairs. It is sport to them. It is death to us.[165]

Moreover, as Hopwood pointed out to Stamfordham,[166] the radicals had ill chosen their battleground, for the First Lord had told the House of Commons how many ships he proposed to build each year and no member of the Cabinet had objected.

When the discussions restarted in mid-January 1914, the estimates had risen to £52,500,000, and it seemed that either the resignation of the First Lord or the dissolution of Parliament was inevitable. These extracts from correspondence between Churchill and Lloyd George show the degree of deadlock reached.

On 26 January the First Lord informed the Chancellor:

> The estimates . . . have been prepared with the strictest economy. For all the expenditure incurred or proposed there is full warrant and good reason. . . . I cannot buy a year of office by a bargain under duress about the Estimates of 1915–16. No forecasts beyond that year have ever been made by my predecessors. . . .
>
> I am now approaching the end of my resources, and I can only await the decision of my colleagues and of the Prime Minister.

---

* In the same letter, Hopwood wrote: 'The Sea Lords should not waste themselves on Winston, but on his successor. . . . if it comes to Winston's resignation he will certainly press them fiercely to go with him'—a completely false statement, as Churchill had written to the First Sea Lord asking the naval members of the Board not to resign on a 'purely political' matter.

Lloyd George replied next day:

... your letter has driven me to despair, and I must now decline
further negotiations, leaving the issue to be decided by the Prime
Minister and the Cabinet.

Your letter warns me—in time—that you can no more be held
bound by your latest figures than you were by your original figure
of £49,966,000. This intimation completely alters the situation. I
now thoroughly appreciate your idea of a bargain: it is an argument which binds the Treasury not even to attempt any further
economies in the interest of the taxpayer, whilst it does not in the
least impose any obligation on the Admiralty not to incur fresh
liabilities.

... I have been repeatedly told that I was being made a fool of;
I declined to believe it. Your candour now forces me to acknowledge the justice of the taunt. ...

Hopwood's information about the attitude of some of the
First Lord's colleagues to his retention in the Cabinet was
accurate. In one pencilled, undated note to the Prime Minister,
probably written in January, John Simon wrote:

Dissolution now, if we are beaten, means the Parliament Act
utterly destroyed ... Home Rule and Welsh disestablishment lost.

The probability of losing the General Election is great ... The
loss of W.C. though regrettable is *not* by any means a splitting of
the party—indeed large Admiralty estimates may be capable of
being carried *only* because W.C. is gone. ...

A majority of the Cabinet certainly take this view.[167]

The crisis was intense. London seethed with political specula-
tion. Delegations waited on Ministers. Articles were written
by the score. Leader-writers thundered. Minutes flew about
Whitehall. Rumour was rife.

After several days of Cabinet meetings—fourteen were
needed in all—the Prime Minister asked the First Lord to take
another look at the Estimates and simultaneously warned his
colleagues of the consequences of a split. A compromise was
reached on 11 February. First, a Supplementary Estimate was
agreed for £2,500,000 to cover the acceleration of the three
ships of the 1913–14 programme already announced, and also
the cost of some of the oil reserves. Then the 1914–15 Estimates

were settled at £51,500,000 and it was agreed to make a substantial reduction—at least £2,000,000—in 1915–16. Three cruisers and twelve small torpedo-boats had been cut, and the reductions in oil reserves maintained.

There is a delightful story, recounted to Randolph Churchill by Lady Megan Lloyd George, about the final decision to compromise.

There were many Cabinets about the Estimates, but the matter was not resolved and Asquith said Lloyd George and WSC must decide between themselves one way or the other. The point had been reached where both were determined to resign rather than yield. Lloyd George said to WSC, 'Come to breakfast tomorrow at No. 11 and we shall settle the matter.' WSC arrived next morning fully expecting that he would have to resign. Lloyd George greeted him and said, 'Oddly enough, my wife spoke to me last night about this Dreadnought business. She said, "You know, my dear, I never interfere in politics; but they say you are having an argument with that nice Mr Churchill about building Dreadnoughts. Of course I don't understand these things, but I should have thought it would be better to have too many rather than too few." So I have decided to let you build them. Let's go in to breakfast.'[168]

The First Lord reckoned that he had gained a victory, and indeed he had. But the lack of both the cruisers and the oil reserves was quickly to be felt in war; whereas it is a remarkable fact that not one of the four battleships which had caused the crisis was ever built! As will be shown later, the war intervened.*

The speech introducing the Estimates on 17 March 1914 was a mammoth effort. The First Lord had spoken on the Supplementary Estimate only two weeks previously, but he embarked on another comprehensive and detailed exposition. The first Opposition speaker, Lee, made a not unfair comment on the speech when he said that the first part had been devoted to appeasing the First Lord's supporters who thought that the Estimates were too large, and the remainder to

---

* Two of the four, the *Renown* and *Repulse*, were redesigned as battle-cruisers in 1915 and completed in 1916.

convincing the Opposition, unsuccessfully in Lee's view, that they were large enough. He added that because the First Lord had emerged semi-victorious from his contest with the Chancellor, he did not propose to abate his criticism. He did not support the admonition: 'Don't shoot at the pianist: he is doing his best.'

The First Lord again explained the difference between Dreadnoughts and super-Dreadnoughts (starting with the *Orion*s with 13·5-inch guns), and it was said that the gap between them was as big as that between the Dreadnoughts and the pre-Dreadnoughts. As well as more money for their capital cost being needed, maintenance costs were also much higher. Then it was that he made his celebrated analogy describing a clash between great modern ironclad ships not as men in armour striking at each other with heavy swords, but rather as a battle between two eggshells striking at each other with hammers. Alas, the *Queen Mary*, the *Invincible*, the *Indefatigable* and the *Hood* were to show that British battle-cruisers could indeed be compared with eggshells; fortunately history has shown that our battleships were made of much tougher stuff.

The First Lord devoted much time to the dominion and colonial navies and to the problems of Fleet dispositions. He explained the paramount importance of maintaining supremacy in the North Sea, the potential battleground, with forces ready *'at the average moment of our power in contrast to the selected moment of another'** and added that, if supremacy was lost there, any dominion ships elsewhere could not survive. They could only 'prolong the agony', for sea-power was world wide. He added: 'If the power of Great Britain were shattered on the sea, the only course for the five million white men in the Pacific would be to seek the protection of the United States.' Prescient words indeed!

The debate was long and bitter, and there was another passage of arms with Lord Charles Beresford, who took the opportunity to attack the oil-fuel policy and to describe the building of the five *Queen Elizabeths* as a 'dangerous experi-

---

* My italics.

ment and gigantic gamble'. History proved Lord Charles wrong on both counts.

The King had followed the long and bitter struggle over the Estimates with deep concern; Churchill had kept him well supplied with information, and Hopwood with gossip. The closing paragraphs of a letter written in the King's own hand from Sandringham on 15 January 1914, at the height of the crisis, show the firmness of his support.

I recognise the difficulties with which you are confronted, but it is you as the head of the Navy, with the assistance of your expert advisers, who are responsible to the Country that the Navy is maintained in such a condition as to be able to carry out what- ever the policy of the Country may necessitate. Since you have been at the Admiralty you have by your zeal and ability done great work for the Navy and I sympathize with you in your present position. I hope the question may be satisfactorily settled and that a solution may be found to the financial problem.[169]

This is, I suggest, a fitting and well-earned epitaph to the testing but fruitful period during which Winston Churchill was First Lord.

Ulster

Winston Churchill took an important political part in the crisis over Home Rule for Ireland which dominated British politics for so many years, and which came to its peak in 1914. He took a diametrically opposite view to that of his father on the Irish question and supported Home Rule, though by 1909 he had agreed to the exclusion of Ulster, at least initially, from the Bill. I have no intention of delving deeply into this political problem, but the outline must be clear if the part played by the Navy, directed by Churchill, is to be understood.

In March the agitation in Ulster against the Home Rule Bill reached a climax. Volunteers enrolled and drilled. Arms were smuggled and the Government 'saw themselves con- fronted with a complete overturn of their authority throughout North-East Ulster'.

As Churchill wrote in *The World Crisis*:

As the peril grew, the small military posts in the North of Ireland, particularly those containing stores of arms, became a source of pre-occupation to the War Office. So also did the position of the troops in Belfast. The Orangemen would never have harmed the Royal forces. It was more than probable that the troops would fraternise with them. In these circumstances, military and naval precautions were indispensable. On 14th March it was determined to protect the military stores at Carrickfergus and certain other places by small reinforcements, and as it was expected that the Great Northern Railway of Ireland would refuse to carry the troops, preparations were made to send them by sea. It was also decided to send a battle squadron and a flotilla from Arosa Bay, where they were cruising, to Lamlash, whence they could rapidly reach Belfast. It was thought that the popularity and influence of the Navy might produce a peaceful solution even if the Army had failed. Beyond this nothing was authorised, but the Military Commanders, seeing themselves confronted with what might well be the opening movements of a civil war, began to study plans of a much more serious character. . . .[170]

These preparations by the Military Commanders produced the Curragh incident, which was thoroughly mismanaged in Whitehall and about which so much has been written.[171] It is clear that many Army officers felt unable to take up arms against their kith and kin in Ulster even if the latter were in revolt against the Crown. What is interesting in the context of this book is to consider the reaction of the Navy to the possibility of using force against Ulster.

First of all, one must recall that a larger proportion of Ulstermen served in the Army than in the Navy. The same was true of Southern Irish Protestants—Wilson, the DMO, and Carson himself, both from the South, were the most fervent supporters of Ulster. Secondly, the Navy in its ships was and still is far more detached from domestic political issues than the Army in its barracks, most of which were in the United Kingdom. Traditionally, too, few naval officers have been interested in politics and in the early years of the century they seem to have been deeply immersed in manœuvres, exercises and technical change, so that the Irish question does not appear to have received much attention. The reaction of most of the senior officers concerned was that it was a job, disagreeable it was true, but it must be done.

Admiral Lewis Bayly, for instance, who was in command of the battle squadron which was diverted from the coast of Spain to Lamlash in the Clyde in order that a strong naval force should be available in the event of serious trouble in Ulster, was ordered to call at Devonport *en route* so that he could receive his orders. He tells his own story.

I knew nothing of what was happening, but assumed that it was probably connected with a possible rising in the North of Ireland, and consequently wirelessed the Admiralty asking that the field-guns belonging to the ships in the squadron should be put on board the *King Edward VII* at Devonport. This was done, and my request was apparently made public, much to my surprise, as I was afterwards told that I was well abused by many newspapers, and that a question was asked about it in the House of Commons.[172]

On the other hand, Admiral de Chair, who was Naval Secretary to Churchill at the time, writes:

On March 24th, 1914, the Director of Operations came into my room and told me that the Third Battle Squadron and two flotillas of destroyers had been ordered to Lamlash, to be ready to move to Belfast and take action. This was a serious step to take and we were determined to stop it.

The Director of Operations managed to persuade the First Sea Lord (Prince Louis) to divert the squadron to Plymouth, as they were passing the Scilly Isles, to fill up with coal. In the meantime I wired to the admiral of the Squadron to come to the Admiralty to see the First Lord.

After a little judicious discussion it was arranged that the men of the Squadron should be given leave. This contretemps ended happily, and I am sure that the First Lord was relieved though I heard afterwards that Lloyd George was furious.*

He adds:

I also heard that the feeling in the Army was dead against fighting in Belfast, and that in general the same feeling permeated the

---

* From the account in *The Curragh Incident*, it is clear that the memory of Admiral de Chair is not faultless and that it was Asquith who ordered the cancellation of the order to the Battle Squadron to proceed to Lamlash. But this does not affect the implication of the story.

Navy. Two Commanders-in-Chief and several Captains had given out that they would resign if orders were given them to take action there. . . .[173]

One admiral, then a junior lieutenant in a destroyer which had been ordered to stand by for the Irish Sea patrol, writes:

In the 7th DF at Plymouth where there were rumours that we were to assist in the blockade of Ulster, at least five young C.O.'s were quite determined not to take part by some means or other; others were considering their position and were quite disturbed. There was even talk, failing other methods of avoiding this duty, of steaming our ships into Belfast or Londonderry to assist Ulster. Perhaps this would not have come off when the question of men's pay was considered . . . Looking back on it now, I wonder we did not go to ask the advice of our new Captain D, but I don't think we ever thought of it.[174]

The task of the historian in getting a true appreciation is difficult. Opinions are so contradictory. There were rumours that ships carrying arms for the rebels were allowed to pass through the destroyer patrols, but no official documents would ever confirm this even if it was true, for the deck log would never have recorded such incidents!

One distinguished admiral, then serving in the Intelligence Division at the Admiralty, writes: 'Except for the legalists, the whole Navy was for Carson. . . . Lewis Bayly and Browning would always side with the law, but they were, in my opinion, in a small minority.' But another experienced officer says that, while there would have been grumbling at a distasteful task, the Navy, which anyhow was 'too busy with exercises to worry about politics', would have carried out its duty.

Meanwhile, the sinister Hopwood was again engaged in attacking the actions and motives of his political chief. In a letter to Stamfordham of 21 March, which he prefaced by a request that neither Prince Louis nor any members of the Government should be told of what he was saying, he reported that:

I find that Churchill is pressing forward secret naval arrangements against Ulster with great vigour, and that a squadron is to

go to Lamlash under Lewis Bayly, destroyers are to be sent to the
Ulster coast and also several small cruisers to blockade. They are
to have precise instructions as to action. L. Bayly has been sent
for to come here tomorrow and he is to be invited to say whether
he and his officers will do their duty and so forth! If he has any
doubts about it, we shall have the proceedings of yesterday [the
Curragh affair] as regards the Army over again. The Naval Lords
tell me, however, that in their opinion the Naval officers will not
follow the line of the Cavalry officers.[175]

The evidence is not decisive, and can therefore only confine myself to the comment that it was a merciful dispensation
that, as events unfolded, no test of the Royal Navy's loyalty
was required.

Churchill was blamed for much of the trouble leading to the
Curragh affair, and was severely criticized for his actions
throughout the crisis. It was also said, for instance, that he
alone had been responsible for the diversion of Admiral
Bayly's battle squadron to Lamlash. But the facts are different
and it is now indisputable that the decision was taken in
Cabinet under the chairmanship of Asquith. Undoubtedly
Churchill made mistakes, but I believe that history will take a
kinder view of his conduct than did the opposition of the
day.

But the arguments were suddenly set aside. In the Cabinet
on 24 July 1914, the Austrian ultimatum to Serbia was reported and discussed. 'The parishes of Fermanagh and Tyrone
faded back into the mists and squalls of Ireland, and a strange
light began, immediately but by perceptible graduations, to
fall and grow upon the map of Europe.'[176]

Three years of achievement

To make a final judgement on Churchill's three years of
peacetime administration at the Admiralty is comparatively
straightforward. He knew what was needed, he knew what was
expected of him, and, by and large, he reached his targets. Only
in the field of staff training and organization did he find that
time was too short. That agonizing cry, 'Fifteen years! And
we were only to have thirty months!' reflects his frustration.
So the Naval War Staff was not efficient at the start of the

war, but I do not think that Churchill can be blamed for this: he did everything and more that man could do.

It would be stupid to pretend that everything was right with the Navy in August 1914. There were many weaknesses, but there were also great strengths, and the improvement since 1911 had been immense. Churchill had grasped the torch of progress lit by Lord Fisher and had carried it bravely forward.

The material deficiencies brought to light by the war fall under three headings. The first was the lack of protection of the Fleet bases from submarine attack, condemning the Grand Fleet to long periods at sea which wore out the machinery. The second was the poor design of the ammunition supply to our turrets, which led to the loss of the *Queen Mary*, the *Indefatigable* and the *Invincible*, and very nearly to the loss of the *Lion*. (Here the Germans were lucky, for they discovered the trouble in the *Seydlitz*, at the Dogger Bank action in 1915, without losing the ship.) The third was the shells, which did not penetrate the enemy armour plate at long range—again due to poor design. I think that it is difficult to blame Churchill for these weaknesses—though it has often been done. Perhaps he must bear most responsibility for the defence of Scapa, and of Rosyth, and here the minutes of the CID meetings show his efforts to get things done against the stone-walling of the Chancellor of the Exchequer and the lethargy of the War Office.

He had faults. Examples of his lack of tact and errors of judgement have already been quoted, and many more could be found, for no great man lacks jealous detractors. Admiral de Chair, who worked closely with him as Naval Secretary, writes in *The Sea is Strong*:

> Winston certainly made us realise that he was clever and hard-working, but he was impulsive, headstrong and even at times obstinate. As a result of this, I as Naval Secretary found it difficult to keep the balance even, especially as he thought he knew more about naval personnel than any of us at the Admiralty . . . and he appeared to have an immense amount of courage and initiative. He could be exceptionally charming and interesting, but at times when crossed or corrected, he could be remarkably trying.

This is probably a reasoned criticism of the less attractive and effective aspects of the young statesman's personality. But the tributes to Churchill's time at the Admiralty during those grim years of approaching conflict are, literally, countless. History has had time, I think, to pass judgement, and Lord Kitchener anticipated the verdict admirably in May 1915, when he went to bid formal farewell of the superseded First Lord. 'There is one thing, at least,' he said, 'they can never take away from you. When the war began, you had the Fleet ready.'

8

THE FIRST FIVE MONTHS

*The War Staff was . . . a body which never was nor ever could
be a war staff as it was deficient in all characteristics that are
needed for staff work. . . . The whole of the work passes
through the Chief of Staff. There is no decentralization, and his
mind has to grapple with every problem that arises even in its
details. . . . The result of this fear to decentralize is that the
First Sea Lord and Chief of Staff are so overworked that they
cannot consider suggestions brought to them and, finally, that a
mass of officers is assembled under the Admiralty roof, many of
whom are wholly unfit for their duties.*[177]

ADMIRAL RICHMOND

BEFORE starting the story of Churchill's time as First
Lord in war, the reader should be reminded that this
book is not a history of the war at sea. Nevertheless, to
gain a comprehension of the issues at stake, one must be
aware of the main features of that struggle from the start
until May 1915. A brief description of the more important
battles and campaigns has therefore been given and the expert
will, I hope, forgive the brevity of the summaries which are
essential as a background to any appreciation of Churchill's
impact on the Royal Navy at war.

The First Sea Lord, Prince Louis, as Director of Naval
Intelligence in 1903–5, had been responsible for mobilization
arrangements, and he was anxious, as soon as he returned to
the Admiralty, that the complicated organization should be
given a peacetime test. With the agreement of the Second Sea
Lord, Jellicoe, he discussed the matter with the First Lord,
who produced in October 1913 a memorandum proposing that
in the interests of economy, instead of the 1914 summer
manœuvres there should be a test mobilization of the 2nd and
3rd Fleets, followed by a review of all three Fleets. This was
agreed by the Board. Parliament was informed in March,
orders were issued in early July, and the mobilization began
on the 15th. The Review was held at Spithead on 17–18 July,*

---

* No less than 406 warships and auxiliaries were present.

and was followed by tactical exercises in the Channel. On 23 July the 3rd Fleet ships dispersed to their home ports with orders to pay off. Thus, when the Austrian note to Serbia was received on Friday 24 July, the Fleet was still on a war footing—a wonderful piece of luck and good management.

The First Lord, after exhaustive discussions on the Saturday with the First Sea Lord and the Chief of Staff, spent the weekend with his family on the East Coast, telephoning Prince Louis at intervals. On Sunday afternoon, 25 July, he decided to return, and arrived at the Admiralty in the evening to find that Prince Louis had stopped the dispersal of the 1st Fleet from Portland. Churchill warmly approved and after he had consulted the Foreign Secretary a communiqué was drafted which announced that manœuvre leave for the 1st Fleet had been stopped and that the 2nd Fleet was remaining at its home ports, near the balance of its crews. The reservists of the 3rd Fleet had, of course, returned to their homes, as general mobilization had not yet been ordered. The situation grew worse, and on the night of 29–30 July, the 1st Fleet left Portland, east about, for Scapa Flow, and the 2nd Fleet was ordered to assemble at Portland. Churchill feared 'to bring this matter before the Cabinet, lest it should be mistakenly considered a provocative action likely to damage the chances of peace. . . . I therefore only informed the Prime Minister, who at once gave his approval.'[178] In this unusual manner, the country was made ready for the war at sea. Churchill was never afraid of taking the initiative!

As the crisis heightened, so the scale of preparation increased. On the evening of 1 August, Germany declared war on Russia, and Churchill, again with the Prime Minister's approval but without Cabinet sanction, called out the Reserves. 'The Prime Minister, who felt himself bound to the Cabinet, said not a single word but it was clear from his look that he was quite content.' Next day the Cabinet ratified the decision and general mobilization was proclaimed.

There was only one more, painful, task to be carried out. Admiral Callaghan, who had trained the Fleet for war for three years, was due to be relieved by Sir John Jellicoe on 1 October. Neither the First Lord nor the First Sea Lord thought that Callaghan's health and strength were equal to the great task facing him in war. Signals were sent to both officers—Sir John was on his way north to join the Fleet as Second-in-Command—that the change must be made at once. Jellicoe protested violently, sending no less than five telegrams, some *en clair* from railway stations on his way, asking for the matter to be reconsidered. Churchill was adamant. It was a hard but correct decision which took courage to impose.[179]

What of Churchill at this moment? He was content, and he had reason to be. The Fleet was at its war station. But Richmond noted on 5 August in his diary: 'Churchill stopped me, saying he wanted to talk about some matters. Said, "Now we have our war. The next thing is to decide how we are going to carry it on." What a statement! The Duke of Newcastle could not have made a more damning confession of inadequate preparation for war.' Here is the first of many examples of the weakness of the War Staff, which should have made firm plans.

What now was the naval situation on the eve of the Armageddon against which the Fleet had prepared for so long?

In August 1914 the High Seas Fleet contained 13 Dreadnought battleships, 4 battle-cruisers (not counting the *Blücher* which operated with them), 16 pre-Dreadnought battleships, 3 cruisers, 15 light cruisers, and 88 destroyers; numbers which were much smaller than those forecast in the pre-war scares.

Jellicoe had under his command in the Grand Fleet 21 Dreadnought battleships, 4 battle-cruisers (3 others were in the Mediterranean, 1 at Queenstown and the *Australia* in her home waters), 8 pre-Dreadnoughts (the 3rd Battle Squadron of *King Edwards*), 8 cruisers, 13 light cruisers and 42 destroyers.

The Channel Fleet consisted mainly of 14 pre-Dreadnoughts and some old cruisers, and the Harwich Force of 2 cruisers and some 40 destroyers. Only in the number of destroyers attached to the Grand Fleet was there any cause for concern; but the demands of local patrols against invasion, and of the escort of the Expeditionary Force to France made it impossible to provide more.

The initial war aims were:

(1) to block the northern and southern entrances to the North Sea, so as to stop enemy warships or commerce entering or leaving;
(2) to prevent invasion;
(3) to transport the Expeditionary Force to France;
(4) to gain control of the High Seas.

A War Staff group was early formed, consisting of the First Lord, the First Sea Lord, the Chief of the War Staff and the Secretary of the Admiralty, which met every forenoon and made plans, sent off telegrams and generally directed operations. Admiral Sir Arthur Wilson had rejoined the Admiralty and acted as an unpaid unofficial adviser when required.*

The first important decision to be taken was over the transport of the Army to France. So complete was the state of readiness, so great the superiority over the enemy, that the Admiralty was able, at the War Council on 5 August, to advise that all the regular divisions available could safely be sent over, leaving the defence from invasion or raids to the Navy and the Territorials. But Kitchener would not agree, and only four divisions and a cavalry division were sent, leaving the 4th and 6th Divisions at home. The operation, covered by the Grand Fleet, went perfectly, and before the Germans realized that the landing had taken place, the British were in the line alongside the French. The 4th Division was sent out in time for the battle of le Cateau, and on 23 August, when the situation in France was desperate, Churchill tried to get the 6th Division sent across, but again he failed. It is now known that the Germans never considered invasion.

And how was the German Fleet employed during the first few weeks of war? On 1 August, the main body was lying in the Jade river, close to Wilhelmshaven, and, contrary to all prediction, there it remained until December.

The Emperor, and the Chancellor, saw the Fleet as a valuable bargaining counter at the peace conference which they thought

---

* Admiral Wilson was anxious to attack and capture Heligoland, and Sturdee complained that he wasted much time opposing this unwise and undesirable project. Jellicoe commented later (May 1915) that Wilson 'has not realized the effect that mines and submarines have on present-day warfare'.

would be the speedy result of the land campaign. Orders were sent to the Commander-in-Chief which stressed the need to avoid risk and to preserve the Fleet. Tirpitz, the Secretary of the Navy, did not agree with this policy, but his office was purely administrative and he was ignored. No attempt was made to interfere with the passage of the Expeditionary Force; indeed, the generals believed that they could destroy the Army on land, so why risk the ships at sea? The Germans also expected a close blockade by the British Fleet and hoped to reduce their inferiority by attrition from mines and destroyer- and submarine-attacks. Thus, both the Grand Fleet and the battle-cruiser force carried out several sweeps of the North Sea during the first three weeks of August without reaction from the enemy, and, surprisingly, the first major clash of the war came in the Mediterranean.

The escape of the Goeben and the Breslau

Shortly after the operation, the First Sea Lord wrote: 'The escape of the *Goeben* must ever remain a shameful episode in the war.' He was referring to the failure of Admiral Troubridge to engage, but later analysis has shown that the whole affair was sadly mismanaged, and its consequences were to have far-reaching effects. The war at sea got off to a very bad start.

Because the scene of action was far from London, and because it was the Senior Officers on the spot who drew up the operation orders and who tried to carry them out, it is not suitable, in a book of this title, to make a detailed analysis. I have no intention, therefore, of subjecting the mismanagement, the errors of judgement and the lack of offensive spirit to the searchlight of criticism. But the guidance and information provided by the Admiralty for the Commander-in-Chief have been widely, and rightly, criticized, and this aspect of the sorry chain of events deserves careful study.

A very short summary is first necessary to provide a background against which decisions may be judged. The story starts six days before the war with Germany opened, when the Admiralty first warned the Commander-in-Chief in the Mediterranean, Sir Archibald Berkeley Milne, that war was possible and that the *Goeben,* a modern battle-cruiser, and the *Breslau,* a light cruiser, were in the Adriatic. It was not known what the ships would do if war came. They might attack the French transports carrying the North African army to Marseilles. They might then break out into the Atlantic. They might break back into the Adriatic in order to support the Austrian Fleet, based on Pola. Doubt about the attitude of Austria and, in particular, Italy, also complicated the issue. But the possibility of the ships sailing to the Dardanelles was never considered.

To deal with these two ships, the Commander-in-Chief had three battle-cruisers, four heavy cruisers, four light cruisers and sixteen destroyers. The French Fleet, the war plan of which was based on protecting the army being transported from North Africa, was reasonably strong in all classes of ship, though there were only one Dreadnought and six other reasonably modern battleships. It would certainly appear that the Allied fleets were more than equal to their task, even assuming that the Austrian Fleet had to be watched.

On 30 July the Admiralty signalled to the Commander-in-Chief that there was a possibility of war, and that his first task was to help defend the French transports by taking up a covering position and trying to bring to action any fast German ship, particularly the *Goeben.* He was also further instructed not to be brought to action at this stage against superior force, unless in a general engagement in which the French were taking part.[180]

The *Goeben* and *Breslau* arrived at Messina on 2 August. They left on 3 August and, at daylight on 4 August, Bône and Philippeville were bombarded. The *Indomitable* and the *Indefatigable* were then north of Bizerte *en route* to Gibraltar, where they had been ordered to prevent a break-out into the Atlantic,* and by the greatest good luck they met the German ships steering east after the bombardment. War had not yet been declared between Britain and Germany and the ships passed tensely with guns trained fore-and-aft. (The Captain of

---

* This fact is not mentioned in 'Naval Operations'. But an account of the *Indomitable*'s part in the action in the *Naval Review* makes it clear.

the *Indomitable* noted regretfully that the German Admiral's flag was not flying—otherwise they would have fired a salute and this might have precipitated battle.) The two battle-cruisers were joined by the light cruiser *Dublin,* and the three shadowed for the rest of the day. Before dark, however, the *Indomitable* and the *Indefatigable* were ordered to break off the chase—and later the *Dublin* lost touch. Both German ships made for Messina, where they coaled. War was declared at 11 p.m. that night, 4 August.

The *Goeben,* designed for twenty-eight knots, had severe boiler trouble which restricted her to a safe speed of eighteen knots. But during the chase she made bursts of twenty-four which were reported as twenty-seven, and so a myth of high speed dominated the chase from then on. As so often happened, the enemy was credited with a higher capability than he possessed. Everything continued to go wrong. Instead of placing a battle-cruiser at each end of the Strait of Messina, the C-in-C sent the *Indomitable* to coal at Bizerte and with the other two ships cruised to the west of Sicily, leaving a light cruiser to watch each end of the strait.

As was made clear to the Captain of the *Indomitable* when coaling at Bizerte, the French had no need for help. Their troop convoys were strongly protected, and they even offered aid to the British C-in-C. But Milne seemed mesmerized by the signal of the 30th, and was further confused by another warning from the Admiralty telling him to respect Italian neutrality and not to allow his ships within six miles of the Italian coast. On the evening of 6 August, the *Goeben* and *Breslau* left Messina by the southern entrance to the strait and, pursued by the *Gloucester,* feinted at the Adriatic, and then altered for Cape Matapan and the eastern Mediterranean.

Between the German ships and their destination was Admiral Troubridge with four armoured cruisers, while the *Dublin* and two destroyers were hurrying from Malta to intercept and attack with torpedoes. The worst part of the 'shameful episode' now followed. Admiral Troubridge, also mesmerized by the instructions to avoid action with superior force, and badly advised by his Flag Captain, refused action, and, what was worse, called off the chase.

The *Dublin* missed the *Goeben*, and the only man to emerge with credit was Captain Howard Kelly in the *Gloucester*, who never lost touch, reported clearly, and had to be ordered to break off near Cape Matapan as his bunkers were almost empty. But even now there was a good chance of catching the Germans. The *Goeben* was only making eighteen knots, and the ships had to stop at Denusa in the Aegean to coal. But the C-in-C showed no sense of urgency. He took all three battle-cruisers into Malta to coal—the *Indomitable* was almost full up and should have been sent on alone, and only the *Indefatigable* was really short. Then fate stepped in again. At 2.30 p.m. on 8 August, a clerk in the Admiralty sent off, in error, a telegram saying that war with Austria had started. In accordance with previous arrangements, the C-in-C broke off the chase and steered for the Adriatic entrance. When the mistake had been made good, more time had been lost. The German ships did not enter the Dardanelles till the evening of the 10th, when they finally escaped for the third time.

Opinions differ on the political effects of the coup. It is now known that although a political agreement was signed between Germany and Turkey on 2 August it was not supported by the Sultan and some of his Ministers, notably the Minister of Marine. From 3 August, when the *Goeben* was ordered to make for the Dardanelles, to the 10th, the German Ambassador in Constantinople could not obtain agreement for the ships to pass the forts at the entrance to the straits, and for two days they had to cruise aimlessly in the Aegean. It is a fair assumption, I think, that if they had been brought to action, and sunk, the pro-Ally faction would have been strengthened and the attitude of Turkey, which did not in the end declare war until 5 November, changed.

The scale of the disaster was not at first understood in the Admiralty, and one early minute talked of the 'harmless fugitives'.[181] After some questioning about some of his actions, the C-in-C's conduct was formally approved—Churchill remarked that 'the explanation is satisfactory; the result unsatisfactory'. Only when Fisher took over as First Sea Lord was the C-in-C's handling criticized, and, allowing for Fisher's known prejudice, it is clear from the detailed analysis that

Milne's performance was very poor*—even after taking into account the muddling signals from London. Troubridge's conduct was castigated from the start. A court of inquiry was quickly appointed, which recommended trial by court martial. But Troubridge was acquitted, to the surprise of the Fleet and the chagrin of the Board, the implied criticism of whose instructions to the senior officers afloat was one of the main reasons for acquittal.

But the most worrying aspect of the affair is the complete lack of any admission of error by the War Staff. I cannot discover who drafted the fatal telegram of 30 July, which so dominated and distorted the conduct of the chase. But the First Lord discussed it with Prince Loiug.† And he must have seen, too, the telegram about not infrinings Italian neutrality. The truth is, I think, that the War Staff was still incompetent, and proper machinery for the direction of the war at sea had still to be constructed. Much blame must be distributed, but it is difficult to decide who should bear the brunt. All concerned must share it.‡

From the Mediterranean, attention must now shift to the North Sea.§

---

* The *National Review* of August 1923 contains a defence of his actions by Milne. It does not convince.

† He also accepted full responsibility for it, remarking, 'So far as the English language may serve as a vehicle of thought, the words employed appear to express the intentions we have formed.'

‡ The more one reads *Naval Operations*, Vols. I and II, the more one realizes how the author was shackled by the Admiralty which resented any criticism of its work or indeed of that of senior officers afloat. There are many omissions of errors and no candid comment.

§ There is a little-known sequel to the escape of the *Goeben* and *Breslau*. In early 1916, after the evacuation of the Gallipoli peninsula, widespread minefields were laid at the entrance to the Dardanelles, watched by a few ships, which were intended to block the exit to any Turkish forces. In January 1918, after a long period of inactivity, the *Goeben* and *Breslau*, accompanied by some Turkish destroyers, sortied from the straits with the aim of sinking any British ships encountered and attacking Mudros Harbour. They gained complete surprise, and sank two small British monitors, but the *Breslau* then struck several mines and swiftly foundered. The *Goeben* came to her aid, but was seriously damaged by

Winston and Jackie

Winston in the cockpit of an early Short biplane

HMS *Queen Elizabeth* at the Dardanelles (from a painting by Charles Dixon, now in the National Maritime Museum, Lambeth)

British Dreadnoughts

The sinking of the *Blücher*

The Prime Minister and Sir Dudley Pound, 1943

The action in the Heligoland Bight

The action off Heligoland on 28 August 1914 was not a major engagement. British losses were insignificant. No ships were lost and only a few damaged, with thirty-five killed and some forty wounded. The Germans lost three light cruisers, a destroyer and over one thousand officers and men, but the effect on the war at sea was out of all proportion to the scale of the encounter. Its most important result was to increase among the German sailors the feeling of inferiority which Berlin had tried to counter by ridiculing the apparent inactivity of the Grand Fleet since the first days of the war. In addition, the sudden appearance of the British off Heligoland confirmed the early view of the Kaiser that the High Seas Fleet should avoid battle and await the attrition of the British from mines and torpedoes.

It all started on 23 August when Keyes, the Commodore 'S' (Submarines) at Harwich, proposed a plan to cut off and destroy the regular patrol of destroyers which operated off Heligoland out of the Ems and Jade rivers. The First Lord supported any scheme savouring of the offensive.

... on 24th, I presided at a meeting in my room between him and Commodore 'T' [Tyrwhitt] and the First Sea Lord and the Chief of the Staff [Sturdee]. The plan which the two Commodores outlined was at once simple and daring. Since the first hours of the war our submarines had prowled about in the Heligoland Bight. They had now accumulated in a period of three weeks accurate information about the dispositions of the enemy. . . . They proposed to take two flotillas (24 boats in each) of our best destroyers and two light cruisers from Harwich by night and to reach just before dawn a point inside the Northern coast of the Heligoland Bight not far from the Island of Sylt. From this point they would make a left-handed scoop. . . .[182]

The details given in *The World Crisis* are not entirely accurate, and also omit any mention, for instance, of Admiral

---

more mines, and retreated through the straits. Owing to a navigational error, the ship grounded in the narrows and remained there for several days, while unsuccessful bombing attacks were made by the Allied air forces. The *Goeben* was towed away, but took no further active part in the war.

Christian with his force 'C' of old cruisers, who was the Senior Officer and who was supposed to control the action—though how he could do so is a mystery still. The preparation of the plan was not properly co-ordinated. The first idea was to station submarines off Heligoland, which were to lure the regular dawn destroyer patrol to the westward, while the attacking force of two flotillas led by Commodore 'T' (Torpedoes) in the *Arethusa* would move down from the north and cut off the enemy. Two battle-cruisers from the Humber were to be stationed north-west of the attacking force in support, while Admiral Christian with his elderly cruisers was to lie off Terschelling, also in support.

As soon as Admiral Jellicoe at Scapa heard of the plan he proposed moving the Grand Fleet down, because operations off Ostend with the Royal Marine Brigade were also in the wind and he thought that the High Seas Fleet might come out. He was told by the Admiralty, however, that the Grand Fleet was not required but that the battle-cruisers might come in support. Accordingly, he decided to send Admiral Beatty in the *Lion*, with two more battle-cruisers and Commodore Goodenough commanding the six ships of the 1st Light Cruiser Squadron to join the two battle-cruisers from the Humber.

Unfortunately, the message from the Admiralty giving news of these additions to the forces engaged, which was sent at noon on 27 August, reached only Admiral Christian, and neither Commodore 'T' nor Commodore 'S' had any idea of the increase in strength. Nor did Admiral Beatty have any inkling of the instructions given to the destroyers or the position of our own submarines. As might be expected under such circumstances, the encounter was very confused, especially as during the night of 27 August the Germans guessed from the increased W/T traffic that some sort of offensive operation was in train and quickly decided to set a trap for the trappers by sending out a far stronger force of cruisers and destroyers than was normal.

The action divides itself into three phases. At dawn (about 06.00 on the 28th) Commodore Tyrwhitt in the *Arethusa* and Captain Blunt in the *Fearless* were leading south as arranged when they fell in with two light cruisers and a number of destroyers. A brisk action at short range followed in which the enemy were severely damaged before Commodore 'T', by now under fire from the guns of Heligoland, withdrew to the westward. One German torpedo boat was then found and sunk.

Shortly afterwards, Commodore 'S' in the *Lurcher*, a destroyer from which he directed his submarines, sighted some cruisers to the north-west of Heligoland, whom he thought to be enemy. They were the *Lowestoft* and the *Nottingham*, which Goodenough had detached to support Commodore 'T' when the signals reporting the action were received. A game of blind-man's buff followed. Keyes shadowed the 'enemy' and Goodenough altered course to support him. It was not until two hours later that Keyes realized that the ships he had been shadowing were British. The last move brought the 1st Light Cruiser Squadron straight over the submarine *E6*, also ignorant of its presence in the area, and Lieutenant-Commander Talbot was just about to fire a torpedo at the *Southampton* when he noticed the white ensign.

The second phase of the battle came between 10.00 and 11.30. Commodore 'T' with his flotilla had stopped for a short time to effect repairs and this had allowed three or four German light cruisers to get uncomfortably close. There was another sharp action in which two of the enemy were damaged and the *Mainz* crippled, but the *Arethusa* was in a bad way and the Commodore called to the battle-cruisers for help.

Beatty had a difficult decision. Neither Keyes nor Tyrwhitt had included their positions in the signals reporting the actions. Nor did he know where his own submarines were. He knew that there might be German U-boats and mines in the area. After consulting his Chief of Staff he decided to support Tyrwhitt, and at once steered for the sound of the guns at full speed. His intervention came at a critical moment. In this third phase the *Lion* and the other battle-cruisers sighted the *Arethusa* at 12.31, opened fire on the *Köln* at 12.38, engaged the *Stettin* at 12.54 and the *Ariadne* at 12.56. By 13.09 Beatty had ordered the 'retire', and it only remained to arrange for the damaged ships to be helped back to harbour.

In the end, the result had been most satisfactory. The enemy had been given a sound beating on his own doorstep and British losses were very slight. In addition to the three light cruisers sunk, three other German light cruisers were badly damaged as well as several destroyers.

But although our ships had shown great dash, and officers and men had fought bravely and with skill, luck had been with us. As Churchill put it: 'Several awkward embarrassments followed from this [bad staff work] and might easily have led to disastrous mistakes. However, fortune was steady, and the initial surprise, together with the resolute offensive, carried us safely through.'[183] But the surprise was not so complete as he believed when he wrote those words.

In his comments on the action, Admiral Jellicoe drew attention to three weaknesses which might easily have led to disaster. The first was the ignorance of the presence of the battle-cruisers and the light cruisers by any of the Harwich force engaged in the action. The second was the lack of information in the signals of Commodore 'T' and Commodore 'S' reporting engagements. They left out their position, course and speed and made it very difficult for Beatty. The third was Beatty's lack of knowledge of the plan, and in particular of the position of the British submarines.

Jellicoe made several recommendations for improvement, most of which were accepted by the Admiralty. But the remarkable feature of the official papers is the complete lack of self-criticism by the War Staff for their appalling staff work. As for the Chief of Staff, Sturdee's only comment was to attack Commodore 'S'. He minuted to the First Sea Lord on 9 September:

> These reports point to the undesirability of a destroyer [*Lurcher*] being allowed to be working independently of the different squadrons taking part in a combined operation.
>
> Personally I believe that the presence of submarines except attached to one of the Squadrons of above water ships is undesirable. If they are present they should not be directed by a surface vessel.
>
> Commodore 'S' in the *Lurcher* did good service in saving life, but his movement confused our forces and it should not be repeated.[184]

This I find self-contradictory and unhelpful comment.

Richmond, who was deputy Director of Operations, was an exception with his strong criticisms of the War Staff, but he complained that no one listened to him. In his diary for 30 August, he writes:

> Anything worse than the orders for the operations last Friday [28th August] I have never seen. A mass of latitudes and longitudes, no expression to show the object of the sweep, and one grievous error in actual position which was over twenty minutes [miles] out of place. Besides this the hasty manner in which, all unknown to the submarines, the 1st Light Cruiser Squadron suddenly turned up in a wholly unexpected direction, thereby running the gravest danger from our own submarines. The weather was fairly foggy, ships came up with one another unexpectedly, and with such omissions and errors in the plan it was truly fortunate that we had no accidents.[185]

The First Lord took a close interest in the analysis of the action, in the improvements to the organization required, in the dispatch to be published in the *London Gazette*, and in the list of awards for the action. He read and initialled every report, he commented on most and he took no complacent view of the outcome, though he viewed Beatty's decision to support the smaller ships well. 'It was a fine feat of arms, vindicated by success.'

Luck had been with the British, for they had made their mistakes but these had not proved expensive. The Naval Staff had undergone its first test of a battle in the North Sea; and not only had it proved incompetent in planning and unhelpful in direction, but it had not realized how seriously it had failed.

Losses from U-boat attack

Not long afterwards, the disaster to the *Hogue*, *Cressy* and *Aboukir* was to confirm that changes of outlook, method and possibly of people were overdue. The Press and many politicians and naval officers accused Churchill of overriding the Naval War Staff and being directly responsible for the disaster. But the facts are quite different, and if the War Staff had listened to the First Lord the tragedy would have been avoided.

During a visit to the Grand Fleet on 17 September the First Lord had heard the expression 'live-bait squadron', and on urgent inquiry found that it referred to cruiser squadron 'C', which made regular routine patrols of the Dogger Bank area and of the Broad Fourteens, off the Dutch coast. On return to the Admiralty, Churchill sent to the First Sea Lord a minute which, among other points, said:

> The 'Bacchantes' ought not to continue on this beat. The risk . . . is not justified by any service they can render. The narrow seas, being the nearest point to the enemy, should be kept by a small number of good modern ships. The 'Bacchantes' should go to the western entrance of the Channel and set Bethell's battleships— and later Wemyss' cruisers—free for convoy and other duties. The first four 'Arethusas' should join the flotillas of the narrow seas.[186]

The First Sea Lord agreed and instructed the Chief of the War Staff to make the necessary arrangements. Next day Admiral Christian, who was on patrol off the Dogger Bank with three *Bacchante* cruisers, but unescorted by destroyers due to the weather, reported that he intended to remain in the area. Before his signal had reached the Admiralty, he had been told: 'The Dogger Bank patrol need not be continued. Weather too bad for destroyers to go to sea. Arrange with cruisers to watch Broad Fourteens.' Simultaneously, Commodore 'T' was told to reinstitute the Broad Fourteens destroyer patrol next morning, so as to protect the cruisers.

By dawn on 20 September, Admiral Christian was off the Maas Light vessel with four cruisers. His flagship was due to coal and the weather was too bad for boatwork, so he left the Senior Officer in charge in the *Aboukir* and returned to harbour. The weather also forced the destroyers which had left Harwich to return. That day, and during the 21st, the cruisers kept their patrol alone. During the night of the 21st an easing of the weather allowed Commodore 'T' to leave harbour, but he was still fifty miles off when, early on the 22nd, the three cruisers were attacked by *U9* and all sunk. They had been steering a steady course at nine knots in line abreast, in weather which had much improved, when the *Aboukir* was torpedoed. The other ships went to her aid and were sunk in turn. In this wholly unnecessary disaster, 60 officers and 1,400 men were lost.

The report of the court of inquiry blamed Captain Drummond, the Senior Officer, for failure to zigzag when the weather moderated and for ordering the other ships to close him after the attack.[187] The Captains of the *Hogue* and the *Cressy* were blamed for stopping their ships to pick up survivors, and all three were blamed for posting insufficient lookouts against submarines.

But paragraphs three and five of the report contain strong criticism of the Admiralty.

3. It is not possible for the Court to measure the degree of blame, if any, attached to those who directed the movements of the three cruisers concerned, since they are not acquainted with the war plans and policy of the Admiralty, but the responsibility for the presence of the cruisers undoubtedly rests with the Admiralty telegram of the 19th September. . . .

5. In the opinion of the Court, a cruiser patrol established in a limited area at so short a distance from the enemy's submarine base was certain to be attacked by submarines . . .

The First Sea Lord took grave exception to these remarks.[188] But the First Lord would not agree to the court being informed that its remarks were 'very improper', for he concurred in their view. He had already sent a number of searching questions to the War Staff on 29 September, one in particular asking why, in view of his minute of 18 September, the cruisers were on the Broad Fourteens.[189] The reply of the Chief of Staff, Sturdee, was unconvincing, and did not answer the main question.[190] It was clear from this reply and from the evidence given at the inquiry that not only should the force have never been there, but also the object of the patrol was not understood and the arrangements for command were imprecise. The Senior Officer in the *Aboukir*, for instance, did not realize that it was his duty to inform the shore when the weather moderated sufficiently to allow destroyers to come out. His movements also showed a complete lack of appreciation of the danger from submarine attack and a lack of guidance from above.

Again, with the exception of the First Lord, and of Richmond, complacency continued.

The attitude of the Chief of Staff seemed to be that it was hard luck on *him*. Leveson [Director of Operations] said in my hearing that 'it couldn't be helped'. We had only to copy the example of the Germans and attach a couple or so of destroyers to each cruiser patrolling, and to avoid regular patrols. Common sense would have told this. I wrote a paper to Leveson some time ago urging that it was dangerous to put vessels on a regular patrol where their movements could be reported but nothing came of it.[191]

Change of First Sea Lord

By the time these operation reports had been dealt with, Churchill had been very active in many other fields. As a personal friend of Sir John French, the Commander-in-Chief in France, he had paid several visits to the Army headquarters,* and as a result the expeditions to Dunkirk and Ostend by the Royal Marine Brigade and to Antwerp by the Royal Naval Division were arranged.† The Navy had also carried out several arduous and valuable 'army-support' operations off the Belgian coast, and two squadrons of the Royal Naval Air Service had been based at Dunkirk, from where they attacked Germany and worked with the Army in the field.

On 3 September the Admiralty accepted responsibility for the air defence of the country—not because it wished to or because it was prepared, but because the War Office and the RFC were even more incapable of doing the job. 'The War Office viewed this development with disfavour, and claimed that they alone should be responsible for home defence. When asked how they proposed to discharge this duty, they admitted sorrowfully that they had not got the machines and could not get the money. They adhered however to the principle.'[192]

---

* Kitchener at first approved, or at least acquiesced in, these trips. Later he came to believe that Churchill was interfering in his affairs, and complained to the Prime Minister.
† The Royal Naval Division was formed at Churchill's request from surplus naval personnel and civilian volunteers.

This added responsibility increased the burden on the Admiralty administration and on the First Lord himself. But I do not intend to discuss at length these affairs, fascinating though they are to read, about which there has been so much argument. Viewed against the background of the whole war at sea, they seem sideshows, though with luck Antwerp might have become decisive.

Churchill has been severely criticized for his conduct of affairs during the Antwerp operation, and many unjust accusations have been made against him—in particular the charge that he went over to Antwerp without permission. The facts are quite different. He was invited by Grey and Lord Kitchener on 3 October to visit the port, and he spent four days in Belgium, virtually taking charge of the operations at Antwerp and offering his resignation as First Lord in order to command in the field—an offer which was refused.

The operations at Antwerp were purely military—the men of the Royal Naval Division which took part had received a very short training as soldiers—and were aimed at prolonging the Allied front line so as to save much of Belgium from the German invader. But other than this brief mention, which explains how Churchill was attacked for his part in the affair, the Antwerp operations have no place in a naval history of the war.

In October, possibly because of apparent Admiralty preoccupation with subsidiary operations, public opinion became restive, and an agitation taking the form of attacks on the First Lord and First Sea Lord was raised. The gutter Press howled at Prince Louis's German birth—a ridiculous charge, for no more loyal subject to the Crown ever lived. The *Globe*, which was the only quality newspaper to join the campaign against Prince Louis, said for example:

We receive day by day a constantly growing stream of correspondence, in which the wisdom of having an officer who is of German birth as the professional head of the Navy is assailed in varying terms. We would glady dismiss all these letters from our mind, but we cannot. They are too numerous, too insistent, and too obviously the expression of a widespread feeling.[194]

There is no doubt, too, that some senior retired officers had always resented Battenberg's position and talents. Prince Louis himself wrote to Fisher in 1906: '. . . I heard by chance what the reasons were which [Admirals] Beresford and Lambton and all the tribe gave out . . . against [me] . . . that I was a d——d German, who had no business in the British Navy and that the Service for that reason did not trust me. . . .'[193]

On the other hand, it must be admitted that there is evidence that Prince Louis was worn out after his time as Second and then First Sea Lord, and that his health had suffered. He took a rather passive role in the direction of Admiralty business and the civilian members of the Board were worried by his inactivity.[195] Lord Esher, too, writes: 'It has been felt for some time that the Board of Admiralty requires renovating. . . . More driving power is required and they [Fisher and Wilson] will supply it.'[196]

Towards the end of October, Churchill asked Prince Louis to resign and on 30 October Lord Fisher was recalled to office.[197] It was just too late to avert disaster.

Coronel

On 1 November, Admiral Sir Christopher Cradock commanding a British force was heavily defeated by a German squadron under Admiral von Spee off the west coast of South America, a reverse which shook the nation's confidence in the Navy and which correspondingly encouraged the Germans.

There can be no doubt that the basic reasons for the disaster must be attributed to the faulty dispositions of the British ships available, but before considering the part which the Admiralty, and the First Lord in particular, played, it is necessary to summarize briefly the course of events.

Cradock's force, consisting of the cruisers *Good Hope* and *Monmouth*, the light cruiser *Glasgow*, and the armed merchant cruiser *Otranto*, confronted the cruisers *Scharnhorst* and *Gneisenau* and the light cruisers *Dresden, Leipzig* and *Nürnberg*. Of Cradock's ships, only the *Glasgow* was modern, well manned and well trained. The *Otranto* was no warship and should never have been in the battle line. The *Good Hope* and

Monmouth were obsolete, elderly ships dragged out of reserve
at the start of the war and manned mainly by reservists, who
were not given the time or opportunity to bring the ships into
an efficient condition by target-practice and exercises. The
Scharnhorst and *Gneisenau* were the crack gunnery ships of the
German Navy, the whole squadron was modern, and the ships
had been long in commission and fully trained. Unless great
luck intervened with a chance hit in a vulnerable spot, there
could only be one result of an action between such disparate
forces. This last possibility must, I think, have been the main
reason why Cradock engaged against such terrible odds, for
he knew that the German ships were far from a repair base
and that even comparatively minor damage might be disastrous for them.

Churchill wrote:

> I cannot accept for the Admiralty any responsibility for what
> followed. The first rule of war is to concentrate superior strength
> for decisive action and to avoid division of forces or engaging in
> detail. The Admiral showed by his telegram that he appreciated
> this. The Admiralty orders explicitly approved his early assertion
> of these elementary principles. We were not, therefore, anxious
> about the safety of Admiral Cradock's squadron.[198]

I believe that this is far too sweeping a statement, and that,
while considerable responsibility must rest with the Admiral
for his gallant but ineffective decision to engage greatly
superior forces, it was due to faulty appreciation in Whitehall
that he was ever placed in such a disastrous position. What is
more, there is no doubt that Churchill himself *was* anxious,
though his fears were not shared by the complacent War Staff.
What is far more interesting is to try to judge how much of this
responsibility must rest on the shoulders of Churchill himself.*

The task of finding and sinking von Spee's squadron, which

---

* I am much indebted to Captain Geoffrey Bennett's *Coronel and the
Falklands* (Batsford, 1962). His account of the complicated events lead-
ing up to the action is very clear, and he gives the most complete account
I have read. I believe that some of his judgements are too hard on the
Admiralty and too kind to those on the spot, but this does not detract
from the excellence of the narrative.

was cruising in the Pacific near the Carolines at the start of the war, was to be immensely complicated by a number of other problems. The departure of the *Emden*, detached by von Spee in mid-August for the Indian Ocean, was one. The need to escort the Australian and New Zealand troop convoys to Europe was another, and the presence of the *Karlsruhe* in the South Atlantic and the *Königsberg* off the East African coast were others. There were military operations in west and south-west Africa to be given naval support and expeditions to be taken to Samoa and German New Guinea. And, finally, the need to watch the Dardanelles for signs of the *Goeben* and *Breslau* diverted further forces.

From the start, it had been appreciated both in the Admiralty and by the senior officers abroad that von Spee's most probable destination was the South American coast. Thence he might either round the Horn or pass through the newly opened Panama Canal. On 1 September, the Admiralty warned Cradock that von Spee was likely to arrive with the *Scharnhorst* and *Gneisenau* at the Magellan Straits or on the west coast of South America, and told him that the *Defence*, a modern armoured cruiser, and the *Canopus*, an old battleship, would be sent to join him. The signal specified:

> Until *Defence* joins, keep at least *Canopus* and one 'county' class with your flagship. As soon as you have superior force, search the Magellan Straits with squadron, being ready to return and cover River Plate or according to information search north as far as Valparaiso. Break up the German trade and destroy the German cruisers.

This signal can be criticized, for it is difficult to see how he could have broken up German trade and destroyed German twenty-three-knot cruisers with a force shackled to a battleship of sixteen knots. But the first serious error was made when, after being 'lost' for some weeks, von Spee gave away his position by bombarding the newly captured Samoa, and then, after feinting to the north-west, steered for Easter Island, far to the eastward.

This feint deceived the War Staff into signalling on 16 September:

Situation changed. *Scharnhorst* and *Gneisenau* appeared off Samoa on 14th September . . . and left steering NW. . . . German trade on west coast of America is to be attacked at once. . . . Cruisers now need not be concentrated. Two cruisers and an armed liner would appear sufficient for Magellan Straits and west coast. Report what you propose about *Canopus*. . . .

However, on 7 October, Cradock received a message from the Admiralty:

. . . it appears that *Scharnhorst* and *Gneisenau* are working across to South America. You must be prepared to meet them in company, possibly with a *Dresden* scouting for them. *Canopus* should accompany *Glasgow*, *Monmouth* and *Otranto*, the ships to search and protect trade in combination. . . . If you propose *Good Hope* to go, leave *Monmouth* on east coast. . . .

In reply, Cradock sent off two signals which were received in London on 12 October. The main features were, firstly, that he had 'ordered *Canopus* to Falkland Islands where I intend to concentrate and avoid division of forces', and secondly, a request for the formation of another squadron, to be stationed on the east coast, large enough to bring the German forces to action if they were able to evade his own squadron.

Churchill was clearly worried by these signals, which were not well worded, and commented:

It would be best for the British ships to keep within supporting distance of one another, whether in the Straits or near the Falklands, and to postpone the cruise along the west coast until the *Scharnhorst-Gneisenau* situation is cleared up. They and not the trade are our quarry for the moment. . . .[199]

But the First Sea Lord was satisfied that Cradock's intentions were to search for the enemy, and a reply was sent on 14 October:

Your combination of *Good Hope, Canopus, Monmouth, Glasgow* and *Otranto* for combined operations concurred in. Stoddart in *Carnarvon* has been ordered to Montevideo. . . . *Defence* ordered to join *Carnarvon*. He will also have *Cornwall, Bristol* (and two armed liners) under his orders. . . .

Thus the Admiralty had accepted Cradock's suggestion of a

second squadron, but at the expense of the *Defence.* The signal was also based on the false assumption that Cradock had concentrated all his ships at the Falklands, whereas only the *Good Hope* and *Canopus* were there.

When the *Canopus* arrived at the Falklands, the Captain reported to Cradock, wrongly, that his ship could only steam at twelve knots, and the Admiralty was so informed.[200]

On 24 October, Cradock signalled that the *Good Hope* had left Port Stanley via Cape Horn, and that the *Canopus* was following with the colliers. Then on 27 October, while coaling on the Chilean coast, he sent:

> . . . with reference to orders to search for enemy and our great desire for early success, consider it impracticable on account of *Canopus*'s slow speed, to find and destroy enemy squadron. Consequently, have ordered *Defence* to join me after calling at Montevideo for orders. *Canopus* will be employed on necessary convoying of colliers. . . .

This, I believe, is the vital signal which should have rung the alarm bells at the Admiralty. Churchill was worried and minuted: 'This telegram is very obscure and I do not understand what Cradock intends or wishes.' But the War Staff were not alarmed and, in reply, minuted complacently on 29 October:

> The situation on the west coast seems safe. If *Gneisenau* and *Scharnhorst* have gone north, they will meet eventually *Idzuma,** *Newcastle* and *Hizen,** moving south and will be forced south on *Glasgow* and *Monmouth* who have good speed and draw them south onto *Good Hope* and *Canopus* who should keep within supporting distance of each other.

So Cradock was told that the *Defence* would not be sent to him, although the signal did not reach him till 1 November. It was too late, and that night the *Good Hope* and *Monmouth* were sunk.

On 30 October, Lord Fisher had become First Sea Lord, and Churchill recounts:

---

* Japanese ships. Both were old and slow and were no match for the German ships.

As soon as he entered the Admiralty, I took him to the War Room and went over with him in two hours the positions and tasks of every vessel. . . . The critical point was clearly in South American waters. Speaking of Admiral Cradock's position, I said 'You don't suppose he'll try to fight them without the *Canopus*?' He did not give any decided reply.[201]

On 3 November, before news of the battle on the 1st had arrived, firm news of the German squadron was received and a signal at once dispatched. '*Defence* has been ordered to join your flag with all dispatch. *Glasgow* should keep in touch with enemy. You should keep in touch with *Glasgow* concentrating the rest of your squadron including *Canopus* . . .' The new First Sea Lord had acted vigorously, but 'we were already talking to a void'.

Criticism of Cradock would be churlish. His motives were magnificent. His courage was complete. He was blamed by the Cabinet for not remaining with the *Canopus*, and this must ever remain the main charge against him. But it is known that he was determined to avoid the fate of a Troubridge, and thus fear of being thought afraid may have sent him and his squadron to their deaths.[202]

A biographer must guard against the danger of whitewashing his subject, but deep reflection reaches the conclusion that Churchill should not be blamed for these appalling blunders. It was he who sounded the first note of warning, and it was the War Staff who complacently advised that all was well. It is easy to criticize a civilian for believing that two old cruisers and a very old and slow battleship could find and destroy von Spee, but there is evidence that his naval advisers believed this too.

The Falkland Islands

One hour after the news of Coronel reached London, Churchill and Fisher were hard at work on the next step. Two possible courses were considered to be open to von Spee—to transit the Panama Canal and operate in the West Indies and North Atlantic, or to pass into the South Atlantic and then attack trade or interfere with the military expeditions to Africa. In fact, he had been advised to make his best way home via the South Atlantic, as all ships were short of ammunition and no reserves were available to him.

To guard against the first possibility, the *Princess Royal* was sent to the western Atlantic from the battle-cruiser force. Churchill would have sent one other battle-cruiser and the *Defence* to guard against the second. But Fisher insisted on sending two capital ships, and Jellicoe was ordered to detach the *Invincible* and the *Inflexible* to Plymouth to prepare for service abroad. After a brush with Devonport dockyard over the time needed for preparation and repairs, the ships sailed on 11 November, two days earlier than forecast. Advised by Fisher, the First Lord had written the signal to Devonport ordering the ships to sail, if necessary with workmen still on board, in his own hand. The new team at the Admiralty had reacted promptly.

Fisher was determined to remove Sturdee from the post of Chief of the War Staff, believing that he was responsible for Coronel. After Sturdee had turned down the job of Commander-in-Chief, Far East, because the headquarters was ashore, Churchill persuaded Fisher to appoint him in command of the forces in the South Atlantic, and accordingly he sailed with his flag in the *Invincible*.

Although the Admiralty had reacted so quickly, and although he had, before sailing, helped Admiral Jackson draft his own instructions for Fisher's approval, Sturdee showed little sense of urgency. He stopped to examine merchant ships *en route*, did not hurry his coaling, and planned a two-day rest at the Abrolhos Rocks. But Captain Luce of the *Glasgow*, who joined him there, persuaded him to sail one day early, and the force arrived just in time.

Entering Port Stanley on the afternoon of 7 December, all ships at once commenced to make good defects and to coal, but only three colliers were available and the process was slow. So, when von Spee arrived off the harbour at dawn next morning, 8 December, the British force was not ready, for only the *Glasgow* and the *Carnarvon* had finished coaling, the *Bristol* had fires died out and the *Cornwall* had an engine opened up for repairs.

As soon as the leading enemy ship, the *Gneisenau*, was in

range, the *Canopus*, which had grounded herself inside the harbour and was acting as a fort, opened fire, the shots falling close. The Germans turned away and shortly after sighted the tripod masts of the battle-cruisers and at once made off. The *Canopus* had prevented an unpleasant situation and given time for the colliers to be cast off and the ships to be got to sea. By ten o'clock the whole squadron, except for the *Bristol*, had left harbour and the chase was on. The result was as inevitable as at Coronel. The *Scharnhorst* and *Gneisenau* were sunk by the *Inflexible* and the *Invincible*. The *Kent* sank the *Nürnberg*, and the *Cornwall* and the *Glasgow* sank the *Leipzig*. Only the *Dresden* escaped, to be sunk three months later by the tenacious *Glasgow*.

The aftermath of this annihilating victory was marred by Fisher's attempts to discredit Sturdee, who only received the honour due to him in 1916. There was a bitter exchange over the search for the *Dresden*, and Fisher was also angry with Sturdee because he had not reprimanded the *Bristol* for errors after the main action. But the First Lord refused to allow Fisher to banish Sturdee by leaving him on the station in a cruiser, and he came home in his flagship, being appointed shortly after to command of a battle squadron in the Grand Fleet.

Sturdee maintained later that his dispatches had been 'doctored', but although he had a justifiable complaint against his cold reception, I do not think the charge is fair. Churchill's minute to the Chief of Staff on the subject (3 Jan. 1915) reads: 'An officer from your department should make a reduced draft of these dispatches and enclosures for publication. Moderate limits to be observed and anything likely to assist enemy omitted.'[203] The task was carried out by Captain Richmond, on behalf of the new Director of Operations, Captain Thomas Jackson.

The results of the battle cheered up the nation and Press criticism was reduced at once. The recall of Lord Fisher seemed to have been justified. Moreover, the *Emden* had been sunk, the *Königsberg* trapped in the Rufiji River and two armed liners sunk. Except for the closely hunted *Dresden* and the *Karlsruhe*, the high seas were clear of enemy surface ships; the

Karlsruhe had in fact been sunk by internal explosion, though this was not then known. Trade could run freely and military expeditions sail unprotected. Thus by December 1914 the first phase, the clearance of the seas, was complete.

The redeployment of the cruisers from foreign stations and the return of the detached battle-cruisers came only just in time to quieten Jellicoe, with whom the First Lord had been conducting a long and rather acrimonious correspondence. Jellicoe was worried by the detachment of three battle-cruisers, and some of his battleships were in trouble with defects.

Fisher, although he had his dark moments when he wanted Jellicoe to avoid action, was sympathetic, but unconvinced by his pleas, and supported the First Lord. He remained, however, in close touch with Jellicoe with whom he corresponded frequently.*

After the war Churchill wrote of these days:

> [Jellicoe] drew severe comparisons between the German Fleet and his own. He was a master of this kind of argument. From his own side, he deducted any ship which had any defect however temporary, however small—even defects which would not have prevented her taking her place in the line in an emergency. He sometimes also deducted two or three of the most powerful battleships in the world which had newly joined his command because they were not trained up to the full level of efficiency of the others. . . . He next proceeded to deal with the enemy. He always credited them with more ships than we now know they had, or were then thought likely to have.[204]

Perhaps this picture is overdrawn. But Jellicoe did suffer from pessimism, and while one must sympathize with his worries the facts as we now know them show that Churchill and Fisher were right. It seems certain that the reaction against Jellicoe which so obsessed Churchill after the war, and which colours his account of Jutland, stems from these long and wearing wrangles about the comparative strengths of the fleets.

---

* One of his first letters after his return includes the words: '. . . at once telegraph me if you want anything or wish anything altered or doubt the wisdom of any orders you get!' (Jellicoe Papers).

The Scarborough Raid

Although not chronologically correct, it is convenient to conclude this chapter with comments on two other actions, both in the North Sea, during which the newly inspired War Staff put up a better performance which was marred only by bad luck and some incompetence among certain of the senior officers afloat. They are the Scarborough raid and the Dogger Bank battle.

Early in December 1914 Fisher had a hunch that the Germans would take advantage of the absence of the three battle-cruisers from the Fleet by carrying out a raid on the East Coast. His instincts were correct, though he did not get the date right, but fortunately on 14 December Room 40, which had been fully operating for only five weeks as a cryptographic intelligence centre, intercepted and decoded the German orders for an offensive operation by the five battle-cruisers of the Striking Group. From them, it was learned that the enemy would leave the Jade early on the 15th and return late on the 16th, but nothing was said about the battleships of the High Seas Fleet.

The Admiralty planned to lay a trap, using the four battle-cruisers available, the 1st Light Cruiser Squadron from Cromarty Firth, and the 2nd Battle Squadron of super-Dreadnoughts from Scapa. The commander of the 2nd Battle Squadron, Admiral Warrender, was to take charge of the operation. Keyes with eight submarines was to be off Terschelling, prepared to attack if the enemy turned south, and Tyrwhitt and the Harwich force of cruisers and destroyers were to be off Yarmouth, ready to go either way.

It was planned that Beatty with the battle-cruisers and cruisers and Warrender with the battleships should rendezvous at dawn on 16 December just south-east of the Dogger Bank, in a position chosen by Jellicoe. It was well chosen, for at 5.15, well before dawn, some of Warrender's destroyers which had become accidentally separated from the battleships met enemy light forces, and a confused mêlée took place.

The whole High Seas Fleet was at sea, and contact had been made with its advanced screen. The situation was extremely dangerous, for the Germans had fourteen Dreadnoughts and

eight pre-Dreadnoughts backed by many cruisers and destroyers to face four battle-cruisers and six battleships. Fortunately, the German C-in-C, Ingenohl, thought that the
Grand Fleet must be out and promptly turned to the south-
east and then to the east, and made his way back to harbour
at best speed.

Warrender, blissfully unaware both of the High Seas Fleet
and of its retreat, had continued to the rendezvous, which he
reached at 7.17. Beatty did not receive the signal reporting the
mêlée at 5.15 until 8.05, when he turned at once to pursue at
best speed. He had no idea that he was chasing the High Seas
Fleet, but his reaction, delayed though it was, was a refreshing
contrast to Warrender's.

Fifty minutes later Beatty received signals indicating that
Scarborough was being shelled by two battle-cruisers, and at
once broke off the chase. He turned to the north-west at 9.09,
followed some time later by Warrender, who did not at first
understand the signal. The situation was now transformed.
Six modern battleships and four battle-cruisers were in a
perfect position to intercept five battle-cruisers. The sea was
calm and the visibility good. A gap between two minefields
gave a good indication of the likely enemy track.

Collision between the two forces seemed inevitable and
tension at the Admiralty grew. Churchill describes the hours
of waiting for news in brilliant prose.[205] But luck intervened.
The weather became worse, the visibility reduced and after a
chapter of accidents, which included a serious error by Goodenough in the *Southampton*, the enemy escaped untouched.

The end of the story is as mortifying as the beginning, for
after Keyes had succeeded in moving four of his submarines
into the Bight to intercept the returning High Seas Fleet,
Nasmith in *E11* fired a torpedo at the Dreadnought *Posen*,
which passed under its target.

Fisher was furious, Churchill extremely disappointed. The
country was alarmed by the bombardment of coastal towns
without redress. Beatty wrote to Jellicoe on 20 December that
'the past has been the blackest week of my life' and added
'next time, come yourself'.[206] Fisher wrote: 'The thick weather
had saved the enemy in the very jaws of death.'

In his official comments on the action, Jellicoe attributed failure to the thick weather. But he was highly critical of Goodenough, who had failed to keep touch with the enemy owing to a misunderstanding over one of Beatty's signals,* and considered too that Warrender should both have reported and taken action when his destroyers met the enemy advanced screen before dawn. This would have given more time to get the submarines into position and to get other ships out of harbour. He also thought that the Admiralty was slow in passing intelligence to the ships at sea. In his private correspondence, he was 'intensely unhappy' about the action, saying that 'we had the opportunity of our lives'. After the war he said that he would have taken the whole Grand Fleet to sea at the start instead of sending only the 2nd Battle Squadron, but this is contrary to his statements at the time.[207]

The Admiralty machine had worked better. Room 40 had had its first success,† though, as Jellicoe said, it should have been better exploited by speedy communications. But things were improving and Oliver was a success as Chief of the War Staff. Churchill himself had little to do during the action, though afterwards he played a moderating part in stopping Fisher sacking all the senior officers who he thought had failed, notably Warrender, Keyes and Goodenough. He would not hear of men being '. . . got rid of for a single failure, unless there are other reasons for thinking they are incompetent. Men often learn by mistakes, and the anxieties of war are such

---

* This was the first example of the deplorable failure of Beatty's Flag Lieutenant (he was not a trained signal officer) to translate Beatty's wishes into clear signals. There were to be other equally grave errors at the Dogger Bank and at Jutland.

† The then DNI, Oliver, had started a cryptographic section in August, which steadily improved its techniques. In October, after the finding of a German Naval signal-book from the wreck of the cruiser *Magdeburg* in the Baltic, success was achieved, and on 8 November the First Lord ordered a member of the War Staff to 'analyse and compare with what followed' the signals decoded. On 16 November Captain Hope joined the team. Knowledge of Room 40 was restricted to a very close circle of senior officers. Admiral James's excellent book on Admiral Hall, *The Eyes of the Navy*, gives a good account of the start and build-up of Room 40.

that leaders must know that they will be supported, and not be worrying about their own positions and feeling themselves in personal jeopardy. . . .'[208] These were wise words, and certainly both Keyes and Goodenough more than justified their retention.*

The Dogger Bank action

Early in the New Year there was widespread dissatisfaction with the performance of the Navy in both Germany and England. In London, Churchill was having a serious disagreement with Jellicoe, who wished to bring Beatty and the battle-cruisers back to Cromarty from the Firth of Forth so that they could work more closely with the Grand Fleet. The First Sea Lord supported Churchill, but rumblings of the quarrel reached the War Council and the First Lord had difficulty in preventing the Prime Minister from sending for Jellicoe for consultation. As he pointed out, the Fleet was at four hours' notice for steam, and the C-in-C must be with his ships.[209]

In Germany, the Naval Staff was advocating more activity by the High Seas Fleet. Instead of 'getting rusty' in harbour, frequent sorties into the North Sea were proposed. But the Kaiser would not hear of any risks being taken.

> The Commander-in-Chief of the High Seas Fleet is hereby authorised to make frequent advances into the North Sea on his own initiative, with the object of meeting advanced enemy forces or attacking them with superior strength. As far as possible the C-in-C is to avoid encounters with superior enemy forces, as in the present circumstances the High Seas Fleet has the added importance of being a valuable political instrument in the hands

---

* It does not seem to have emerged in the reports of the action that ships of the 2nd Battle Squadron sighted German cruisers and destroyers at a range of only 11,000 yards at one stage of the operation but that because the flagship had not seen the enemy the other ships did not engage, though all ready to open fire. The reason was that they were waiting for the (Squadron) Admiral, Warrender, to give the signal! See also *Sea Heritage*, by Admiral Sir Frederick Dreyer, who was Captain of the *Orion*, one of the ships concerned, and whose (Divisional) Admiral ordered him to *'wait for the signal'*.

of the All Highest War Lord; an unfavourable outcome of a naval action would therefore be a particularly serious matter. Proposed advances on a large scale as far as the enemy's coast are to be reported beforehand to his Majesty the Kaiser.[210]

The German Naval Staff was disappointed at this ruling. But when the Chief of the Staff of the Fleet proposed a sortie into the North Sea to mop up any fishing-boats or light forces encountered near the Dogger Bank, the C-in-C agreed, despite the Kaiser's orders and despite the absence in the Baltic of most of the battleships of the Fleet for gunnery practice.

On 23 January 1915, at 10.25, a signal was sent to Admiral Hipper ordering a reconnaissance of the Dogger Bank by the 1st and 2nd Striking Forces. By noon, the signal had been decoded.

The ensuing scene is well described in the *World Crisis*.

. . . the door opened quickly and in marched Sir Arthur Wilson unannounced. He looked at me intently and there was a glow in his eye. Behind him came Oliver with charts and compasses.
'First Lord, these fellows are coming out again.'
'When?'
'Tonight. We have just got time to get Beatty there.'[211]

Orders were at once sent to all forces concerned to raise steam, and plans made for Beatty, leading five battle-cruisers and the 1st Light Cruiser Squadron from the Forth, to meet Tyrwhitt, with three cruisers and thirty-five destroyers from Harwich, on the Dogger Bank at 7.00 on the 24th. The 3rd Battle Squadron of pre-Dreadnoughts from the Forth was to be thirty miles north-west of the rendezvous in case Hipper turned north, and Keyes and four submarines were sent into the Bight to attack the enemy on his return. Finally the Grand Fleet was ordered to sail after dark, though it has never been clear why its departure was so delayed.

Thus, the British forces left harbour before their German opponents. Before dawn all forces were in their positions, and the trap, again, seemed securely set.

Just after the rendezvous had been reached, the *Arethusa* sighted enemy ships (at 7.15). They were the port wing of Hipper's screen, and the German Admiral promptly turned away to the south-east, with Beatty in hot chase. The British ships steamed magnificently, several exceeding their designed speed, and gradually overtook the Germans. The day was clear, the sea was calm, and the scene set for victory for Beatty with his five battle-cruisers against the three (and the *Blücher*) of the Germans. (The *von der Tann* had been damaged in a collision during the confusion caused by a British air-raid on Cuxhaven on Christmas Day, and was absent.)

At first, all went well. The *Seydlitz*, Hipper's flagship, was hit near a magazine. Flames spread and both after turrets were destroyed with great loss of life. The ship was only saved from destruction by the prompt flooding of the magazines.*

Then two tragic errors brought frustration. The *Tiger* left the *Moltke* unfired at, and the *Lion* was severely hit and had to leave the line. Shortly after, Beatty altered course ninety degrees to port to avoid what he believed were submarine torpedoes and his signal to the remaining ships of the squadron to continue the chase was misunderstood. Instead, they circled the rear enemy ship, the already crippled *Blücher*, and the remaining enemy escaped. The *Lion* was towed home by the *Indomitable*, screened by no less than fifty-six destroyers under Tyrwhitt, and although Press and public claimed a victory, post-action analysis proved painful.

Beatty was very disappointed, though with his usual generosity he did not comment on the conduct of his second-in-command, Moore, who broke off the chase after the *Lion* had been disabled. Fisher thought Moore's conduct had been 'despicable'. 'No signals (often unintentionally ambiguous in the heat of action) can ever justify the abandonment of certain victory such as offered itself here. . . .' In his official comments on the action Jellicoe criticized Moore, and also believed that the Captain of the *Tiger*, Pelly, was much to blame. He found Pelly's excuses unconvincing. Moore himself, in his report of 25 January, expressed no regret and did not seem to appreciate

---

* Thus the Germans learnt, at small cost, the lesson which the British were to learn at Jutland with the loss of three battle-cruisers: that the anti-flash precautions were useless.

his mistake. Fisher wanted disciplinary action taken against him, but the First Lord again exerted a moderating influence. 'I do not propose to deal with the matter in a disciplinary way. An appointment of a more suitable character has been found for Admiral Moore; and there is therefore no need to enter into an argument on the facts; nor is it intended to prefer any charges.'[212] Moore was quietly relieved by Pakenham and sent to an old cruiser squadron in the Atlantic. And when Fisher also demanded the removal of Pelly from the *Tiger*, the First Lord minuted: 'I do not see any great advantage in pursuing this matter further. The future and the present claim all our attention.'[213] Here, however, the direct outcome was disappointing, as the *Tiger*'s gunnery was still poor at Jutland, fifteen months later.

But it is easy to criticize. A modern flag officer sits in a quiet and comfortable operations room, examining a radar screen or considering a neatly drawn electronic plot of the situation. At the Dogger Bank the mistakes were made by officers standing on bridges, exposed to the icy wind and spray and subjected to the devastating effect not only of the enemy's fire but of the blast and flash of the forward gun-turrets. There is no more shattering experience than to be near the muzzles of great naval guns, and the interval between the sounding of the warning 'fire' bell and the explosion prohibits constructive thought.

One more result of the battle was to persuade the First Lord, again supported by Fisher, to press Jellicoe to bring his fleet to the Firth of Forth and to move the battle-cruisers to the Humber, where they would be so much closer to Germany and to the High Seas Fleet if it sortied again. But Jellicoe feared the fogs of the Forth, and Beatty, who at first supported the plan, changed his mind because he was afraid of being 'mined in'. As a result the First Lord had to minute on 3 March: 'The Commander-in-Chief's view must prevail, and in consequence I consider that the land defences of Scapa should immediately be begun on an emergency but semi-permanent scale.'

It was not until 1917 that the Grand Fleet was moved to the Firth of Forth.

Conclusion

In *The World Crisis* Churchill admirably sums up the situation, after describing the strains of the first six months.

> Then suddenly all over the world the tension was relaxed. One after another the German cruisers and commerce destroyers were blocked in or hunted down. The great convoys arrived. The Expeditions were safely landed. Ocean after ocean became clear. The boom defences of our harbours were completed. A score of measures for coping with the submarine were set on foot. Large reinforcements of new ships of the highest quality and of every class began to join the Fleet. The attack on the Suez Canal was stemmed. The rebellion in South Africa was quelled. The dangers of invasion, if such there were, diminished every day with the increasing efficiency of the Territorials and the New Armies. The great battle for the Channel ports ended in decisive and ever glorious victory. And finally with the Battle of the Falkland Islands the clearance of the oceans was complete, and soon, except in the land-locked Baltic and Black Seas and in the defended area of the Heligoland Bight, the German flag had ceased to fly on any vessel in any quarter of the world.*
>
> As December passed a sense of indescribable relief stole over the Admiralty. We had made the great transition from peace to war without disaster, almost without mishap.[214]

To the historian, the most striking feature of Churchill's first few months of war was his astonishing activity. He never seemed to stop. His mind covered a variety of subjects, not all naval by any means, and his keen brain produced a stream of exhortations and ideas. Not only did he allow no part of Admiralty business to remain unsupervised, but he spent many days in France and Belgium on what were primarily military matters. He was also closely involved in the air defence of the country. From his adventures in France with the RNAS emerged the armoured car and the tank. He was the first to propose the use of 'noxious gases'. He raised and nurtured the Royal Naval Division.

---

* The *Dresden* and two armed merchant cruisers were alive for a few weeks more, but in complete inactivity.

Churchill took a more active part in the day-to-day running of the war at sea than any First Lord in history. His were many of the ideas for action; it was he who drafted many of the signals to the ships. He studied and analysed each operation with great care, and there is hardly a report, however unimportant, on which his initials cannot be found. His moderating influence on Fisher has already been remarked. And no reader of the first volume of Randolph Churchill's biography of his father will be surprised to learn that the First Lord spent much time considering questions connected with honours and awards. After each of the early actions he decided the number of awards to be granted, and his comments are shrewd and fair. His sense of social justice was unchanged, as is shown by his remark after the Heligoland Bight: 'In the despatches of the action in the Heligoland Bight only six warrant officers and naval ratings are recommended for reward while at least 17 officers are put forward. It is most important that the lower ranks should receive a full and fair recognition.' And his sense of proportion was shown by: 'I have been looking at the despatches on the Heligoland Bight action. They are all right as far as they go but we must be careful not to make too much of it in view of the enormous casualties and practically unnoted heroism of regimental officers and men of the Army.'[215]

His methods of work have been severely criticized. In 1923 Lord Selborne, a former Tory First Lord and a well-informed critic of Churchill, wrote in a review of the first volume of *The World Crisis*:

'It was no part of my duty to deal with the routine movements of the Fleet and its squadrons, but only to exercise a general supervision.' These are Mr Churchill's own words, and yet his book is one long record of constant interference in routine and consequent failure of supervision. The fundamental fault of his system is its restlessness. Great as his services were, they would have been greater if he could have refrained from trying to do his colleagues' and his subordinates' work as well as his own. The result was a diminution of his otherwise splendid driving power and a grievous injury to the value of his supervision. For what is the value of a man's criticism, when the order has been drafted by himself; or his supervision, when he himself is the author, approver, and executor of the policy?*[216]

There were also many complaints about the First Lord's facility in discussion. Admiral Hall, the Director of Naval Intelligence, tells a delightful tale.

Once, I remember, I was sent for by Mr Churchill very late at night. He wished to discuss some point or other with me—at once. To be candid, I have not the slightest recollection what it was: I only know that his views and mine were diametrically opposed. We argued at some length. I *knew* I was right, but Mr Churchill was determined to bring me round to his point of view, and he continued his argument in the most brilliant fashion. It was long after midnight, and I was dreadfully tired, but nothing seemed to tire the First Lord. He continued to talk, and I distinctly recall the odd feeling that although it would be wholly against my will, I should in a very short while be agreeing with everything that he said. But a bit of me still rebelled, and recalling the incident of the broken shard in Kipling's 'Kim', I began to mutter to myself: 'My name is Hall, my name is Hall. . . .'

Suddenly he broke off to look frowningly at me. 'What's that you're muttering to yourself?' he demanded.

'I'm saying,' I told him, 'that my name is Hall because if I listen to you much longer I shall be convinced that it's Brown.'

'Then you don't agree with what I've been saying?' He was laughing heartily.

'First Lord,' said I, 'I don't agree with one word of it, but I can't argue with you, I've not had the training.'

So the matter dropped and I went to bed.[217]

Similarly, when Lord Fisher returned to the Admiralty, he was soon complaining to Jellicoe:

My beloved Jellicoe—I find much difficulty in snatching even a few moments in which to write to you—Winston has so mono-

---

* Lord Selborne added some further advice, and the reader will be able to judge later if, in the Second World War, it was taken. 'If any future First Lord finds himself in that great position in another Armageddon, I hope that the courage of Mr Churchill will wrap him as a cloak, but I hope also that he will shun as poison the temptation to do the work of his naval and technical advisers, of his administrative officers and of the Secretariat, as well as his own.'

polised all initiative in the Admiralty and fires off such a multitude of departmental memos; (his power of work is absolutely amazing!) that my colleages are no longer 'Superintending Lords' but only the First Lord's registry! I told Winston this yesterday and he did not like it at all.[218]

This letter was headed, as were many others, *Please burn at once*, and I think it must not be taken too seriously, since this tempestuous genius did not always mean every word he said. Later in the letter, for instance, he talked about the German battle-cruisers attacking Folkestone and Portsmouth and then returning home via the coast of Ireland and round Iceland north about! But it gives a good impression of current opinion.

I must confess that, accustomed to such judgements, I approached this chapter with set ideas, rather like the Admiral who said, 'My mind is made up. Do not confuse me with the facts.' I proposed to indict Churchill for uncalled-for interference with matters of which he had no expert knowledge and to castigate a military mind which could not understand the difference between operations on land and sea.

But when the protecting cloak of *Naval Operations* Vols. I and II was penetrated, and when the true facts of the direction of the naval war were known, then a complete reversal of judgement took place. The weakness of the Naval War Staff, and indeed of almost every officer concerned with the Admiralty direction of the war, was so great that *someone* had to take action to provide the imagination so lacking, to inculcate the spirit of the offensive and, above all, to build up an efficient machine for the direction of operations. Other than Richmond, and one or two other more junior officers like Bellairs, no one seemed to appreciate the weaknesses. Complacency reigned. Admiral Wemyss, writing in 1919, said: 'The Admiralty needs a large and efficient staff organization. At the commencement of the war this was, I am afraid, lamentably inadequate. . . .'[219] In the absence of an adequate team, the First Lord grasped the need, and one can only wonder that he did so well. Perhaps the worst feature of the system was the lack of any delegation of work. Instead of the commanders drafting minutes or signals and then submitting them for discussion, alteration if necessary, and then approval, the Chief of Staff or the Director of Operations used laboriously to write the papers. When such senior officers had committed themselves to a view, therefore, it was not easy for their juniors to disagree. Many diaries and recollections of the time complain that captains and commanders were used to keep charts up to date and to act as glorified messengers.

When Fisher was recalled, things improved and a tremendous sense of urgency swept through the Admiralty. Fisher had always opposed the idea of a naval staff in peace, but now he found himself quickly absorbed in the great task of ordering the new ships which he knew were needed. So he had to rely on the staff, to which he gave a thorough shake-up, for the detailed control of operations. Oliver quickly relieved Sturdee. Thomas Jackson relieved Leveson. Admiral Sir Arthur Wilson, for some problems, Admiral Sir Henry Jackson and Commodore Bartolome, the Naval Secretary, were brought in to the War Staff Group, and the Second Sea Lord faded out.

It was all the more tragic that the excellent start made by the Churchill–Fisher team was soon to degenerate into dissension over the Dardanelles. For until this clash caused Churchill to assume many of the First Sea Lord's duties, there was every prospect of forging a reliable and competent machine to direct operations at sea, and I do not accept the theory that this strongly contrasted pair of geniuses could never have continued to work harmoniously together.

9

THE SEARCH FOR THE OFFENSIVE

Although it would be grossly unfair to heap the blame for the Gallipoli disaster on Churchill, it is equally foolish to contend, as some of his more apoplectic admirers have done, and still do, that his part was uniformly wise and justified by events.[220]

R. RHODES JAMES

AS soon as the clearance of the oceans was complete, the First Lord turned to the subject nearest to his heart—the use of the Navy for an offensive against Germany.

One of the undoubted weaknesses of his work at the Admiralty in war was his restlessness. He was not content that German trade, except in the Baltic, had come to a halt, that British commerce moved freely all over the oceans, and that German naval activity was restricted to submarine and mine attacks in coastal waters and to occasional raids on the East Coast, such as those on Yarmouth in November and on Scarborough in December. Most naval leaders, particularly Jellicoe, although they sought battle with the High Seas Fleet on ground of their own choosing and not in the mine-infested waters of the Heligoland Bight, were content with the situation; Churchill wanted more. His reading of history had convinced him, rightly, that the Navy must be used to land armies on the flank or in the rear of the enemy, and he was ever seeking to accomplish this aim.

Prompted by Fisher, whose brainchild the project had been for many years, he wished to secure naval command of the Baltic and so to allow Russian armies to land and attack the heart of Germany.

On the eve of war, Churchill had resurrected a study by Admiral Bayly, commissioned in January 1913, of the use of the Fleet in capturing forward bases near Germany.[221] A series of reports was produced in the summer of 1913, but did not receive a very favourable reception either in the Admiralty or in the Fleet. The capture of the islands of Borkum, off the Ems River, Sylt, off the Schleswig-Holstein coast, the Danish Esbjerg and the Dutch Ameland, was considered. An attack on Heligoland was also examined and rejected.

One of the weaknesses of these schemes was that they represented a return to the policy of close blockade, which had been decisively rejected in 1912 for very good reasons. It is true that one of these was that no forward base would be available for the destroyers and submarines needed, but the other reasons—dangers from U-boats and from mines and difficulty over fuel supply—still held good. Churchill had cogently argued the merits of the distant blockade, but its somewhat passive method of application evidently did not satisfy him.

The Bayly proposals fared no better under the new examination than in 1913. The War Staff were least critical of the Borkum plan, but they were firm in their opinion that a decisive action between the two fleets was necessary before any such operations were possible. The First Lord, however, was not to be put off so easily by his advisers, and he formally proposed, on 9 August, the capture of Ameland and the establishment of a flotilla base in the Born Deep. He estimated that three thousand Marines in two transports, together with destroyers, cruisers and submarines, would be needed, with the Channel Fleet in 'reserve support'. But naval opinion was, rightly, against the operation, and he had to drop it.

There were other ideas in the background. Admiral Sir Arthur Wilson had for years believed that Heligoland could be captured and held without excessive loss. Even the fire-eating Bayly had concluded that the cost would be prohibitive, and all other naval authorities agreed; but Wilson was not to be put off. From the start of the war, he urged that Heligoland should be attacked. He was rebuffed when, on 27 September, a conference of flag officers of the Grand Fleet, which was attended by the First Lord and by Prince Louis, rejected the scheme as utterly impracticable, but when he was made a member of the War Staff Group on Fisher's recall he raised the question yet again. Yet again, he was unanimously defeated, both by the War Staff and by the C-in-C Channel Fleet who would have had to carry out the operation.* It should be noted that one of the main reasons given was that ships were at such a disadvantage when engaging forts, especially strong ones like those on Heligoland. Spotting was more difficult for the ships, and the shore guns could easily be protected.

So by December the Heligoland scheme had ceased to be a runner, and the First Lord turned back to Borkum, which had been the least criticized of Bayly's choices.

On his recall, Fisher had at once revived his Baltic project, and had set in train a vast building programme of monitors, landing-barges and light-draught ships with which to carry it out. He favoured a direct attack on the Baltic without any preliminary seizure of an island to command the Heligoland Bight and without the neutralizing of the High Seas Fleet, and it does not appear that he ever really faced this risk, nor the problem of supplying the Fleet once it had entered the Baltic. Churchill wrote:

> Again and again, orally and in writing, I confronted him with the issue: 'Before you enter the Baltic you must first block up the Elbe. How are you going to do this? Are you ready to take the islands and fight the fleet action necessary to block the Elbe? Can you divide the fleet and enter the Baltic with a part while the Germans are free to sally out with their whole strength from either end of the Kiel Canal?' . . . he would never face this pretty obvious question.[222]

Fisher was not enthusiastic about the Borkum project, but he agreed in November to let the War Staff re-examine it and prepare plans. Bayly was then appointed as Commander-in-Chief Channel Fleet, and Borkum again became a runner.

The First Lord's strategic instincts were sound.

> . . . I think it quite possible that neither side will have the strength to penetrate the other's lines in the Western theatre. Belgium particularly, which it is vital to Germany to hold as a peace-counter, has no doubt been made into a mere succession of fortified lines. . . . my impression is that the position of both

---

* Writing to McKenna about Wilson in May 1915, Jellicoe said: 'We one and all doubted Sir A's sanity. . . . Anyone who could put forward the proposition as he put it forward is capable of *anything*.'

armies is not likely to undergo any decisive change—although no doubt several hundred thousand men will be spent to satisfy the military mind on the point.

He did not believe that a decision could be reached on the Russian Front either: '. . . a similar stalemate seems likely to be reached in the Eastern theatre. When the Russians come in contact with the German railway system, they are heavily thrown back. On the other hand, withdrawn into their own country they can hold their own.' He had found allies, too, in his search for a means of breaking the stalemate on the Western Front, for Lloyd George had come to a similar conclusion and was suggesting a move in Salonika to help the Serbians, while Hankey had circulated a cogent paper calling for activity in the eastern Mediterranean, where he believed decisive action against Turkey was possible. So, in two closely written letters, the First Lord pressed the Prime Minister for an offensive against Germany elsewhere than on the Western Front. In the first, written on 29 December and quoted above, he said: 'Are there not other alternatives than sending our armies to chew barbed wire in Flanders? Further, cannot the power of the Navy be brought more directly to bear upon the enemy?'

He wanted to invade Schleswig-Holstein with a view to neutralizing the Kiel Canal and then going round into the Baltic.

The essential preliminary is the blocking of the Heligoland debouch. The capture of a German island for an oversea base is the first indispensable step to all these possibilities. It alone can guarantee Great Britain from raid or invasion [the reverse of the argument which he had been using recently!]. It enables the power of our flotillas to be applied. Its retention by us would be intolerable to the enemy, and would in all probability bring about the sea battle.

He ended dramatically and, in the light of events, prophetically.

We ought not to drift. We ought now to consider while time remains the scope and character we wish to impart to the war in the early summer. We ought to concert our action with our allies, and particularly with Russia. We ought to form a scheme for a continuous and progressive offensive, and be ready with this new alternative when and if the direct frontal attacks in France on the German lines and Belgium have failed, as fail I fear they will. Without your direct guidance and initiative, none of these things will be done; and a succession of bloody checks in the West and in the East will leave the Allies dashed in spirit and bankrupt in policy.[223]

How true it was, and how tragic that there was no one man and no organization capable of, and charged with, the consideration of the conduct of the war as a whole! No Chiefs-of-Staff Committee nor Combined Chiefs of Staff organization, such as in the Second World War co-ordinated and planned Allied victory, existed, merely an ardent First Lord writing to a militarily ignorant Prime Minister.

In a second letter, on 31 December, he repeated a number of the arguments for action and gave a more detailed description of the plans and objects of the Borkum expedition. He ended: 'Detailed plans for the operation will be submitted if the principle is approved. Upon these plans being found satisfactory the adoption or rejection of this enterprise will depend.' He added a request for daily meetings of the War Council for a week as: 'No topic can be pursued to a fruitful result at weekly intervals.'

A few days later, on 3 January 1915, he was urging the Naval Staff to capture the island of Sylt, despite objections from the experts. He proposed to land eight to twelve thousand good infantry under cover of a bombardment which would have subdued the batteries. But again his advisers would not agree, and he was forced to give up the idea. Oliver remarked of this period: 'Churchill would often look in on his way to bed to tell me how he would capture Borkum or Sylt. If I did not interrupt or ask questions, he would capture Borkum in twenty minutes!'[224]

There had been another very strong runner in the field, which had the unique distinction of receiving support from Churchill, Fisher, Wilson and Jellicoe. It was a landing at Zeebrugge, first proposed by the Commander-in-Chief in France, to be carried out in conjunction with advances by the British and Belgian armies on the left flank of the Allied line.

When Zeebrugge and Ostend had been evacuated, the port

installations had been left intact because the Army thought that they would soon return. When it became obvious that the line was becoming stabilized about Nieuwpoort, Zeebrugge was bombarded by old battleships (23 November), but the results were not significant, and both the Navy and the Army were worried by the prospect of the use of Zeebrugge (and Bruges, a few miles up the canal) as U-boat bases. The danger to the cross-channel supply routes and to the Channel Fleet was emphasized by the loss of the *Formidable* off Start Point on 1 January 1915 to a U-boat's torpedo, and all concerned seemed agreed on the merits of the plan. But Kitchener then had second thoughts and decided that the troops would not be available for a landing, the French Commander-in-Chief made difficulties, and the plan was soon forgotten.

During January the Borkum, Sylt and Zeebrugge schemes faded out. Bayly had been removed from the Channel Fleet after the unnecessary loss of the *Formidable*, and the main naval supporter of Borkum had been quietened. But, more important still, the dangers to be faced in capturing either of the islands, and, what was even more difficult, the problem of retaining them, had become clear to the War Staff. The Chief of Staff was opposed to both operations, because of the strong defences and because the islands could be dominated by long-range guns from the mainland. The assistant director of operations, Richmond, produced a devastating criticism of the Borkum plan.

> The batteries are not visible from the sea in the clearest weather conditions, and aeroplane spotting is as yet untested in connection with moving ships. . . .
> Until the batteries covering the approaches where you want the transport to go are destroyed, you have not got command of the sea. All ideas of rushing past them by smoke screens are impracticable, as you cannot tell off the wind to blow how you want it to blow. Also, until you have made the navigation safe as regards both mines and sandbanks, you cannot bring the transports in. You cannot remove the mines except by sweeping and you cannot sweep till the batteries are destroyed. Whichever way you work at it, it comes back to that in every case—the batteries must be destroyed as a first measure . . .[225]

Jellicoe was against the plan from the start, and wrote afterwards: 'To suggest that we could mine them in their harbours *as the result of the capture of Borkum* is ludicrous, as is the idea that the capture of Borkum, even if it could be held, would have assisted us in a military attack on Schleswig-Holstein.'[226]

The First Sea Lord, Fisher, was lukewarm—as Churchill complained: 'He spoke a great deal about Borkum, its importance and its difficulties; but he did not give that strong professional impulsion to the staffs necessary to secure the thorough exploration of the plan.'[227] And finally, and most important, all eyes were turning eastwards.

Dardanelles—the inception

The First Lord was well informed of the difficulties of an operation against the Dardanelles. In particular, he was aware of the conclusions of a joint naval-military group which had studied the problem in 1906, and which led to the conclusions of the 107th meeting of the CID on 28 February 1907 that '. . . the operation of landing an expeditionary force on or across the Gallipoli peninsula would involve great risk, and should not be undertaken if other means of bringing pressure to bear on Turkey were available'.

Action by the Fleet alone had been ruled out altogether. Moreover, in March 1911 Churchill had, as we have seen, written to McKenna, saying, 'It is no longer possible to force the Dardanelles, and nobody could expose a modern fleet to such perils.'[228]

From the start of the war, he was involved in negotiations with Turkey. He personally directed the taking-over of the two Turkish battleships building in Britain, for example, and he had strong views, after his service in India, on the dangers of a clash with a Muslim power. But when it was clear that the Turks would not intern the *Goeben* and the *Breslau* it became certain that trouble could not be avoided, and, with Kitchener's support, he commissioned a joint plan for the seizure of the Gallipoli peninsula by the Greek Army, aided by the British Fleet. Nothing came of the proposal, though Churchill later quoted it to the Dardanelles Commission as proof that he favoured a joint attack.

The British ultimatum to Turkey expired on 31 October 1914,* and the Admiralty promptly directed that, as a demonstration, a bombardment of the outer forts of the Dardanelles should be carried with the object of 'testing the effective range of the guns of the forts'.[229] The plan was 'to do as much damage as possible in a short time with a limited number of rounds and to turn away before the fire from the forts became effective'.[230] But the War Council was not informed of this move by the Admiralty! An odd way of waging war.

On 3 November an Anglo-French squadron carried out the operation in favourable weather conditions with some success. In fact, more damage was done in this attack than in any other, including the final naval attack of 18 March 1915, but the Turks were alerted, and by February all damage had been made good and the defences considerably improved. There was no evidence that the object—to test the effective range of the forts—was ever mentioned again, and it is now clear that this bombardment was a serious mistake. Afterwards, in evidence to the Dardanelles Commission and in post-war writing, many officers criticized the operation as premature, but there were no dissenting voices at the time.[231]

On 25 November, at the War Council, Churchill, with the hearty concurrence of the First Sea Lord, proposed a joint attack on the Dardanelles as the best defence of Egypt, which was then under discussion, but Kitchener declared that no troops were available and that was that. On 2 January the problem was raised again in dramatic form, when the Russian Commander-in-Chief, the Grand Duke Nicholas, appealed for a demonstration against Turkey, either naval or military, to take the pressure off his armies in the Caucasus. Kitchener discussed the matter with Churchill and then sent a telegram via the Foreign Office promising to make a demonstration. He believed that 'the only place that a demonstration might have some effect in stopping reinforcements going east [to the Caucasus] would be the Dardanelles',[232] and he insisted that it

* War was not declared till 5 November.

must be a naval operation because the troops would not be available 'for some months'.*

This, I believe, was the signal which released the safety catch of an operation which was to fail with such grievous losses, and which was to bring such glory to the fighting men and such discredit on those who directed them. The story of the momentous months which followed has been told and retold. With the passage of time, more and more documents have been made available to the historian and it is unlikely that anything more of importance will be unearthed.

Churchill's words—'Those terrible "ifs" accumulate'—are only too true. There were numbers of moments when, if events had taken another turn, if advice had been accepted or rejected, or if decisions had been made instead of shelved, history would have been written altogether differently. But one of the most striking features of the many accounts of the campaign is that each authority seems to choose his own turning-points, and hardly any two are the same.[233]

Instead, therefore, of attempting a narrative of the operations and of the events leading up to them, I propose to examine, in rough chronological order, the main 'turning-points' of the campaign, on the assumption that the reader will know enough of the march of events to follow my analysis.

But we have already passed one turning-point, for if any high authority had, on 2 January, replied to Lord Kitchener: 'Please look at the report of 1906; it concludes that a joint attack is very hazardous and a naval attack on its own would be out of the question,' surely sounder counsels would have prevailed.

By a coincidence, the First Lord received next day, 3 January, Fisher's proposals for a *joint* attack on the Dardanelles, using British troops from France, Indian troops and a Greek contingent, supported by battleships of the elderly *Majestic* and *Canopus* classes, which were simultaneously to force the straits.

Churchill ignored Fisher's requirement that the troops hold

---

* Ironically, the need vanished with the collapse of the Turkish offensive on 4 January, but the Russian C-in-C did not pass on the news.

the high land dominating the straits while the Fleet forced the passage, and saw his chance to urge a naval attack. With Fisher's concurrence, he signalled Carden, the Admiral commanding the Anglo-French squadron: 'Do you think that it is a practicable operation to force the Dardanelles by the use of ships alone? It is assumed that older battleships would be used. . . . The importance of the result would justify severe loss.' Carden replied on 5 January: 'I do not think that the Dardanelles can be rushed, but they might be forced by extended operations with a large number of ships.'

If Carden had been supplied with better intelligence of the improvement to the defences since his November bombardment, it seems unlikely that his reply would have been so optimistic. But Churchill was delighted and replied on 6 January: 'High authorities here concur in your opinion. Forward detailed particulars showing what force would be required for extended operations. How do you think it should be employed, and what results could be gained?'[234]

Fisher afterwards said that he knew of the signal but did not see it, and Churchill does not claim that he was one of the high authorities referred to. He relied on Oliver and Sir Henry Jackson for his support. And here we reach another great 'if'. What would have happened if, before 12 January, the Naval War Staff had had the courage to confront Churchill with the facts of 'ships versus forts'? But on 12 January Fisher offered the *Queen Elizabeth*, which was proving her new fifteen-inch guns in the calm waters of the Mediterranean, so 'firing all her ammunition at the Dardanelles forts instead of uselessly into the sea'. This offer had an electrifying effect on the First Lord, for after his struggles in 1912 to introduce this gun he felt a parent's pride in the weapon, and in his imagination he credited it with almost supernatural powers of destruction.

At the end of a long meeting on 13 January, he brought up before the War Council the plan for a naval attack. Hankey wrote:

> The idea caught on at once. The whole atmosphere changed. Fatigue was forgotten. The War Council turned eagerly from the dreary vista of a 'slogging match' on the Western Front to brighter prospects, as they seemed in the Mediterranean. The

Navy, in whom every one had implicit confidence and whose opportunities had so far been few and far between, was to come into the front line.[235]

In his official minute, he recorded:

This plan was based on the fact that the Dardanelles forts are armed mainly with old guns of only thirty-five calibre. These would be outranged by the guns of the ships, which would effect their object without coming into range. . . . The Admiralty were studying the question and believed that a plan could be made for systematically reducing all the forts within a few weeks. Once the forts were reduced the minefields would be cleared, and the fleet would proceed up to Constantinople and destroy the *Goeben*. They would have nothing to fear from field guns or rifles which would be merely an inconvenience.

Churchill and Kitchener were enthusiastic about Carden's plan, Fisher and Wilson were silent, and the War Council gave provisional approval that 'the Admiralty should prepare for a naval expedition in February to bombard and take the Gallipoli Peninsula with Constantinople as its objective'.

Both this conclusion and Hankey's minute are redolent of facile optimism. Certainly ships' guns might outrange the guns of the forts, but there was no evidence that they could hit them—the reverse was the case. And how could the Navy alone 'take the Gallipoli Peninsula'?

We have reached another turning point. There is more than one 'if' to discuss. What would have been the result if the Prime Minister had asked the advice of Fisher or Wilson or even General Murray, the CIGS?* What would

---

* Unfortunately Murray was dominated by Kitchener and seldom expressed his opinion.

The names of the four Chiefs of the Imperial General Staff who served Lord Kitchener during the first two years of the war have baffled most historians. General Sir Charles Douglas, in office at the start, died on 25 October 1914. He was relieved by General Sir James Wolfe Murray, who in turn was relieved by General Sir Archibald Murray in September 1915. Sir Archibald was succeeded by General Sir William Robertson in December 1915. Sir James Wolfe Murray was in office during the inception of the Dardanelles Campaign.

211   P

have happened if there had been some body of experts, naval and military, to whom the proposal could have been remitted for study?

Why did not the Prime Minister or one of the other Ministers interrogate Kitchener closely about the statement that no troops were available? There were plenty to spare, in fact, but no one dared to argue with the great man. He had a unique and impregnable position. As Churchill told the Dardanelles Commission: 'When he gave a decision, it was invariably accepted as final. He was never, to my belief, overruled by the War Council or the Cabinet in any matter, great or small. Scarcely anyone ventured to argue with him in Council. . . . All-powerful imperturbable, reserved, he dominated absolutely our counsels at that time.'

In the days after the Council of 13 January, preparations were hastened. Signals passed constantly between Carden and the Admiralty. The French offered their support. The Grand Duke Nicholas was informed. Sir Percy Scott was offered the command—he refused, as he did not consider that the expedition could succeed.

But, slowly and steadily, Fisher's opposition grew, and on 25 January he produced a long memorandum to the Prime Minister, with a copy to the First Lord, in which he explained, for the first time, his objections.[236] They were basically three: that the Navy was better employed elsewhere (i.e., in the Baltic); that the operation would weaken the Grand Fleet; and that the expedition should be joint and not solely naval. But unfortunately his main stress was on the weakening of the Fleet in Home Waters, and in a covering letter to the Prime Minister the First Lord was able easily to point out that the old ships which would be included were of no use to Jellicoe, who had received great accretions in strength since November.[237]

As a result of these two papers and of another threat of resignation from Fisher ('I am very reluctant to leave the First Lord. I have a great personal affection and admiration for him, but I see no possibility of a union of ideas and unity is essential in war, so I refrain from remaining a stumbling block'), Asquith called Churchill and Fisher to his room immediately before the next War Council on 28 January. After listening to both sides, Asquith said: 'I am the arbitrator. I have heard Mr Winston Churchill, and I have heard you and now I am going to give my decision. Zeebrugge* will not be done; the Dardanelles will go on.'[238]

At the War Council which followed, on 28 January, Churchill opened by describing the preparations for the naval attack, about which he was confident. Fisher interjected that he had understood that the matter was not to be raised, but was over-ruled by the Prime Minister. He started for the door, but was intercepted by Kitchener, who persuaded him to resume his seat. As Fisher put it later: 'I said to myself after some delay, "Well, we can withdraw the ships at any moment, so long as the Military don't land," and I succumbed.'[239]

Kitchener was enthusiastic for the naval attack. Balfour and Grey supported the project, and the meeting adjourned. After lunch Churchill persuaded Fisher to lend his support, and when the War Council resumed in the evening he announced on behalf of the Board of Admiralty that they had decided to undertake the task with which the War Council had charged them, *subject to the right to break off the operation.* The War Council gave the 'go ahead', and another turning-point had been reached, with the 'ifs' proliferating like ants.

If only Fisher had made it clearer to Asquith that it was technical reasons which put him against the plan, just as much as fear of weakening the Grand Fleet or the merits of the Baltic project. Asquith thought that it was the petulance of a veteran sailor thwarted of his brainchild. If only Ministers had interrogated Fisher when he tried to leave the Council. But, astonishingly, Balfour, Haldane and Asquith in their later evidence said that they did not notice the scene.

In the proceedings of the Dardanelles Commission, and in the many post-mortems after the war, there was much discussion of the position of the military advisers in the War Council. While Fisher and Wilson stuck rigidly to their conviction that their job was to support their political chiefs and only to open their mouths if asked a question, the politicians

---

*See pp. 205–6.

concerned were unanimous that it was the duty of the military experts to speak up if they disagreed fundamentally with anything that their Minister said. The Commission discussed this important point of principle at great length and agreed with the politicians' claims, although three dissenting opinions were written.*

The Commissioners concluded by criticizing Asquith, who 'should have encouraged the experts present to give their opinions, and, indeed, should have insisted upon their doing so. . . . What actually happened was that the stress laid upon the unquestionable advantages which would accrue from success was so great that the disadvantages which would arise in the not improbable case of failure were insufficiently considered.'[240] This I believe is a monumental example of the 'non sequitur'. It seems to me that the lack of expert opinion was responsible, not for the *disadvantages* of failure being forgotten, but for the *improbability* of success not being understood.

They also thought that Churchill was not blameless in this matter. Instead of asking his advisers to speak their minds at the Council, he gave the impression that his view was the considered view of the Board as a whole, which was not the case.

So here we find another 'if'. If only Churchill had given his colleagues any inkling of the informal opposition of which he must have been aware. Sir Percy Scott, a genuine expert, had refused to co-operate; the Third Sea Lord, Tudor, another gunnery officer, and the Second Sea Lord, Hamilton, had both disagreed in casual conversation.[241] Here, again, there has been criticism of Churchill because of the exclusion of the junior Sea Lords from the direction of affairs, in order that they could concentrate on their supply function in the field of personnel, ships and stores. But this exclusion was the policy of the First Sea Lord, who did not like control by committee, and the First Lord cannot be blamed—if, indeed, blame is needed.

But one must conclude, I think, that the First Lord was so seized of the benefits which success would bring, and so

---

* By Sir Andrew Fisher, Sir Thomas Mackenzie and Walter Roch.

determined to give the plan a trial—and remember, at this stage it was always assumed that the Fleet could withdraw if difficulties were met—that he minimized to the point of deception the degree of opposition among the experts.

Dardanelles—the execution

After the War Council of 28 January, preparation continued in the eastern Mediterranean, accompanied by new developments in London. Opposition among the Naval War Staff crystallized, but Churchill rejected the advice of Oliver and Richmond to send out the Royal Naval Division to help the Fleet. Instead, only two battalions of Royal Marines were sent to cover the demolition of the guns of the forts.

On the other hand Kitchener was becoming more convinced of the merit of the operation, and on 9 February he declared that troops would be made available if they were later needed. At a War Council on 16 February he offered the 29th Division —a well-trained regular formation—and thus the character of the operation started to change. But Kitchener withdrew his offer on 19 February, and, worse still, he also cancelled, without informing the First Lord, the assembly of the transports to carry it out to the Mediterranean. There was thus a further delay when he finally agreed on 10 March to the dispatch of the 29th Division.

There was a startling episode at the War Council of 26 February which has received less attention in histories than it deserves. The First Lord had protested against the half-hearted measures of military co-operation proposed, and he 'formally recorded his dissent at the 29th Division being retained in this country', adding that 'he must disclaim all responsibility if disaster occurred in Turkey owing to the insufficiency of troops'.[242]

His argument was, it seems, that either a full-blooded effort by the Army, including the 29th Division, should be made, or else the Navy must be left to try alone. Then in case of failure the operation could easily be called off, whereas if the military intervened it would be far more difficult to withdraw. But his words had no effect on Kitchener until 10 March, when it was too late.

On 19 February the first attack on the outer forts was made, and, with intervals due to bad weather, attacks continued spasmodically until 5 March, when, with little success, the intermediate forts were first engaged. The parties which had landed from the ships to demolish the guns of the outer forts had met gradually increasing opposition from the Turkish Army and it had not been possible to destroy all the guns. They were silent, but they were to be used again. Operations against the minefields, covered by ships' guns, continued until the eve of the naval attack of 18 March, but with no success, for the minesweepers were unsuitable craft for the task and their fisherman crews were untrained. On 16 March Admiral Carden went sick, and his second-in-command de Robeck was appointed in his place.

On 18 March the great naval attack on the main forts, which had roused so many high hopes, took place. But after a promising start three battleships were sunk by mines, and two others seriously damaged, leaving the guns of the forts comparatively untouched, though damage had been done to the ramparts and ammunition had run short.

Next day de Robeck decided to reorganize and improve the minesweeping force before trying again, but on 22 March he had an important meeting with General Hamilton and General Birdwood,* who had watched the bombardment and who had both come to the conclusion that the Fleet could not get through alone. Knowing that the 29th Division was on its way, and that the Royal Naval Division and the Australian and New Zealand Corps would also be available, the meeting came to the conclusion that it would be right to wait for the land forces, and then to carry out a deliberate joint operation.

Churchill was furious at the news and tried to persuade the Naval War Staff to order de Robeck to try again at once. 'Not to persevere—that was the crime,' was his later comment. But Fisher was adamant that the decision of the men on the spot must be respected. On 29 March he reluctantly agreed to

* General Hamilton had just arrived as Commander of the Land Forces. General Birdwood had been sent from Egypt to survey the situation. He had expected to get the Command, but was relegated to a Corps.

a probing signal to de Robeck inquiring why he had changed his mind, but this did not affect the decision of de Robeck, who replied firmly that he intended to wait till the Army was ready, which he hoped would be on 14 April. But it was then discovered that the 29th Division transports were not 'combat loaded', and it was necessary to send them on to Alexandria—seven hundred miles away—to be sorted out.

The joint attack did not take place till 25 April, achieving but limited success, and so the long and bloody process of military operations had started and the main control now shifted from the Admiralty to the War Office. This outcome was a dreadful disappointment to the First Lord, who wrote:

Henceforth the defences of the Dardanelles were to be reinforced by an insurmountable mental barrier. A wall of crystal, utterly immovable, began to tower up in the Narrows, and against this wall of inhibition, no weapon could be employed. The 'No' principle had become established in men's minds, and nothing could ever eradicate it. . . . [Instead of renewing the naval attack upon the Narrows] they waited for nine months the spectators of the sufferings, the immense losses and the imperishable glories of the Army; always hoping that their hour of intervention would come . . . until in the end they had the sorrow and mortification of taking the remains of the Army off and steaming away under cloak of darkness from the scene of irretrievable failure.[243]

This epitaph cannot be bettered.

It is difficult to pick out the 'ifs' associated with this period because they are so numerous. But the turning-point stands out starkly. After the failure of the naval attack on 18 March it would still have been possible to call off the operation and to divert the forces involved, both naval and military, to some other objective in the eastern Mediterranean, where Alexandretta was a favourite choice. There was much talk of the loss of prestige thereby entailed, but the Dardanelles Commission certainly did not agree that this was a dominating factor.

By 19 March it was clear to observers on the spot that naval guns at long range were not accurate enough to hit the guns in the forts. To do this, it was necessary for the ships to close to point-blank range, and this they could not do without braving the perils of the minefields. The mines which did the damage on 18 March had been laid, recently and unobserved, in one line *along* the straits, but there were several other known minefields laid *across* the straits. It was found by experience that minesweepers could not work until the forts had been silenced, and so the plan entered a vicious circle from which there seemed to be no escape.

There were many—and Churchill and Keyes are prominent among them—who believed that just one more effort would have brought success. They quote the shortage of ammunition in the forts and the demoralization of the defenders. But there is much evidence available now which was not known at the time to those who believed that one more try would be successful. The reports of the Mitchell Committee of 1919 and the statements of Turkish and German officers all seem to me to provide overwhelming evidence to the contrary.

More ammunition was on its way, and, anyhow, the mobile howitzers which were so difficult to find and to hit had plenty of ammunition. The minefields were untouched, and the minesweepers unprepared and untrained. If some of the naval force had succeeded in forcing the Narrows (only three-quarters of a mile across), how would their communications have been secured, in the absence of military forces to occupy the peninsula and subdue the fire of the forts and the mobile guns on both sides? What is more, many responsible Turkish and German observers affirm that the failure of the naval attack on 18 March raised rather than lowered morale.

There is only one certainty—that it would have been perfectly possible to withdraw altogether after 19 March. But no War Council was held until 14 May. There was no cool appraisal, no thorough discussion, and a policy of drift allowed the operation to roll doggedly onwards, impelled by its own momentum and the enthusiasm of a few men in London.

The 'ifs' accumulate. What if Kitchener had not changed his mind about the dispatch of the 29th Division, and if the ships had been loaded for an immediate landing? If the Russian Government had not vetoed a Greek offer on 1 March to provide three divisions of troops for the Gallipoli peninsula? All the evidence points to the narrow margin by which the defenders completed their new measures. An attack made only a few days earlier might have succeeded.

And in the more technical fields, one must ask what the result of a number of alternatives would have been. If the eight *Beagle*-class destroyers had been converted to minesweeping before 18 March and so employed their discipline, training and high speed; or if, in a more general sense, an efficient force of sweepers had been sent out earlier? If aircraft with a better performance had been sent for spotting? (The *Ark Royal*'s seaplanes could not get high enough to dodge the rifle fire.) If ships and aircraft had practised bombardment together? If Mudros harbour had had good facilities for handling ships, so that it would not have been necessary to send the 29th Division to Alexandria? And if a more determined character than Carden had been in command? Birdwood (like many others) was very critical of his competence.

Rivers of ink have flowed in attempts to allocate blame. At the time, and for many years after, Churchill was saddled by the Press and by public opinion with the greatest share. The Dardanelles Commissioners let him down rather lightly, though Walter Roch's dissenting report is more critical. The official Australian military historian is in no doubt that Churchill should take most of the responsibility.[244]

He was indicted on two counts. The first, that he interfered with the operation unnecessarily and that in his enthusiasm he misled his colleagues about the facts and about the opinions of his expert advisers; the second, that the expedition was a strategic mistake, that it diverted effort from the vital theatre and was an expensive sideline of no real military significance.

To take the second point first: there has been a reversal of opinion, and historians and strategists now agree that Churchill and Lloyd George were right in their search for offensives elsewhere than in the mud of France and Flanders, and that, as a skilfully handled joint enterprise, the operation might have shortened the war and saved millions of lives. I agree with this judgement. As to the first count, I have made it clear that I believe that Churchill *was* guilty of deception, albeit unconscious, in his efforts to gain approval for his schemes, and that there can be no doubt that in the later stages he usurped many of the First Sea Lord's functions, though he was always careful to obtain his assent, however reluctantly given.

Some considerable measure of blame must rest therefore on him. But Admiral Wemyss has given a sound judgement, and there can be no one better qualified, by reason of his position at Mudros, to pronounce: 'The blame for this tragedy cannot be laid at the door of any one individual, but must be attributed to a system. . . .' And one's only comment is that it was the *lack* of a system which was the trouble.

The Dardanelles Commissioners, sitting in the shadow of the loss of Lord Kitchener in the *Hampshire*, were inclined to treat him very generously, though they criticized his method of centralized control and his disregard of his staff.* But I believe that he must bear a large share of responsibility for the disaster. His enthusiasm for the naval attack swayed the Cabinet. His unnecessary refusal to provide troops made the naval attack inevitable. His vacillation over the 29th Division and his dispersal of the assembled transports may have been decisive. His insistence on sending out General Hamilton with confused instructions, with a totally inadequate staff and with none of the intelligence of the peninsula available in the War Office was an astonishing error. It can only be understood as made by a man overburdened, of his own choice, with work which should have been done by others.

Asquith, too, was blamed by the Dardanelles Commission for allowing events to take charge and a policy of drift to dominate the counsels. The Commissioners were very critical of the lack of any War Council between 19 March and 14 May, and evidently thought that better decisions would have been taken if the Council had met to consider the failure of the naval attack. Thereafter history records grim struggles on the peninsula which ended, after many hopes had been raised, in final evacuation. The story of the endurance and the courage

---

* For example (para. 105): 'It is with great reluctance and hesitation that we comment on these proceedings, for it is obvious that Lord Kitchener was mainly responsible for the decisions taken during the critical period between February 16th and March 10th and it is quite possible that were he alive he might be able to throw a new light on them.'

of the soldiers is the most moving of a war dominated by courage and carnage. The survivors and the relatives of the fallen may take some consolation from the conviction of both Asquith and Grey, expressed eloquently to the Dardanelles Commissioners, that although the expedition failed, it had played a vital part in diverting large Turkish forces from other theatres of war.

The May crisis—dismissal

Before the crisis of May 1915 there had been signs that the Churchill–Fisher team, which had made such a good start, was becoming an uneasy partnership. Fisher had been irked by the First Lord's refusal to agree to a clean sweep of the senior officers whom he considered to have failed. There had been friction over the measures needed against Zeppelin attack; Fisher had resigned but had been persuaded to stay. Moreover, the contrasting methods of work of the two men began to grate. Churchill rose late, took a short nap after lunch and did his best work after a good dinner; he seldom turned in until the small hours. On the other hand, Fisher retired early— he was seventy-four and never went to his office after dinner— but got up early and did his best work before breakfast. At first this went well—there was talk of a twenty-four-hour watch by the pair—but gradually the First Sea Lord became irritated by the stream of memoranda, instructions and draft signals which he found waiting for him when he woke up, some with the First Lord's ink only just dry on the paper.

During the Dardanelles operation, Fisher's frustration grew. He was worried by the comparative strengths of the fleets in Home Waters, or at least he thought he was, and he saw his Baltic project fading away and his great ship-building programme wasted with the drain to the Dardanelles. He found, too, that the First Lord was taking more and more of the day-to-day direction of affairs out of his hands. Constitutionally, Churchill had this power, but no First Lord in history had ever so monopolized the powers of the professional head of the Navy.

The crisis rose to a peak very quickly. By 9 May the Army on the Gallipoli peninsula was deadlocked, and de Robeck made a qualified proposal for a renewal of the naval attack, which led to a sharp clash between Churchill and Fisher on the reply to be sent. With the support of the junior Sea Lords, Fisher persuaded the First Lord to instruct de Robeck to wait for the Army. On 12 May the sinking of the battleship *Goliath* by a German-manned Turkish destroyer alarmed Fisher, who at once demanded the recall of the *Queen Elizabeth* from the danger-zone; another argument followed in which Churchill again gave way. At the War Council on 14 May Kitchener complained formally about the withdrawal of the *Queen Elizabeth*, almost accusing the Navy of deserting its colleagues, and Fisher intervened to say that he had been against the operation from the start. The meeting adjourned in deep gloom.

Fisher had considered 'packing up' that evening, but a talk with Churchill calmed him. However, next morning, 15 May, he awoke to be handed four minutes by the First Lord, one of which, as he thought, demanded greater diversions of ships to the Mediterranean than he had agreed to the night before. He saw the end of the Baltic scheme. It was the last straw. Before breakfast he had written out his resignation (his ninth!), and he left his office that forenoon, never to return.

The story of the events which followed reads like a brightly coloured political romance. It is well told by Marder,[245] and the account need not be repeated here. There were all the elements of high drama—a move towards a Coalition Government, the Conservative refusal to serve with Churchill, public reaction to the loss of Lord Fisher, political intrigues at many levels, rumours of shell shortage in France and Flanders, the increasing disenchantment of the Junior Sea Lords with Lord Fisher, a firm conviction on the part of Churchill that he himself was the right man for the Admiralty, and, finally, a quixotic gesture by Sir Arthur Wilson, who refused to serve with any other First Lord. And in the middle of it all, there was a sally by the High Seas Fleet which at first promised to bring about the 'great battle', but which proved only to be a covering operation for minelaying near the Dogger Bank.

The letters exchanged between the First Lord and the

Prime Minister make painful reading. A few extracts will suffice.

> Above all things I should like to stay and complete my work—the most difficult part of which is ended. . . . The German Fleet are out in full strength and all our ships are at sea. It is possible that the afternoon may produce events. (*18 May*)

> I have your letter. You must take it as settled that you are not to remain at the Admiralty. . . . I hope to retain your services as a member of the new Cabinet. . . . (*20 May*)

> What makes me anxious is the arrival of German submarines in the Eastern Mediterranean. . . . My responsibility is terrible. But I know I could sustain it, and without the slightest impairment of our margin here, could bring this vast Dardanelles business safely through in spite of the submarines. Arthur Wilson and I can do it. We alone know the whole position. It is no clinging to office . . . which seizes me. I am clinging to my *task* and to my *duty*. . . . (*21 May*)[246]

Once it was certain that he could not remain at the Admiralty, Churchill showed a warm-hearted and selfless acceptance of the decision, offering to take any position, whether in office in London or in the field in France. He also pressed for Balfour to succeed him, for, in this way, he hoped the Dardanelles project would be sympathetically handled by one who had been enthusiastic from the beginning.

Then he considered the next First Sea Lord. Fisher would not serve with Balfour, but in any case his retention in office was out of the question, because of his desertion of his post and because of a subsequent letter in which he had demanded of the Prime Minister dictatorial powers if he was to remain in office.* Churchill next suggested Wilson, not realizing, I think, the distrust which the latter's policies roused in the Fleet, but Wilson would only serve under Churchill. So Sir Henry Jackson, who had been at the Admiralty since the start of the war, was chosen as the next best alternative.

Thus was formed the Balfour–Jackson team of the

---

* Churchill was not aware of this astonishing document until after the war.

philosopher-statesman allied with the scientist-sailor; a team which was to bring lethargy to the Admiralty in the place of imagination and drive.

But there is no doubt that the change was welcomed in the Navy. Churchill's faults were remembered, especially his tactlessness, his urge to probe the smallest details, his intolerance and his occasional bombastic moments. His merits were forgotten and his part in preparing the Fleet for war was taken for granted. In the Fleet, the general belief was that the war would now be run by professionals, and that all would be well, but I am afraid that the belief was unfounded and that a naval equivalent of the saying that 'war is too important to be entrusted to the generals would be only too true.

At the end of May Churchill accepted the sinecure post of Chancellor of the Duchy of Lancaster, retaining a seat in the Cabinet and also on the Dardanelles Committee, which had replaced the War Council in the Coalition Government's organization. But although he was at first kept busy on papers and discussions connected with the conduct of the war in general, and the Dardanelles in particular, his influence was steadily waning. In the late summer the Salonika expedition started to divert effort from the Dardanelles, and a move towards evacuation of the peninsula began. A proposal by Keyes, supported by Wemyss but opposed by de Robeck, for another naval attack was turned down. Churchill's period of power was coming to an end, and when, in a further reorganization in November, he was left out of the new War Committee which was to be responsible for the conduct of the war, he resigned from the Government and immediately left for regimental duty in France.

While still in the Government, however, he wrote several accounts of his stewardship at the Admiralty, which are impressive and convincing documents, filled with facts and figures. After reading them, I reflected deeply on the events which led to this tragedy; for tragedy it was, both for Churchill himself and for the country which could ill afford the loss of one who had 'the supreme quality which I venture to say very few of your present or future Cabinet possess—the power, the imagination, the deadliness to fight Germany'.[247]

I believe that there was one cardinal error which pervaded his policies and which more than any other factor was responsible for his dismissal. It stemmed directly from his military background and education. Rightly imbued with the urge for the offensive in war and the need for *doing something* rather than waiting passively for the enemy to strike, Churchill did not understand that the hold of the Grand Fleet on the North Sea was an offensive act in itself. He confused the Germans' policy of remaining in their harbours—a policy which led directly to the loss of morale and mutinies of later years—with the apparent inactivity of the Grand Fleet, which, however, exercised at sea and sallied forth from time to time into the North Sea, maintaining a complete stranglehold on German shipping.

Certainly a decisive battle in the North Sea was most desirable, and every officer and man in the Grand Fleet longed for it, but offensive planning should have led to this outcome and not to operations in the shallow coastal waters off Germany, which could only bring disaster to the Grand Fleet.

It was this constant urge for action, whether in the Heligoland Bight, off Borkum or Sylt or in the Baltic, which wore down his naval colleagues and which sapped confidence in his judgement. When the proposal for the Dardanelles operation was produced, it became only 'another of Winston's schemes'. and so the only truly brilliant and practicable strategical concept of the First War received lukewarm support in its inception and was disgracefully bungled in its execution.

To the reader whose mind keeps leaping ahead to 1939-45, there is a particularly revealing passage in Churchill's indictment of the 'negative' attitude of the admirals in *The World Crisis*.

Through the greater part of 1915, peace brooded on the seas; through the greater part of 1916, apart from the Battle of Jutland, there was comparative peace. But thereafter there was a change which came near to our complete undoing. . . .

Yet even in their extreme danger [from the U-boats] the negative school of Admirals and those who followed their advice resigned themselves to defensive measures either of an active or passive character, such as eating less bread, ploughing up the land, cutting down the forests, dispersing thousands of guns on merchant ships, building more merchantmen for submarines to sink, strewing the seas with mines, *consuming hundreds of destroyers and thousands of small craft on escort** and submarine hunting; . . . they continued to strengthen the Grand Fleet— even when all the power of the American Navy was added to their own. And by all these means they drew upon our limited resources to such an extent that in 1918 the equivalent in men and material of fifteen or twenty divisions was denied to the hard-pressed fighting line on land; and Fisher had to coin the biting sentence, 'Can the Army win the war before the Navy loses it?'

Nevertheless . . . the Navy eventually crushed the U-boat. But how narrowly and at what cost! It was left to Admiral Keyes to show at Zeebrugge that there were other ways of making war from the sea.

This is a thoroughly misinformed statement which is, I think, the genesis of many of the worst mistakes of the direction of the war at sea in 1939–45. It was not until 1942— nearly too late—that Churchill was at last persuaded that escorted convoy was the only solution to the German attack on shipping, and that the system was not purely 'defensive'. As a result, many thousands of tons of bombs were wasted, and many useless miles of sea patrolled by 'offensive' hunting-groups, before the attack was defeated. And as for Zeebrugge —it was a gallant and well-executed enterprise which raised morale at a moment when the spirits of the country were low. But Churchill knew that it hardly hampered the U-boats it was designed to stop. His remarks are difficult to justify and, again, I think we can find here the reasons for some of the wasted efforts and unused plans for similar operations in the Second World War.

* My italics.

10

DOLDRUMS AND STORMS, NOVEMBER 1915—AUGUST 1939

The task is not yet done. The greatest exertions must continue to be made over a long period of years. The danger of war has by no means passed from the world. Old antagonisms are sleeping, and the drumbeat of new antagonisms is already heard. The anxieties of France and the resentments of Germany are only partly removed.[248]

WSC

THIS book is a study of Churchill's impact and influence on the Royal Navy, and not a history of his life. This chapter will touch on periods of his career when he was in office, in Opposition, in the trenches and in comparative obscurity. Through much of the time his official contacts with the Navy were few, though he kept in informal touch through friends and he was able to retain his interest in technical development. In the writing of history, too, both *The World Crisis* and *Marlborough: His Life and Times,* he was brought face to face with the problems of maritime war in the days of steam and of sail.

The aim of the chapter will be to examine the incidents and influences which affected his views and opinions on naval affairs and, conversely, the influence which in a period of oscillating fortune he brought to bear on the Navy—an influence which was inevitably somewhat spasmodic. Events will be considered in rough chronological order but many important milestones will be omitted and only a few of the political changes will be included so as to act as markers over the twenty-four years so lightly covered.

The trenches

Churchill's resignation speech was unexceptionable, and was received with sympathy. He gave a confident account of his stewardship at the Admiralty, denied vehemently that the Dardanelles had been a 'civilian plan foisted by a political amateur on reluctant officers and experts' and ended optimistically:

There is no reason to be discouraged about the progress of the war. We are passing through a bad time now, and it will probably be worse before it is better, but that it will be better if we only endure and persevere, I have no doubt whatever. Sir, the old wars were decided by their episodes rather than their tendencies. In this war the tendencies are far more important than the episodes. Without winning any sensational victories, we may win this war. We may win it even during a continuance of extremely disappointing and vexatious events.

During his time in France, he brooded deeply on the war in general, and on methods of breaking the deadlock in the trenches in particular. His mind returned to the tank, and naval problems were thrust into the background. There they remained until he came to London on leave in early March 1916, unaware, according to one account, that the Naval Estimates were shortly to be debated. But friends asked him to lead the opposition to Government policy.[249]

The result, on 7 March, was a disaster which gravely damaged his chances of returning to office. He started his speech with a bitter attack on the Admiralty conduct of the war: 'I wish to place on record that the late Board would certainly not have been content with an attitude of pure passivity. . . .' He called for more action, giving a seaplane raid on Germany as an example, and ended with the astonishing demand for the recall of Lord Fisher.

Balfour's reply was simple and devastating. He pointed out that Churchill had admitted that he believed Lord Fisher had failed in his duty over the Dardanelles operation. He had dismissed him at the start of the speech and asked for him back at the end. Balfour castigated him for his attack on Sir Henry Jackson, the First Sea Lord, and criticized his efforts 'to arouse doubts, misgivings and suspicions about the strength of the Fleet and the energy of the present Board'.

After his speech, Churchill determined to resign from the Army and return to politics, but he was persuaded to return to France and to his duty. But it was only for a few weeks, for his battalion was soon amalgamated with another and he lost his post. This time his resignation was accepted and he returned to political life.

Return to politics

From May 1916 until July 1917, when he became Minister of Munitions, he led an unsettled, unproductive and unhappy life. Much of the time was taken up by advocacy of a public inquiry into the Dardanelles expedition and by the production of written and verbal evidence for the Commission. There were many objections, political and official, to a public inquiry. The Foreign Office wished to retain diplomatic secrecy and the service ministries believed that the enemy would learn much useful information. Lord Hankey wrote in his diary on 5 June 1916:

> In the evening Winston Churchill turned up at the office to give me his views on these wretched Dardanelles papers. I gave him my views on the objections from the point of view of public policy to laying papers. He became quite furious and asked where he came in. 'Whenever I open my mouth in Parliament,' he said, 'someone shouts out that I am the man who let us in for the Dardanelles mistake, and the papers are perpetually repeating it. My usefulness in Parliament is entirely ruined until my responsibility is cleared. . . .'

But eventually the Commission was set up and, as we have seen already, Churchill was able at least to share some of the blame with others.

He also resumed his journalism—the loss of office brought a sharp reduction in income—and, as with the speech of 7 March in the House, the results did not enhance his reputation. He showed an extraordinary inconsistency in argument, particularly in a series of articles in the *London Magazine* between October 1916 and March 1917. In the first, he said: 'If Germany had never built a Dreadnought or if the German Dreadnoughts had all been sunk, the control and authority of the British Navy could not have been more effective,' and went on to say that the Fleet was being offensive by doing nothing and that battles were a luxury; he made no mention of offensive operations. But in December he was saying that the Germans would not accept battle except on their own doorstep and that other means must be found to promote a clash. By January he was urging the Admiralty to take the offensive, adding that

'Monitors were not built to be tied up like cows to defend East Coast municipalities'.

In three months, therefore, there was a complete change of tune, and I think that the most charitable explanation is that he started the series in a spirit of loyalty to the current Admiralty policy, but soon reverted to his own strong convictions on the right way to wage the war.

Churchill had retained his contacts with Lloyd George throughout this sterile interlude, and was able to lend him support and ideas. The Prime Minister wanted to use his talents. 'His fertile mind, his undoubted courage, his untiring industry, and his thorough study of the art of war, would have made him a useful member of a War Cabinet. Here his more erratic impulses could have been kept under control and his judgement supervised and checked. . . .' But: 'For days I discussed with one or other of my colleagues Churchill, his gifts, his shortcomings, his mistakes, especially the latter. Some of them were more excited about his appointment than about the War. . . .'

The Tories, particularly, distrusted and disliked him:

May I again and for the last time urge you to think well before you make the appointment (WSC) which we have more than once discussed? . . . . X tells me that it will be intensely unpopular in the Army. I have every reason to believe the same of the Navy. . . . He is a potential danger in opposition. In the opinion of all of us, he will as a member of the Government be an active danger in our midst.

The Prime Minister chose the moment when Northcliffe was in Washington and appointed Churchill Minister of Munitions. Later he recorded: 'I took the risk, and although I had some reason to regret my trust, I am convinced I was right . . . for Churchill rendered conspicuous service in increasing the output of munitions when an overwhelming supply was essential to victory.'[250]

Minister of Munitions

Churchill took over from Addison on 18 July 1917, and, paradoxically, one of his first troubles was the efficiency with which the Admiralty controlled the production of specialized steel, aero-engines and other important items. Something of a monopoly had been established, and the new Minister found difficulty in getting fair shares for the Army and the Royal Flying Corps. As Lloyd George puts it in his *War Memoirs*: 'The Navy . . . being an essentially mechanised service started with a priority of claim and a superior army of mechanised talent.'

In fact, Churchill's especial protégé, the Royal Naval Air Service, had continued to make great progress after he had left the Admiralty, despite the fact that Balfour, his successor, had promptly handed over its flourishing ancillary activities like the armoured cars, the armoured trains and the anti-aircraft defence units to the War Office.

Due to the lack of suitable aircraft and of ships from which to operate them, air operations over the sea were seldom practicable in the early days of the war, so the RNAS, which was firmly imbued with Churchill's aggressive spirit, turned instead to the bombing of Germany. The bombing raid or the seaplane sheds at Cuxhaven on Christmas Day 1914 gained some successes; other aircraft operating from France and Belgium had attacked Cologne; and yet another operation had been launched against the Zeppelin sheds at Friedrichshafen.

Up to 1917, it was the RNAS which had supported and carried out a policy of strategic bombing, and the Royal Flying Corps which had rejected this policy and concentrated on Army support: a striking comparison with the views of the Royal Air Force in the Second World War.

But the greatest expansion of the RNAS came with the aircraft and airships needed for the defence of shipping against U-boat attack. The first U-boat was sunk by an aircraft in May 1917, and five more were sunk by the same means before the end of the year. Even more important was the effect of aircraft in the role of convoy escort, for it was soon found that convoys which were provided with air escort were virtually immune from attack.

By the end of the war, there were 285 aeroplanes, 291 seaplanes and flying-boats and 103 airships employed on anti-submarine duties in Home Waters alone, and these machines played an indispensable part in the protection of shipping. Thus it can be seen that the inspiration and impetus which Churchill gave the RNAS in its early days had a lasting effect.

But the rivalry between the RFC and the RNAS, and also the technical inferiority of the former's aircraft, led to the Smuts Report on Air Organization, which recommended the amalgamation of the RFC and the RNAS into one independent service, controlled by an Air Ministry. At the Cabinet meeting on 24 August 1917 at which these proposals were discussed, Churchill as Minister of Munitions was invited to attend.

At the meeting, Geddes, the First Lord, expressed misgivings about the introduction of a third ministry on to the service scene. The Admiralty had always insisted that the RNAS was an integral part of the Navy. However, he recognized that:

> There were strong reasons in favour of a development of Air Policy, and they accepted without question the views of those who had investigated it—that there is a definitive future for an aerial offensive apart from the Army and Navy. It did not appear practicable to them that such operations however should take place over the sea without being part of naval operations and under naval command. Consequently they considered at this stage it would be perfectly simple for the Air Ministry to adopt its proposed functions for the Army and for the Ministry independently, leaving the Royal Naval Air Service as it exists today. . . .[251]

The First Lord went on to say, however, that if his proposals were not accepted—and he seemed to assume that they would fail—then the 'naval aerial work' should be done by machines approved by the Admiralty and operated by pilots and observers trained on lines laid down by the Board, and that such units should be under naval command.*

Churchill supported the Admiralty contention that naval airmen required a longer training than others, but he also said that 'he himself strongly favoured the formation of an Air

---

* There is a lesson here for all negotiators—'never let it be known that you are going into conference with detailed second or third alternative plans in your pocket'.

Ministry. . . . Speaking from his own considerable experience, he was confident that there were natural and intimate bonds linking the two services. . . .'[252]

Thus by agreeing to an independent air force, guided by a specialized air staff to operate the growing number of aircraft which it was wrongly believed would be produced surplus to purely Army and Navy requirements,* he was sounding the death-knell of the RNAS, which he had done so much to nurture. And, although the Cabinet conclusions included a provision that air units provided by the RAF for operation with the Navy were to be placed under naval control,[253] this was forgotten when Coastal Area (later Coastal Command) was formed in peacetime. It was not until 1941, under the demands of war, that the Admiralty regained operational control of all maritime aircraft.

Lloyd George was highly critical of the Admiralty obstruction of attempts in 1916 and 1917 to pool the production of airframes and aero-engines. Maybe he was right in the broader picture. But there was no doubt that the Board was right in asserting that naval aircraft would suffer in a unified supply organization. From a superior position of owning the best aircraft, the Navy gradually suffered a decline in quality until in the years between the wars its aircraft were humiliatingly inferior—a fate which was avoided by the Fleet Air Arms of both America and Japan, countries which each retained a separate naval air organization.

I cannot agree with the views of those who, after the First War, wished to abolish the RAF and return the separate components to their old services. If this mistake had been made, I do not believe that the Battle of Britain of 1940 would have been won, for the service made responsible for Air Defence would not have diverted the resources necessary from its own traditional naval or military functions.

But, equally, I believe that the Battle of the Atlantic would never have reached a critical stage if some compromise scheme had been evolved by which the Navy would have been made

---

* Production estimates were extremely optimistic and bore no relation to facts.

233

responsible for the Fleet Air Arm and for all anti-submarine aircraft. As it was, the decisions of 1937 (to give the Navy control of its air arm) and 1941 (to place operational control of Coastal Command under the Admiralty) came too late.

Minister for War and for Air

Soon after the end of the war, Lloyd George re-formed the Coalition Government and offered Churchill the choice of the Admiralty or the War Office, adding that the Air Ministry would go with whichever Churchill accepted, as he did not want separate ministers for each of the three services.

Churchill, after a night's reflection, decided to accept the Admiralty, but next day events combined to persuade the Prime Minister that he must be sent to the War Office, and thus he became responsible for the Air Ministry also. Demobilization plans had not been successful, owing to the unfair rules for release. Unrest was widespread, and mutinies had occurred in some army units. A strong man was needed to settle affairs, and this, with a combination of firmness and of a revision of the rules in favour of 'first in, first out', Churchill proceeded swiftly to accomplish.

He has been criticized for his failure to reshape the army on modern lines, and for his drastic reductions in the size of the Air Force.[254] But he succeeded in keeping the Air Force in being, and this must be considered his main achievement—despite *The Times*'s comment on his period at the Air Ministry: 'He leaves the body of military flying at that last gasp when a military funeral would be all that would be left for it.'

Naval efforts to gain control of shipborne aircraft

In February 1919, soon after Churchill had taken over the Air Ministry, he recalled Trenchard as Chief of the Air Staff. He believed that Trenchard, who had resigned the post only eighteen months earlier, was the best man available to consolidate the new service, and he seems to have been so impressed by the obstruction of aviation by the older services, especially by the War Office, that he was determined to maintain a separate Royal Air Force, independent of the Army and Navy.

In the years following, both as Air Minister and as Secretary for the Colonies, he remained a faithful supporter of the new force, and did much to frustrate the efforts of those who wished to partition the RAF between the Army and Navy.[255] The years 1919–37 also saw an unedifying struggle between the Navy and the Air Force for the control of aircraft flying over the sea on naval missions, both from shore bases and from ships.

On many occasions—at the start of the Bonar Law Government of 1922,* during the Geddes economy committee† and during the Salisbury committees of 1923 and 1928—when the question of naval control was discussed, Churchill supported the RAF, because, I believe, he thought that any move to take away aircraft would lead to the disintegration of the RAF as an independent service.

Only in 1937, when the Whitehall atmosphere was quite different, when rearmament was under way and when the RAF was impregnably established, did he come round. Sir Thomas Inskip had been appointed to adjudicate on this contentious issue, arguments over which had wasted so much valuable Whitehall time since 1919. He asked Churchill's advice and was given a memorandum which 'was eventually adopted almost word for word by His Majesty's Government'.[257]

Churchill has been criticized by the advocates of the Royal Air Force for his part in this vital change of policy, and he has even been accused of bias against the concept of an independent air force. But such accusations are unfounded, and the story shows that his influence weighed heavily in favour of its survival.

The Memo is too long to reproduce, but extracts will show the sense of his views.

---

* Bonar Law had come to power with the aim of abolishing the RAF but the Minister, Hoare, with Churchill's support, managed to get him to change his mind.
† In evidence to the Geddes Committee, Churchill also pleaded for reductions in the Naval cuts.[256]

1. It is impossible to resist an admiral's claim that he must have complete control of, and confidence in, the aircraft of the battle fleet, whether used for reconnaissance, gun-fire, or air attack on a hostile fleet. These are his very eyes. Therefore the Admiralty view must prevail in all that is required to secure this result.

[2.] ... all functions which require aircraft of any description ... to be carried regularly in warships or in aircraft-carriers naturally fall to the naval sphere.

7. What is conceded to the Navy should, within the limits assigned, be fully given. The Admiralty should have plenary control and provide the entire personnel of the Fleet Air Arm. ...

10. The Air Ministry have as clear a title to control active anti-air defence as have the Navy to their own 'eyes'. . . .[258]

It is most surprising to find no mention whatever of the control of aircraft operating from shore bases on purely naval missions, whether against surface ships or on anti-submarine operations. It must have reflected a lack of knowledge of the predominant part played by shore-based aircraft and airships in the anti-submarine campaign of 1917 and 1918, and must also have stemmed from Churchill's dislike of the convoy system.* But the Admiralty was also much to blame for not pressing harder for the return of all maritime aircraft to the Navy, and there was the same lack of knowledge in the Naval Staff. This failure was to produce serious weaknesses in the early years of the war, which were only put right when Coastal Command was placed under the operational control of the Admiralty in 1941.

The return of naval aircraft to Admiralty control came too late to build up a fully integrated service before the outbreak of war, but it was better than to refuse to change. I believe that analysis of the results of maritime air operations in the Second World War shows conclusively that the Navy with its own air arm fared better than the Navy supported by an independent air force.

The disappointing results of the co-operation between the Luftwaffe and the German Navy, and the failure of the Italian

---

* See p. 227.

Navy to obtain effective help from the Regia Aeronautica, contrast sharply with the signal success of Japanese, American and, indeed, British naval aviation, despite the latter's late revival.

Minister for the Colonies

Churchill became Colonial Secretary in 1921 and was at once busily engaged in dealing with Middle East problems and with the Irish troubles. The Turkish crisis of 1922 provided the nearest approach to a close involvement in naval affairs.

> I found myself in this business with a small group of resolute men: the Prime Minister, Lord Balfour, Mr. Austen Chamberlain, Lord Birkenhead, Sir Laming Worthington Evans, with the technical assistance, willingly proffered, of the three Chiefs of Staff, Beatty, Cavan and Trenchard. . . .
>
> . . . The British Mediterranean Fleet lay in the Marmora, and its flotillas swept to and fro through the Dardanelles and the Bosphorus. No army could pass from Asia into Europe except piecemeal and clandestinely, at night. But, it was said, the Turks will bring cannon to the Asiatic shores . . . But Beatty said the Navy would put up with that; also that they would fire back.[259]

Fortunately, due to the firm but unprovocative handling of the situation by General Harrington, the Army Commander on the spot, it was not necessary to test the validity of naval confidence, and the crisis was settled satisfactorily without bloodshed.*

As Minister for the Colonies, Churchill remained a member of the CID and continued as a regular attender and frequent contributor to the discussions.†

At the first post-war meeting, Churchill asked for a Joint

---

* Churchill's method of dealing with the dominions during the crisis has been much criticized.

† When the CID was re-established after the war, a small subcommittee was formed, with the Prime Minister as nominal Chairman and the Service Ministers and Chiefs of Staff as members. This subcommittee acted for the CID and its minutes were later included in the full series.

Staff College to be set up (the Imperial Defence College was established shortly after), and he continued to urge the importance of joint staff training. Indeed, in the report of the committee on the Geddes proposals on national expenditure, he advocated a Ministry of Defence and the amalgamation of the 'common services' such as transport, food, stores and supplies.

And the CID minutes show that on questions of inter-service discussion—the future of the capital ship and the pre-parations for the Washington Conference on naval disarma-ment—he was particularly prominent.

He took a fairly consistent line—he was anxious to protect the Air Force from partition, but he was determined to keep a strong Navy. He irritated Lord Beatty by demanding that fresh minds be brought to bear on naval questions and sug-gesting that Admirals Richmond, Duff and Tyrwhitt, none of whom were members of the current Admiralty 'establishment', should be consulted. 'He himself was trying to keep an open mind on the subject [the future of the capital ship], though his ideas were at present strongly on the side of the Admiralty. He would however welcome any views which would tend to shake his opinion.'

Beatty said that:

> He [Beatty] himself could give the Committee the opinions held by Admirals Duff, Tyrwhitt, Keyes and Richmond. The Ad-miralty were not hidebound in their views. . . . He would add that if the Battle of Jutland had been carried forward to the conclusion to which it should have been carried, and had resulted in the destruction of the German Fleet, this question of the Capital Ship being superseded by the Submarine would never have arisen.[260]

Churchill ended his contribution by comparing the capital-ship controversy with the question of tanks versus cavalry. But he re-established himself with Beatty at a later meeting when, in commenting on Air Force claims, he said that he:

> . . . did not share the apprehensions of the Chief of the Air Staff as regards the great moral effect of the bombing of London. He considered that a potential enemy would be better advised to

concentrate on dockyards, magazines, etc., and other objects, the destruction of which would paralyse the organisation by which this country would transform itself from a peace to war footing.[261]

He tried also to gain agreement between Beatty and Trenchard on the relations between the Navy and the Air Force, but without success, and he reported in August 1922 that while the two sides had drawn together on material matters, on personnel no agreement could be found.[262]

There can be no doubt that the Admiralty, in their fight to gain control of aircraft flying over the sea, indulged in some bitter battles with the Air Force as a whole. There were faults on both sides, however, and exaggerated claims by the new service were responsible for much of the trouble.

In a paper by the Chief of the Air Staff on 'the part of the Air Force of the Future in Imperial Defence', which was discussed at the 137th meeting in May 1921, for example, the claim was made that the Air Force should assume responsibility for the 'defence of these islands from invasion by air; their protection against invasion by surface ships; and coastal defence'. The argument used was that 'as the Navy could only deal with attacks from the sea, while the Air Force could deal with attacks from both the air and the sea, it was logical that the control of the defence should rest with the Air Force'.

The task of the Army in resisting invasion does not seem to have been considered, and the thought that the problem was a joint operation which depended on close co-operation between the three services was ignored.

Amery, who was first Financial Secretary and later First Lord of the Admiralty, writes of his fierce fights with Churchill over naval economies,[263] and there can be no doubt that the latter had reverted to his 1909 ideas of a strong Navy, but not as strong as the Admiralty wanted. In the subcommittee of which he was Chairman which was set up to review the recommendations of the Geddes Report on national expenditure, however, Churchill saved the Navy from real disaster.

The gist of the Geddes recommendations on the Navy was a cut of £21,000,000 on the Estimates of £81,000,000 with the additional proviso that if the Washington Conference succeeded in reducing the capital-ship programme further cuts would be applied. What was even more serious, it was proposed to cut naval manpower from 121,000 to 88,000.[264]

The review-subcommittee report is full of Churchillian phrases. It demanded a 'one-power standard' with the United States Navy more for prestige reasons than from any fear of war: a forerunner of the 'seat-at-the-top-table' argument of today. It referred to the growing menace of Japan, and recommended a discreet building-up of the Singapore base complex. It refused to accept the Geddes cut in manpower and recommended instead a ceiling of 100,000, being 'convinced that the one-power standard could not be maintained on such a basis'. The Estimates were cut to £62,000,000 instead of the £60,000,000 recommended—a sharp reduction: but the Committee declined to proceed with the further cut consequent on the success of the Washington Conference in reducing big-ship building from four to two.

Defeat in an election

In December 1922 Churchill was defeated in the General Election, and another forced interlude of over a year intervened. He employed it profitably in writing a history of the war which (despite Balfour's remark, 'Winston has written an enormous book about himself and called it *The World Crisis*') must rank high in the lists of military literature of all nations.

I have already commented on a few of the concepts of war which reveal themselves from his writing,* and it may be remembered that the soundness of some is suspect. But the most important outcome of the long and thorough study of the course of the war was a conviction that the Dardanelles operation, which promised so much, had been ruined by feeble execution and supervision, as well as by poor planning. From this conviction stemmed a determination—subconscious perhaps—that in comparable circumstances in the future no such weakness would be tolerated.

His agony at the timidity and irresolution of the commanders, his pleas to be allowed to go to the Gallipoli peninsula

* See p. 226.

himself, his certainty that with more drive a brilliant victory could have been gained—these thoughts permeated his mind and he never forgot them. In the Second World War they were responsible, I am sure, for the constant journeys to the Middle East, for the goading of the commanders and for the lack of confidence in them shown in some of his signals. So when one criticizes the absurdity of the spurring of Admiral Sir Andrew Cunningham, the Commander-in-Chief in the Mediterranean, who of all men represented the essence of the offensive spirit, one must remember the agony of the Dardanelles, which had left a scar on Churchill's mind which never healed. And the ruthless dismissal of High Commanders—that of Wavell is the saddest example—must have stemmed from memories of those incompetents who by their indecision and inertia on the Gallipoli peninsula missed so many opportunities; men, moreover, who were allowed to remain in command to repeat their mistakes and to shed more unnecessary blood.

The Douglas libel case

There occurred, in 1923, a bizarre affair which might have damaged Churchill's reputation, but from which, fortunately, he emerged unscathed. It was the libel action brought by the Crown against Lord Alfred Douglas.

When, on 2 June 1916, the first communiqué on Jutland had been issued, the immediate effect of its stark language and open admission of serious losses was catastrophic. Balfour himself had written this first communiqué, as well as a second later in the day which gave an amplifying report. But when information about the German losses started to filter through from intelligence sources and it was realized that the High Seas Fleet would be out of action for some weeks, whereas the Grand Fleet had reported 'ready for sea' as soon as coaling had been completed after the battle, and was eager for a fresh attempt to crush the Germans, a different atmosphere prevailed. Balfour understood that his first words had been too gloomy, and that it was necessary to correct the mendacious accounts put out by German propaganda.

Accordingly, he invited Churchill, a political opponent but a personal friend, to visit the Admiralty and, after receiving all the available information about the damage to both sides, to draft an appreciation for immediate publication. Churchill wrote a short note which put the battle in its correct perspective. It stated: 'Our margin of superiority is in no way impaired,' and it ended with: '. . . in a blue-water action, which, as it is studied, will more and more be found to be a definite step towards the attainment of complete victory.'

There the matter rested for some years, until Lord Alfred Douglas, who had been the defender (and prosecutor) in more than one libel action, published an attack on Churchill in which he accused him of laying a plot with Sir Ernest Cassel. A false communiqué had been issued, he claimed,which brought about a panic-stricken fall on the Stock Exchange, both in London and New York; vast numbers of shares had been bought at the low price, and then the Churchill appreciation was issued which caused a rise in prices and gained Cassel a profit of £18,000,000. Churchill was advised by the Law Officers to disregard this ridiculous story, but a libel action by Douglas against the *Morning Post* on a different issue brought public attention to the matter, and so, in October 1923, the Government sued Lord Alfred Douglas for libel.

The account of the case makes gripping reading.[265] Much public interest was aroused. A number of prominent men, among them Balfour, Admiral Oliver and Admiral Jackson, gave evidence for the prosecution, and Churchill was the star witness. The two main defence witnesses proved unreliable and discredited (one had been certified insane), and the defendant's appearance in the witness box was laughable, so the jury needed only eight minutes to find him guilty, and Churchill's reputation was, rightly, saved. But it had been an anxious time, for mud, even when thrown by lunatics, is inclined to cling.

Chancellor of the Exchequer

The widespread criticism of Churchill's financial policies during his five years as Chancellor has received ample publicity. It is a less well-known paradox of this remarkable man's personality that his influence on the three services during these years was equally disastrous in its effect.

In 1919, he had supported Lloyd George's ruling that the Service Estimates should be framed on the assumption that 'the British Empire will not be engaged in any great war during the next ten years, and that no Expeditionary Force will be required'. On arrival at the Treasury in November 1924, one of his first acts was to ask for a review of this ruling—with a view to its extension—but no change was made except an application of the rule to Japan. In 1927, the War Office asked that the ruling should now cover only the ten years 'from the present date' but the Chancellor fought this proposal and in July 1928 the 'advancing' ten-year rule was affirmed by the Cabinet, with the proviso that the matter should be reviewed annually by the CID.[266]

Churchill defends his policy. 'Up till . . . 1929 I felt so hopeful that the peace of the world would be maintained that I saw no reason to take any new decision; nor in the event was I proved wrong. War did not break out till the autumn of 1939.'[267] But this is not altogether convincing, and the rule remained in force, in fact, till 1932. There is no doubt that, armed with such a weapon of policy, his task of attacking the Service Estimates from the Treasury was much simplified.

Having for so long pressed for the tank, and for mechanized warfare, he allowed the supporters of the horse to obstruct the mechanization of the Army under the guise of economy.[268] He cut the planned RAF expansion programme savagely, and although he had supported the efforts of the airmen to take over military policing duties in Iraq, Egypt and in India, he starved the Home Air Force.

For the Navy, he reserved his fiercest proposals for economy, and strongly opposed the cruiser-building programme, the first instalment of which had been drawn up before his arrival at the Treasury.* He claimed that the design of the ships was unsuitable for their task, but it was economy which really dominated his mind. After a bitter struggle and threats of resignation by the Board of Admiralty, a further programme of four 'county-class' cruisers was approved in February 1925,

---

* *Berwick, Cornwall, Cumberland, Kent, Suffolk.*

R

and these ships,* although much criticized at the time and subject to serious teething troubles, gave valuable service during the war.†

A few extracts from letters by Beatty, then First Sea Lord, illuminate the atmosphere of the times.

> That extraordinary fellow Winston has gone mad. Economically mad and no sacrifice is too great to achieve what in his short-sightedness is the panacea for all evil—to take a shilling off the Income Tax. As we the Admiralty are the principle spending department he attacks us with virulence. (*26 January 1925*)

> This Government . . . is actually behaving worse to us than the Labour Party. Of course it is all Winston as Chancellor. He has gone economy mad and the result is that the Government are not proposing to build any cruisers at all. (*1 February 1925*)

> I think that I have overcome them now and saved the situation . . . the way is clear to an understanding. (*14 February 1925*)[269]

The story of those five years tells of bitter battles with the Admiralty over ship-building and is punctuated by constant reductions and cancellations. In the 1926–7 estimates, for example, a five-year building programme was published which included, among others, the proposal to lay down a new aircraft-carrier in 1929. But nothing was heard of this ship until 1934–5 when the *Ark Royal* was approved.

In other ways, too, the Chancellor reduced the effectiveness of the Fleet by economies in the expenditure of oil fuel and practice ammunition; always an unprofitable exercise which leads to inertia and inefficiency.

Explanations of the apparent inconsistency of his policies towards the services in general and the Navy in particular are difficult to find. We have already seen the pattern. Economy in

---

* *London, Devonshire, Shropshire, Sussex.* The Royal Australian Navy also ordered the *Australia* and the *Canberra* of the same class.
† Due to the Washington Treaty, the new cruisers' size was limited to 10,000 tons displacement, and the resulting attempts to fit the maximum armament and the highest speed into such a hull produced a lightly protected ship with a large silhouette, so his criticisms had some force.

the defence departments in 1910 to help the schemes for social security, immediately followed in 1912 by a large expansion of ship-building. Now we have savage cuts in 1925 to be followed by demands for rearmament in the 1930s. One explanation must be that Churchill became absorbed in his task, whatever it was, and fitted himself with mental blinkers which allowed him to appreciate no one else's point of view. He then pursued his policies regardless of opposition and focused every energy on the task to be done. Despite his previous pre-occupation with welfare services, for instance, he seemed totally to ignore the damage to them caused by the expansion of the Naval Votes in 1912. And in the years 1925–9 he mercilessly reduced all three services, despite his admitted preoccupation with the dangers of a resurgent Germany.

Another possibility, suggested by an experienced elder statesman, is that he was no economist and did not pretend fully to understand the intricacies of finance and fiscal policy. As Chancellor, therefore, he was much in the hands of his permanent officials at the Treasury and the Bank of England, at a time when economy in public spending was still thought to be the key to success and the theories of Keynes had failed to win approval.

Out of office in 1930, with blinkers discarded, he saw the danger at once and started to preach rearmament. But it is, I think, a fair criticism that the deplorable condition of the nation's defences, which he struggled so hard to restore in the thirties, was due in considerable measure to his own policies in the twenties.

In the shadows again

When, in 1929, the Labour Government again took office, Churchill joined the Shadow Cabinet, but differences with his party leaders over policy towards self-government for India led him to resign, and gradually he became an independent back-bencher, only nominally supporting the Conservatives. He was not given office when the National Government was formed in 1931, and he remained an outsider, albeit an outsider of influence, until the outbreak of war.

Throughout the period, he retained a close interest in

defence questions—both Ramsay MacDonald and Neville Chamberlain allowed him to see CID papers—and he was anxious for office, preferably as First Lord. In 1936 it was thought that he would be given the newly created post of Minister for the Co-ordination of Defence, but Sir Thomas Inskip, who was singularly unqualified for the job, was appointed. Pressure to use Churchill's talents continued, but Baldwin, the Prime Minister, whose influence had been waning, recovered his strength during the Abdication Crisis, when Churchill supported the King, and felt enough confidence to continue without his experience and administrative ability.

But these years were not wasted, though Churchill found them bitter and frustrating and more than once despairingly described himself as 'one of the has-beens'. His production of *Marlborough: His Life and Times* absorbed his energies from 1933 and helped to keep his mind tuned and his analytical qualities keen. His great ancestor had been a capable wielder of sea-power. Marlborough's handling of the Mediterranean campaigns had been masterly, and he had understood, as few did, the benefits to be reaped from the intelligent use of a maritime strategy. Indeed he was more far-seeing than his admirals, who constantly complained about the diversion of resources from the 'main theatre'—i.e., the Home Station—to the Mediterranean, a complaint which the author must have found familiar.

> In the War of the Spanish Succession, the energies of the fleet were devoted to fighting purposes to a far higher degree than ever before or since. Sir George Rooke was the chief opponent of this view. He resisted at every stage and by every means the policy of dominating the Mediterranean. Arrogant, crafty . . . he saw no prize worth the risk and trouble in securing an overseas base in the Iberian Peninsula; still less was he attracted by prospects of such a base being used to draw the main fleet into the Mediterranean.[270]

Churchill's study of Marlborough's strategic concepts can only have confirmed him in the view that his own strategy in relation to the Dardanelles had been correct; and to it can be ascribed the genesis of the 'soft-underbelly' policy, the courageous reinforcement of the Middle East in the Second

World War and the unswerving determination to use pressure on the flanks rather than in the centre to bring victory.

It was a remarkable feature of British political life that, in 1935, Churchill was invited, as a back-bencher with most critical views of Government policy, to join the Air Defence Research Committee. From then on he took a prominent part in the development of air defence, and of course in the exploitation of radar for this and for other important purposes.

By then, too, Churchill was deeply worried by German rearmament and by the threat of air attack on this country by a modern German air force. He resented his political isolation and his lack of power directly to influence policy, and he would gladly have accepted office. But each time that it appeared probable that an offer was coming, something intervened. As he mentioned in *The Second World War*, this was fortunate for him in the end, for, when the call came, he was free from responsibility for the errors of the thirties, he was known as a consistent champion of rearmament, and he started off in office with a clean sheet.[271]

He pressed strongly for the formation of a Ministry of Supply, for he believed that the Air Ministry and War Office were not capable of organizing the production drive required, but it was not until he became Prime Minister in 1940 that he was able to form a Ministry of Aircraft Production, while the Ministry of Supply was set up too late (spring of 1939) to provide the weapons required for the Army.

As the menace of war drew nearer, his interest in the Navy increased. Admiral Fraser, for example, recalls that in 1939 Churchill drew his attention to the possibilities of naval exploitation of radar—a development of which Fraser, only recently appointed Controller of the Navy, was as yet unaware.[272] In this way, Churchill encouraged the development of radar for detecting surface targets as well as aircraft, for directing the armament at night and when the target could not be seen, and for other purposes.

In 1936 he engaged, as a back-bencher, in a lengthy correspondence with the Admiralty on the question of the size and number of the guns to be fitted in the new battleships, five of which were to be laid down to replace the elderly

Royal Sovereigns, for which Churchill had been responsible in 1913.

In his enthusiasm, he was inclined to look back instead of forward, and in later years he admitted that: 'I did not sufficiently measure the danger to, or the consequent deterrent upon, British warships from air attack.'[273] And I think it is true that he accepted too easily the Admiralty confidence that the guns and protection of warships would provide sufficient defence against air attack—a confidence which was quickly lost by those at sea during the Norwegian campaign of 1940.

Churchill also visited the anti-submarine training establishment at Portland and went to sea to witness A/S exercises. He was much impressed by the results. 'What surprised me was the clarity and force of the [Asdic] indications. I had imagined something almost imperceptible, certainly vague and doubtful. I never imagined that I should hear one of those creatures asking to be destroyed. It is a marvellous system and achievement.'[274]

But he was lucky in watching exercises carried out in perfect conditions. No mention was made of those days when water conditions made Asdic detection (also known as 'Sonar') extremely difficult, nor of the problem of detecting submarines operating on the surface at night, when the Asdic was of little use. He came away with too optimistic a picture of the efficiency of this system, which coloured his appreciation of warships' immunity to submarine attack.

In general, then, his contacts with the Admiralty in these years, reinforced by his natural trust in the battleship which stemmed from his years as First Lord, gave him too rosy an appreciation of the Fleet's ability to operate in the face of submarine and air attack. This distorted his subsequent judgement, and led to the failure off Norway and the disaster off the Malayan coast in 1941.

Many authorities, among them Sir Basil Liddell Hart and the Air Marshals and their chroniclers, have criticized Churchill for his support of the battleship-replacement programme in the thirties. It is easy, in the light of the fate of the *Prince of Wales* in the Second World War, to say that the

Admiralty was wrong to build the five *King George V*s, the first of which became operational in 1940 and the last in 1942. But I believe the critics forget some inconvenient facts. The alternative choice was, clearly, to build more aircraft-carriers and to rely on aircraft, both carrier-borne and shore-based, for the destruction of enemy battleships and cruisers. For the potential enemy, German, Italian or Japanese, showed no signs of wishing to dispense with these ships. But this argument ignores the fact that aircraft could only operate effectively in daylight during the first years of the war. Until radar and other navigational aids had been fitted they could not fly from carriers at night or in thick weather, so at night carriers became defenceless targets, requiring their protection to be provided by another source, and this could only be the battleship.

Moreover, without radar, aircraft could not find their quarry by night or in poor visibility, and they could not hit it once it was found. It was the fitting of radar to carriers and to carrier-borne aircraft which turned them into all-weather weapons and so allowed them to provide both for their own protection and for attacks on the enemy, by night and by day. But this could not have been foreseen in 1936. Indeed, in the first years of the war, the carriers could not face, at night, ships like the *Bismarck*, the *Scharnhorst* and the *Gneisenau*. They had to be kept out of their way, and this situation would not have been altered if there had been more of them. Modern, fast battleships were needed.

Before the war the Admiralty gravely underestimated the air threat to ships, and the Naval Staff was slow to understand, in the early stages, that the situation had changed. Moreover, the enthusiasm of the specialists was responsible for too optimistic a view of the capability of the Asdic to defend both warships and convoys.

In the light of full after-knowledge, however, I cannot agree that the decision to build the *King George V*s was a mistake. Perhaps five was too many. But they filled a gap, short but important, when the carrier was unable to provide its own protection, and I tremble to think what would have happened if in 1940 the fleets had had to rely on the *Nelson* and the *Rodney,* on the *Queen Elizabeths* and the *Royal Sovereigns,* for their main source of strength.

In 1945, in the Pacific, the modern battleship was a useful adjunct to the carrier. In 1940 the battleship was an indispensable defence, and sometimes a substitute for the carrier on the many occasions when aircraft could not effectively operate.

The eve of war

As the beating of the drums calling the nations to war grew louder, so Churchill's involvement in defence affairs increased. He was becoming an unofficial adviser to the Government. His counsel during the Abyssinian Crisis of 1936 had been ambivalent. He was obsessed by the menace of Hitler and he did not want a war with Italy and the weakening of our position in the Mediterranean which he feared might result. He had been slow to realize the danger of Mussolini's policy, and he hated the thought of fighting the Italian people. His analysis of the times in Volume I of *The Second World War* indicates that he thought he had listened too carefully to the alarmists and should have sought the opinion of the Commander-in-Chief in the Mediterranean, who was in no doubt whatever as to the outcome of any clash with Italy.

But at the time of the Munich Crisis he was as firm as a rock. He advised the Government to bring forward the Reserve Fleet on 31 August 1938—the Fleet was mobilized on 28 September. He was one of the few members of Parliament who did not acclaim Chamberlain's return from Munich with 'peace in our time'. He worked incessantly to confront Hitler and to seek strong allies, notably the Russians.

When the Italian Army invaded Albania, in early April 1939,* he complained bitterly about the dispersed state of the Mediterranean Fleet. 'Of our five great capital ships, one was at Gibraltar, another in the Eastern Mediterranean, and the remaining three were lolling about inside or outside widely-separated Italian ports, two of them not protected by their flotillas.'[275] And in a letter to Lord Halifax, the Foreign

---

* The 'Easter Sunday Invasion'.

Secretary, a few days after the invasion, he also warned him of the unreadiness of the Home Fleet, whose ships were semi-immobilized by a leave period and whose minesweepers were refitting.[276] His mind must have returned to the days of Agadir and of Lord Charles Beresford's warning of unreadiness. On 15 May instructions were issued for the call-up of 15,000 reservists in order to man the Reserve Fleet by 15 June, and his advice, again, had proved useful.

From then on, he was increasingly consulted by the Government, and it was clear that, if war came, he would be called upon. In August the French Army invited him to tour the Franco-German frontier, and he says that he came away with a strong impression of defeatism and of the acceptance of the defensive which may have been generated in the Maginot Line.[277]

With this up-to-date knowledge of the French Army, with the grasp of the problems of air defence gained in the Air Defence Research Committee, and with his continuing contacts with naval affairs, he was, by the end of August 1939, well equipped for the trials ahead. As a final comment, it is well to note that on 5 August he made, in a letter to Sir Kingsley Wood, the Secretary of State for Air, a most accurate forecast of the future development of nuclear energy—a letter intended to prevent a sudden scare which might '. . . induce us by means of . . . threat to accept another surrender'.*[278]

But this time there was to be no surrender.

---

* In an article in the *Strand Magazine* of December 1931, Churchill had foretold both the peaceful and the warlike uses of Atomic Energy.

11

FIRST LORD AGAIN

*My thoughts went back a quarter of a century to that other
September when I had last visited Sir John Jellicoe and his
captains in this very bay, and had found them with their long
lines of battleships and cruisers drawn out at anchor, a prey to
the same uncertainties as now afflicted us . . . but now all these
were new figures and new faces. The perfect discipline, style,
and bearing, the ceremonial routine—all were unchanged. But
an entirely different generation filled the uniforms and the
posts. Only the ships had most of them been laid down in my
tenure. None of them was new.*[279]

WSC

'Winston is back'

THE signal *'Winston is back'* was received in the Navy
with great satisfaction. Officers and men, young and
old, all were delighted and believed that now we had a
man who would infuse some 'zip' into our affairs. The Navy
had not been fortunate in its political heads since the First
World War. None had been outstanding. Few had shown much
real interest in the service or in its people, and one or two, in
the thirties, had appeared bored stiff. So the knowledge that
Churchill, whose experience of the Admiralty was so great and
who had almost alone preached of the dangers of the coming
war, would be directing the Navy came as a great encouragement.

But this reflects an interesting change of heart. When
Churchill left the Admiralty in 1915, relief was general, and
when it was rumoured that Lloyd George was considering
his return to the Admiralty in 1917 a 'resistance movement'
was at once formed. And as Chancellor, from 1925 to 1929,
he had been no friend to the Navy. But it was known that
he was a 'character' who 'did things', even if sometimes mistakenly, that he was full of zeal and enthusiasm; and it was
thought that after his warnings of war and his appeals for rearmament, he should be given a chance to put his theories into
practice.

The most important requirement for any First Lord's capable control of the Admiralty is a satisfactory relationship with his principal naval adviser, the First Sea Lord. Churchill's memories of Wilson, Bridgeman and Battenberg were vivid, and his desertion by Fisher was forgiven but not forgotten. Mutual confidence was essential, and from the Navy's point of view the First Sea Lord had to be firm and clear in argument to defeat many of the wild schemes which would emerge from the First Lord's fertile mind.

Churchill started off with some prejudice against Admiral Pound, whom he believed, mistakenly, to have been negligent during the Albanian Crisis of 1939 in allowing the Mediterranean Fleet to be dispersed in several Italian ports when the crisis broke. Intelligence of the move had been lacking and the Government was equally caught unprepared. But a most satisfactory relationship was quickly formed. Pound was imperturbable, determined in discussion and a master of the details of his profession—his knowledge of the work of the main fleets was probably unequalled. Called unexpectedly to the Admiralty from the Mediterranean on the illness of Sir Roger Backhouse in the summer of 1939, he had only three months in Whitehall before the start of the war. His principal assistant in operational matters, Rear-Admiral Phillips, had arrived with him, so that there had been little time to settle down, but both men were experienced in Admiralty business and by September the machine was working smoothly.

No biography of Admiral Pound has yet appeared. He was a reserved, rather remote man, who needed knowing before the humanity and humour emerged. He was extremely hardworking and was quite selfless—when appointed to succeed Admiral Fisher in the Mediterranean at the time of the Abyssinian Crisis he had volunteered to serve as Chief of Staff so that Fisher could continue in command. An assessment of his stature must wait some years, but for this study it is enough to say that, for the first year of the war, at least, he was the ideal foil for Churchill, whose confidence and trust he quickly acquired. His complete loyalty soon aroused affection, and his dogged determination to defeat the First Lord's wilder schemes laid the foundation of a sound administration. It will be seen later that Pound was stricken by a fatal illness, but during the period we are now considering he was tireless, fit and alert.

The Navy as a whole was in excellent heart, and the dress rehearsal of Munich had shown many mistakes which had been put right. The mobilization of the Reserve Fleet in June had ensured a speedy deployment of the Navy to its war stations, and, as in 1914, it was well prepared all over the world. In numbers, it was much reduced compared to 1914, but the enemy strength was also much weaker. There were 10 battle-ships, 2 battle-cruisers and 6 aircraft-carriers operational. The cruiser force consisted of 49 ships, together with 8 from Australia and New Zealand. There were 162 destroyers to-gether with 11 from Australia and Canada, 54 escort vessels, and 69 submarines.

Probably the three weakest features were the shortage of escorts for convoys, the small numbers and poor performance of the naval aircraft embarked in the carriers, and the com-plete lack of ships and craft for amphibious warfare. The unsatisfactory aircraft provided for the Navy by the Air Ministry had formed one of the many reasons for the decision to transfer to the Admiralty full control of its aviation. But two years were too short, and it was not until American aircraft were obtained that naval aircrew were enabled to fight on equal terms with the enemy. The basis of carrier-borne aircraft in 1939 was the Swordfish, which was a reliable, rugged torpedo carrier with a tremendous capacity for load-carrying and achieved a wide range of functions. But it was very slow, and an easy target for enemy fighters or anti-aircraft fire. Despite this, it performed nobly and remained in operation till the last year of the war, the need for an A/S machine which could operate at night having extended its life considerably.

For the shortage of convoy escorts, however, the Admiralty must bear direct responsibility, and there can be little excuse. Despite the lessons of the years 1917 and 1918, when sinkings of merchant ships by U-boats had threatened to bring the war to an end due to a shortage of supplies for the Western Allies, commerce protection had not received the attention it de-served. Between the wars, far too much time had been devoted to Jutland and the controversies which followed; far too little to the problems of the defence of convoys, and any convoy situations which were discussed related to attacks by surface raiders. The U-boat war on shipping had been a shameful episode in our naval history, for the Admiralty had been slow to adopt the convoy system in 1917 and the process of persuading it to do so had been painful. It is evident now that the instinct was to forget such disagreeable affairs and concentrate on 'proper' naval operations such as the clashes between great fleets. This attitude was encouraged by two other factors—the wishful thinking of those who declared that never again would Germany resort to unrestricted warfare against shipping, and the opinion that convoy was a defensive system. As a result, trade defence became something to be left to the second team; the glamour lay in the main fleets and there were to be found the best officers.

Consequently in 1939 the Navy was unprepared psychologically as well as materially for an attack on trade. There was no 'doctrine' of convoy defence, no tactics had been evolved, the potential escort commander had no guidance as to his duties and the historians had paid little attention to the tragic story of trade protection. The importance of aircraft in the defence of convoys against U-boat attack had been entirely forgotten, and here the Air Ministry was no less at fault.*

It was also a grave reflection on the inter-service co-operation between the wars that so little had been done to prepare for the 'combined operations' which had formed a regular feature of our past history, and of which Gallipoli was such a recent example. Perhaps, as with the U-boat war, disappointment had banished this episode from men's minds. At any rate, in 1939 only a few assault-craft were being laid down, exercises had been few and on a small scale, and little study had been devoted to the art of amphibious warfare.

In many other aspects of naval warfare, the lessons of the First World War had been assimilated. Night fighting was

---

* The last two volumes of the *History of the War in the Air* gave clear descriptions of the value of the work of aircraft in trade defence. But the last volume was not issued till 1937 and this came too late.

rigorously exercised under realistic conditions. Surface gunnery was effective and the shells were efficient, though the aircraft bombs were unreliable. British torpedoes were trustworthy, though a little slow and short-ranged. British propulsion machinery was rugged and reliable, if somewhat old-fashioned.

In the detection of submarines British science led the world, though the enthusiasm of the experts had caused exaggerated claims and there was a lack of knowledge of the weakness of 'Sonar' under some conditions.*

It was unfortunate that the anti-submarine branch of the Navy was not strong; it was comparatively new and had not attracted enough really good officers to gain the drive and enthusiasm needed. Worse still, Commander Walker, the most able officer in the branch, had been 'passed over' for promotion to Captain and as a result started the war in a shore job, in which his talents and leadership were not used to the best advantage. Later, he was to prove an unequalled killer of U-boats and a magnificent convoy escort commander. But he was not able to develop his potential in peacetime.

In the very important matter of the provision of shore-based aircraft of the Royal Air Force for work with the Navy, the situation was not promising. A force of 291 aircraft had been allocated, but less than two-thirds of this number was available. There were very few suitable machines, and not until the Hudson was bought from America and the Sunderland flying-boat came along in quantity did the quality measure up to the task. Most of the training was aimed at intercepting surface raiders, and the problems of convoy defence had been neglected. There was no effective weapon for use by aircraft against submarines. In the words of Roskill, 'Coastal Command had always been the Cinderella of its own service.'

As we have already seen, there was also much overconfidence in the ability of ships to defend themselves against air attack with their own guns. Anti-aircraft control was poor—the Italians already had a far better system. The eight-barrelled

---

* The passage of sound-waves through water is quite different from that of radar-waves through the atmosphere. Sound-waves are easily deflected by various phenomena, while radar-waves are consistently straight.

pompom, on which so much reliance was placed, had more bark than bite, and the arrangements for dealing with low-flying torpedo-carrying aircraft were primitive.

In 1939 radar was fitted in only two ships and was used only for warning against the approach of aircraft. The days when it could detect surface targets, aim and fire the guns and explode the shells near their targets were still to come.

The Royal Navy at the start of the war creaked a little, and it still suffered from the financial stringencies of the twenties and early thirties. But morale was high, the fleets were well trained, and the knowledge that a large building programme of 6 aircraft-carriers, 5 battleships, 19 cruisers and 30 destroyers or escorts was under way added to the general confidence.

Other navies

The German Navy was only a shadow of its first-war self. The core of the Fleet consisted of the 2 new battle-cruisers *Scharnhorst* and *Gneisenau* and 3 pocket-battleships with eleven-inch guns and a large radius of action. There were 6 cruisers, 20 destroyers, 14 torpedo boats and many small craft. The U-boat fleet totalled 56 boats (the Admiralty had been deceived by a clever ruse and thought the number was higher). Of these 26 were ocean-going and 30 were coastal types of small displacement. All these ships were new, and there was a building programme which included 2 battleships, 3 cruisers and 1 aircraft-carrier (which was never completed).

During August 1939 eleven U-boats sailed for their war stations and the pocket battleships *Graf Spee* and *Deutschland*, together with their supply ships, were passed into the Atlantic. None of these moves was known to British Intelligence.

The German naval leaders were well aware that they could not directly challenge the Royal Navy, but they were determined to attack trade from the start with U-boats, aircraft, mines and surface raiders. Hitler, however, for political reasons issued very restrictive orders for the first few months of the war—the pocket-battleships were not allowed to attack trade, for instance. Indeed, the sinking on 3 September of the liner *Athenia* by a U-boat, with heavy loss of life, was a mistake made contrary to orders. It was a fortunate error for the

Admiralty, for it convinced the doubters that convoys must at once be instituted.

The German Navy was modern, efficient and well led, and its ships well designed and built. The U-boat crews were well trained, and the gunnery standard of the surface ships was high. Good progress had been made with radar for use against ships, though less for the detection of aircraft, and in its use to assist gunnery fire-control the Germans were well ahead of the British.[280] But after the British invention of the Magnetron, which allowed centimetric radar with close discrimination, they were soon outstripped in every aspect of the use of radar and never again even reached parity.

In one other important part of sea warfare the Germans were unexpectedly proficient—in obtaining information from the codes and cipher signals of the enemy. It is clear from Admiral Doenitz's *Memoirs** that until the summer of 1943 the German 'B' service was able to read most of the signals giving the position of British ships, convoys and submarines, and this was a very great advantage, especially as it was not suspected that the codes were being broken. On the British side the cryptographers were 'not inactive', as the official historian puts it, but no details are available for security reasons.

There were, fortunately, some grave weaknesses on the German side. The machinery of some of the cruisers and of all the destroyers was brand new and of high performance. But it had not been properly tested at sea, teething-troubles were serious, and many ships were out of action for long periods for repairs. German torpedoes, though of high performance, did not keep their depth and were fitted with warheads of advanced design which did not work. The story of the Norwegian campaign would have been very different if the U-boat torpedoes had been effective.

The French Navy was modern and well trained, and its strength was roughly comparable with that of the Italian Fleet. Co-operation with the British had been worked out in considerable detail before the war, and relations between the two services were good. During the months in which the French

* Weidenfeld and Nicolson, 1959.

and British operated together, harmony was complete, especially off Norway, yet the French, by chance, did not have any opportunity to win great distinction.

Of the potential enemies, Italy, with a medium-sized modern fleet, was obviously unready for war, but it was equally clear that Mussolini would seize any chance to pick up an easy prize. The attitude of Japan was difficult to assess: Japanese eyes looked across the Pacific, and the United States was very strong.

The impact on administration

There is no doubt that Churchill's arrival brought a blast of fresh air down the corridors of the Admiralty. His satisfaction at finding his office unchanged and his own chart of the North Sea lying undisturbed in an alcove, his first meeting with the Sea Lords—all have been described more than once. The same stream of minutes started to pour out, each demanding information on every conceivable subject or suggesting action. These missives soon became known as 'daily prayers'.

By his interest in technological development he did much to persuade the senior officers of the supreme importance of technical advance, and although some needed no urging there were others who were not fully aware of the march of science. The first losses from magnetic mines, for example, were suspected in early September and confirmed on the 16th. Churchill was then at his best. He encouraged every type of antidote. He helped to set up an organization to plan and produce counter-measures. And when, on 23 November, a complete mine was recovered from the mud of the Thames and the solution had been found, he saw personally that everyone concerned, naval or civilian, understood the importance of driving on with the production of sweeping-gear and with the fitting of all ships with 'degaussing' protection. The story of the battle against the magnetic mine in the first three months of the war tells of a miracle of improvisation which produced effective permanent measures for defence against mines of all types.

In personnel questions, the First Lord resumed his interest in the senior appointments and vetted personally each flag officer proposed for a new post. He had not forgotten his fight for improving conditions of service on the lower deck, and he was also as keen as ever to produce conditions by which the abler men could become officers and ferreted out one or two branches where this was not possible. He issued many 'prayers' on personnel questions, and there is one when he overrode the Board over the granting of cadetships.

> I have seen the three candidates. Considering that these three boys were 5th, 8th and 17th in the educational competitive examination . . . I see no reason why they should have been described as unfit for the naval service. It is quite true that A. . . . has a slight cockney accent, and that the other two are the sons of a Chief Petty Officer and an engineer in the merchant service. But the whole intention of competitive examination is to open the career to ability, irrespective of class or fortune.

He ended the minute: 'Cadetships are to be given in the three cases I have mentioned.'[281]

It has proved possible to trace the careers of these three officers. Two are still serving, and after useful, honourable careers have reached the rank of Commander.* The third resigned his commission in 1948 after service in which he always received reports of above average merit, and the fact that he was wounded in action during the war may have influenced his decision to leave the Navy. None of the three served in the seaman branch.

It is clear that the First Lord was right and the Board wrong.

His energy seemed unimpaired and he succeeded, with the aid of his afternoon siesta, in cramming a vast amount of work into each day. He paid a series of visits to the Fleet, to the dockyards, to Scapa and other ports, and to training establishments and experimental stations, so that it was crystal clear to the whole Navy that the First Lord was genuinely interested in every facet of the service and especially in the officers and men. He was quick to praise a victory or some exceptional exploit, and he often met or sent for those responsible, so that he could hear their story personally.

* 1967.

Admiral James recalls how the First Lord decided to abolish the automatic court martial on the captain of a ship which had been lost in action, because he thought that the practice was bad for morale.[282]

Finally, by his broadcasts, he was gradually establishing himself as the spokesman of the nation. The tone was exactly right, and there was none of the bombast which had marred his speeches in 1914. He paid tribute to the enemy fighting men when tribute was due, and he castigated Hitler and his lackeys in terms which have never been bettered.

The quest for the offensive

The transport of the British Expeditionary Force to France had gone smoothly, and thereafter there was inaction on the Continent. The War Cabinet had decided against the bombing of land targets for fear of retaliation against Allied cities, and although the RAF made some attacks on German ships in the first weeks the operations were so expensive in aircraft and disappointing in results that there was no repetition. Thus the Navy was the only service fully engaged from the start, and there was no twilight war at sea. This fact was agreeable to the First Lord and it helped him to achieve a pre-eminent position in the War Cabinet and in the committees directing the war effort.

But operations were mainly defensive—the protection of shipping from every type of attack—and although this used up much energy and consumed much time, it did not satisfy the First Lord, who longed for an offensive against the enemy vitals. His mind returned to the First War; and his first scheme, which he pursued with great determination, was for a sortie into the Baltic, the object of which was to gain control of this sea and, among other advantages, to cut off the iron-ore traffic from Sweden to Germany.

Plan 'Catherine' envisaged the transformation of two of the old *R*-class battleships into super-monitors, with heavily armoured decks and a light draught produced by lashing caissons on either beam. A dozen minesweepers were to clear a passage for the battleships, and the force was to be fuelled by 'turtle-back blistered tankers', carrying enough oil for three months. There were also to be cruisers, destroyers, submarines and depot ships, and: 'An aircraft-carrier could be sent in at the same time. . . .' The expedition was to set off after the ice had melted in the spring of 1940.[283]

The plan was hopelessly impracticable, and ignored the inability of the Fleet to operate in waters dominated by the enemy force. 'A heavy attack from the air must be countered by the combined batteries of the fleet,' was pure wishful thinking. Only a few days after the First Lord's plan had been launched, it was proved conclusively that the guns of the Fleet were ineffective against air attack; the dive-bombers, in particular, had caught the AA controls unprepared.[284]

Naval staff opinion was initially encouraging, but as the implications, especially the effect on the ship-building programme, became clear, it changed to opposition. The material work involved was immense and would have occupied much ship-building and repair capacity; and it was doubtful, anyhow, if the work could have been finished in time. More important still, the object of the plan—to stop the summer iron-ore traffic from Sweden—was unimportant compared with the risks to be taken. In 1914 Fisher had at least wished to land a Russian army in Pomerania; in 1939 the Russians were unfriendly neutrals.

Much effort was expended by busy technical staffs in examining the proposals and much time was expended by the operational staffs in arguing against the plan. Naval opinion was unanimously unfavourable.[285] Eventually, and reluctantly, the First Lord gave way. But at what cost in wasted effort! It is noteworthy that the official history of the war does not even mention Plan 'Catherine'; it is a record of events rather than of aspirations. Lord Fraser, who was then Controller of the Navy, recalls that one bonus was obtained. Almost the only material progress with the plan was the conversion of four cargo liners to armoured ammunition and supply ships, and these ships, pre-eminent among them the *Breconshire*, were later to be found invaluable in many operations in the Mediterranean.[286]

Another offensive idea which consumed much effort was Operation 'Royal Marine', which was to involve laying floating mines in the Rhine to be carried downstream by the current and bring all traffic in its German waters to a halt. Unfortunately the French would not agree to this project for fear of retribution, and it was overtaken by the invasion of France in 1940. Yet another brainwave had a purely military use. A machine called 'Cultivator' was designed by the naval constructors to dig trenches through the enemy lines and so breach the strongest defences. But the German Panzers found a better way by outflanking the lines, and so the scheme died a natural death in the spring of 1940. The concept was exactly parallel to the mechanized tractor of 1914 which turned into the tank. But this was the only example of 'interference' in another service. There were none of those private visits to France which so enraged Lord Kitchener, and the First Lord's journeys were all made in company with the Prime Minister to Allied War Councils, at which he maintained a surprising silence.

Yet another diversion related to the Fleet Air Arm. The First Lord was worried by the cost of naval aviation and by the fact that, owing to the circumstances of the twilight war, naval aircraft were not engaged in offensive operations against the enemy coast. The seaplane raid on Christmas Day 1914 must have been a vivid memory. He therefore produced a plan to '. . . liberate the RAF from all ordinary coastal duties in the Narrow Waters and the North Sea, and to assume the responsibility for the Fleet Air Arm'. To achieve this, he wanted to reduce the aircraft complements of the carriers in order to form squadrons to operate in coastal waters from shore bases. As he says in *The Second World War*, this plan was swept away by events. Behind the scheme may have been the wish to take over Coastal Command—long an Admiralty goal—but to divest the carriers of their aircraft was not the right way to go about it.

Of all the 'offensive' hares, the most dangerous was the First Lord's prejudice against the convoy system and his obsession with 'patrolling forces, sweeping the seas of U-boats'. In November 1939 he was writing to the First Sea Lord:

I am deeply concerned at the immense slowing down of trade, both in imports and exports, which has resulted from our struggle during the first ten weeks of the war. . . . We shall have failed in our task if we merely substitute delays for sinkings. . . . We must secretly loosen up the convoy system (while boasting about it publicly), especially on the outer routes . . . a higher degree of risk must be accepted. . . . [Our ships] can go in smaller parties. Even across the Atlantic we may have to apply this principle to a refinement . . .[287]

This minute shows a lack of comprehension of the fundamentals of the convoy system, one of which was that for a U-boat in the wide oceans a convoy was only marginally easier to find than a single ship. Later in the month, he wrote:

Nothing can be more important in the anti-submarine war than to try to obtain an independent flotilla which could work like a cavalry division on the approaches without worrying about the traffic or U-boat sinkings, but could systematically search large areas over a wide front. In this way these areas would become untenable to U-boats . . .[288]

This too reveals the old obsession with military tactics, but the imagery aroused by this picture gave a totally false impression of dash, action and the spirit of the offensive. It ignored the fact that random sweeping for U-boats was like searching for a needle in a haystack. Even when the water conditions were good, the chances of success were very small indeed.* There was no doubt that the best place to find U-boats was around the convoys which they must attack if they were to succeed. There they could be destroyed, if possible before they attacked, but if necessary afterwards. This was the true offensive. The diversion of the precious convoy escorts to offensive sweeps left the convoys lamentably weak—some were escorted by one destroyer or even by one trawler—and it totally failed to sink U-boats.

In a footnote to his minute quoted above, Churchill wrote in 1948: 'This policy [of forming independent flotillas] did not become possible until a later phase in the war.'[289] This, I am afraid, shows that he never understood the functions of the support groups which were formed in late 1942 and early 1943. They were intended to strengthen the escort of convoys which

---

* See p. 248.

were threatened or attacked, or, when *accurate* intelligence of a U-boat was known, to seek it out and destroy it. Support groups never aimlessly swept the ocean; they were kept in positions from which they could best reinforce convoys, and it was near convoys that they scored their greatest successes.

It was only in 1942, when the pioneers of operational research led by Professor Blackett thoroughly investigated the early period of the U-boat war, that clear proof of the efficacy of the convoy system was accepted by Churchill; he then agreed that the bigger the convoy, the better the result, and that independent sailings, except for very fast liners, were extremely dangerous. But many ships, lives and cargoes were lost unnecessarily before this fact was understood.

In September 1939 a committee under Admiral Binney had observed that '. . . the best position for anti-submarine vessels is in company with a convoy', recommending that 'every anti-submarine vessel with sufficiently good sea-keeping qualities should be employed with convoys rather than dispersed in hunting units'.[290] This conclusion was endorsed by the Vice-Chief of the Naval Staff. It is therefore surprising to find that almost exactly the opposite policy was adopted in practice, and that no guidance on these lines was sent to the Commanders-in-Chief concerned. It would be unfair to saddle the First Lord with all the blame. His naval advisers were also gravely responsible, for, despite the recommendations of the Binney Committee, the Naval Staff too was mesmerized by the concept of offensive sweeps—a concept which received temporary encouragement from some early claims of successes against U-boats which later proved to be unfounded. But Churchill's restless search for 'action' and his cavalry background encouraged these fallacies instead of killing them.

It must be recorded, however, that from the start the First Lord understood the vital importance of trade defence to the nation, and that he never forgot it, whatever the circumstances of the war. Although the threat from the German U-boats was small at the outbreak of war, he foresaw the great U-boat building programme and he laid plans to foil the offensive to come. His early minutes are full of warnings about the dangers ahead, and he saw that an emergency programme of trawler conversions to A/S work was given high priority, and laid the foundations of a sound programme of escort-vessel construction. What is more, he ordered the move of the Western Approaches Command Headquarters from Plymouth to Liverpool, where it was much better placed to control operations, and although the move was opposed in the Admiralty it was more than justified by events.

One point which it is difficult to understand, however, is his insistence on publishing figures of the sinking of U-boats which were much higher than those presented to him by his Intelligence advisers. He had urged realistic claims of enemy damage from the start, yet he ignored his own instructions over the U-boat casualties, an inconsistency which, I believe, stems from the advice given him by Professor Lindemann, who distrusted all Intelligence reports. Lindemann was often right, but the U-boat assessment committee was remarkably accurate throughout the war.

The control of operations

In 1914–15, one of the main criticisms of the First Lord was that he interfered in the control of operations. In 1939–40 he took the closest interest in whatever was going on at sea, and he was a regular visitor to the Operational Intelligence Centre (or War Room) where control was exercised. Pound kept a firm hand on the direction of affairs, however, and there were few examples of signals being sent out by the First Lord himself. Only when political factors intruded, as during the *Altmark* incident and the Norwegian campaign, did he act himself.

Indeed Pound, who had always preferred to draft his own signals, was a great centralizer, and kept a very firm hand on the movements of the Home Fleet, much to the fury of the Commander-in-Chief, who protested vigorously. The reasons advanced for tight control from London were twofold: that the Admiralty had the best Intelligence available, and that the Commander-in-Chief needed to keep radio silence. But the unhappy results of over-centralization were to be seen later in the disaster to convoy PQ 17. Historians now agree that it would have been better—as was done in the Mediterranean—to feed all the information available to the man on the spot

An ocean convoy exercising an emergency turn

The Swordfish

HMS *Nelson* at Loch Ewe

HMS *Prince of Wales*

HMS *Repulse*

and leave him to do his best with it. As it was, it was not unknown for ships to be ordered to steer a certain course by
London! Yet the paradox remains that the rigid control
exercised by Pound had the effect of restraining interference
by the First Lord. There was no doubt, either, that on naval
matters the First Lord would eventually yield if his advisers
had a convincing case and were prepared to persevere with
their opposition, and the only important exception was the
dispatch of the *Prince of Wales* and the *Repulse* to the Far
East.

It is interesting to examine some of the events of the first
few months of the sea war in order to compare Churchill's
performance in 1914–15 with what he did in 1939–40.

The sinking of the Courageous

In September, the two aircraft-carriers *Ark Royal* and
Courageous, together with some destroyers, were detached
from the Home Fleet to take part in U-boat-hunting operations
in the Western Approaches. The *Ark Royal* was narrowly
missed by several torpedoes on 14 September, the U-boat
responsible being sunk by the escort, and on 17 September the
Courageous was torpedoed and sunk with heavy loss of life.
On this occasion the U-boat escaped.

The Cabinet, rightly, advised the withdrawal of fleet
carriers from submarine-hunting work. The official historian's
comments on this folly are discreet. 'Our weakness in that class
of ship, of which only the *Ark Royal* was of modern design,
and the obvious danger to which submarine hunting would
expose them, now makes it seem surprising that they should
have been risked on that type of duty.'[291] I am sure that he is
right. It was disgraceful that the Naval Staff should have been
so ignorant of the capabilities of the Sonar set as to expose
these priceless ships to such danger. No experienced A/S expert
would have claimed one-hundred-per-cent success in detecting
a submerged U-boat approaching a heavy ship, but given a
strong and well-trained escort he would guarantee the destruction of the offender after its attack. This wholly unnecessary disaster was brought about by a combination of the
urge for the offensive and overconfidence in the A/S methods

available. Churchill wrote afterwards: 'This was a risk which it was right to run.'[292] But he had been misinformed and was quite wrong.

The loss of the Royal Oak

Scapa Flow had been finally chosen in April 1938 as the main Fleet base in a war against Germany; previously, Rosyth would have been used. The *Royal Oak* was torpedoed and sunk with large loss of life while at anchor in Scapa Flow on the night of 13–14 October 1939. *U47* had skilfully penetrated the defences through an unblocked entrance in the east—Kirk Sound—and had escaped unharmed by the same route.

This disaster must be chiefly the responsibility of the Government, which in peace did not ensure that the main Fleet base was secure. The weakness of the defence against both submarine and air attack was well known. Churchill records his anxiety at the state of the base which he learned at a long conference held in the Admiralty on 5 September. 'I was surprised to learn at my conference that more precautions had not been taken in both cases [i.e. air and submarine] to prepare the defences against modern forms of attack. . . . As a result of the conference on my second evening at the Admiralty many orders were given for additional nets and blockings.'[293]

But it was too late, though only by a narrow margin, for the blockship designed to be sunk in the channel through which *U47* entered arrived the day after the *Royal Oak* had been sunk.

The disaster was not the only one—though it was the most serious—caused by the lack of a secure Fleet base, for Loch Ewe and Rosyth had to be used as temporary alternatives. They were unsatisfactory: the Fleet flagship *Nelson* was mined in the approaches to the Loch, and the cruiser *Belfast* in the Firth of Forth, both ships being out of action for long periods.

The Graf Spee operations

Rounding up the surface raiders presented a puzzling problem. Neither of the pocket-battleships *Graf Spee* and

Deutschland, although both in the Atlantic, attacked a ship until the end of September and their position was unknown. The *Deutschland* sank only two ships before being recalled to Germany for refit in mid-October, for Hitler feared the effect on morale if a ship of that name was to be sunk.[294] Her name was changed to *Lützow* as soon as she arrived home.

As soon as the first news of a raider's attack was received, when the *St. Clement*'s boats were sighted on 6 October, no less than eight hunting-groups were formed—British and French—consisting of combinations of cruisers, battle-cruisers and aircraft-carriers.

The *Graf Spee* was well handled by her commander and sank several merchant ships in the South Atlantic and Indian Ocean. She had been lucky from the start, when she evaded the cruiser *Cumberland,* which her seaplane sighted in time for her to turn away,* but her luck did not hold. After some intelligent anticipation by Commodore Harwood she was encountered by the *Exeter, Ajax* and *Achilles* off the entrance to the River Plate on 13 December. After a skilfully fought action by the three cruisers, during which the *Graf Spee* scored many hits, she was forced to take refuge in Montevideo harbour. It had been a most successful engagement, as the eleven-inch guns of the pocket-battleship could outrange the eight-inch and six-inch guns of the British ships.

After much diplomatic activity, the Germans were persuaded that a large fleet, including the *Ark Royal* and *Renown,* was lying off the entrance to the Plate (these two ships were actually many thousand miles away), and approval was signalled to Captain Langsdorf to scuttle his ship outside Montevideo harbour.[295] Churchill had followed the action attentively and had been ready with many suggestions. Afterwards, he was full of advice on the redisposition of the ships.

Now that the South Atlantic is practically clear except for the *Altmark,* it seems of high importance to bring home the *Renown* and *Ark Royal,* together with at least one of the 8-inch-gun cruisers. . . . It would be very convenient if, as you proposed,

* The *Graf Spee*'s supply ship, the *Altmark,* was also lucky, and by claiming to be the steamer *Delmar* she escaped destruction.

Neptune relieved *Ajax* as soon as the triumphal entry into [Montevideo harbour] is over; and it would be very good if all the returning forces could scrub and search the South Atlantic on their way home for the *Altmark*. . . .[296]

He succeeded also in vetoing a proposal that the gravely damaged *Exeter* should be left at the Falkland Islands, and she was brought home to receive a hero's welcome, and was repaired to fight another day.

The Altmark *episode*

By remaining in the South Atlantic longer than expected— she did not start for home until 22 January 1940—the *Altmark* evaded the forces searching for her and passed through the gap between the Faeroes and Iceland undetected. On the evening of 15 February it became known that she had passed Bergen, southward bound, at noon. A search was organized, using ships already in the area; she was sighted on 16 February, and attempts were made to board by destroyers, but she made good her escape into Josingfjord, escorted by a Norwegian torpedo-boat. The Norwegian commanding officer declared that the ship had been boarded at Bergen, was unarmed and had been given permission to use territorial waters. So Captain Vian, who was senior officer of the British force, withdrew outside Norwegian waters and reported the situation to the Admiralty. 'At this juncture the First Lord himself took charge and, after communicating with the Foreign Secretary, told Captain Vian to offer the Norwegians joint escort of the *Altmark* back to Bergen. If this was refused, he was to board her, and, if the prisoners were found, she was to be seized in prize.'[297]

That evening, Captain Vian took the *Cossack* into the fjord, boarded the *Altmark*, and released 299 prisoners, thus refuting the Norwegian claim. The prisoners were safely landed next day in Scotland, none the worse for their ordeal.

There was a complaint from the Commander-in-Chief that the Admiralty had interfered by sending signals direct to Vian, but it was clear that only the Government could take the responsibility for entering territorial waters and threatening force against the Norwegian ship. Vian was left in no doubt as to his orders and the operation was a complete success. Of no great strategical importance, it came as a great encouragement to the nation when prospects were gloomy and achievements few.

The Norwegian campaign

By March 1940 a situation approaching stability had been reached on the high seas. The British Army was settled in France with supplies assured, the Canadian troops had been brought safely across the Atlantic to train in Britain and the Australians and New Zealanders had been transported to the Middle East. All the German merchant ships had been captured, sunk or interned, and the surface raiders had, for the moment, been neutralized. The magnetic mine had been countered and the first attack by the U-boats had been satisfactorily repulsed. The convoys to Norway were well organized and protected and the flow of trade to and from Scandinavia had been maintained, despite German efforts to interfere. The Fleet had been lucky, during its sorties into the North Sea, to avoid serious losses from air attack, and the weakness of gun defences against both high-level bombing and dive-bombers was well understood at sea. At the Admiralty, however, this important fact of life does not seem to have been appreciated by many of the senior officers.

The situation was strikingly similar to that at the start of 1915, when stability had been reached, the seas had been cleared of the enemy and Churchill was searching feverishly for an offensive role for the Navy, which he had found in the Dardanelles operations.

From the start of the war the First Lord had pondered deeply on the possibility of cutting the supply of iron ore from Sweden to Germany. Normally the iron ore came from Luleå through the Baltic direct to the North German ports; when the ice prevented navigation it was sent by rail to Narvik and thence shipped through Norwegian territorial waters to German North Sea ports.[298] Churchill called this route through the Inner Leads the 'covered way'. With the French iron ore from Lorraine no longer available, the commodity could quickly become critical to the German war effort, especially as reserves were known to be low. But Intelligence reports stressed that early action was necessary as the Baltic ice would melt in April at the latest, and then, unless Plan 'Catherine' was successful, ample supplies would be available for many months.

In mid-September 1939 Churchill first called the attention of the War Cabinet to the problem, suggesting, among other measures, that minefields should be laid in the Inner Leads to force the ships carrying the ore into the open sea where they could be intercepted.[299] The Cabinet was interested and asked for specific proposals, but the Foreign Office would not agree to the infringement of Norway's neutrality and the plan was dropped. In December, when a plan to use Narvik as a base through which to pass Allied troops to Finland was being considered, the First Lord again raised the plan to mine the Leads, and again, the Cabinet refused to authorize any action.[300]

Churchill had considered German reactions with accuracy.

. . . if Germany thinks it her interest to dominate forcibly the Scandinavian peninsula. In that case the war would spread to Norway and Sweden, and with our command of the seas there is no reason why French and British troops should not meet German invaders on Scandinavian soil. At any rate, we can certainly take and hold whatever islands or suitable points on the Norwegian coast we choose. Our northern blockade of Germany would then become absolute. We could, for instance, occupy Narvik and Bergen, and keep them open for our own trade while closing them completely to Germany. It cannot be too strongly emphasised that British control of the Norwegian coast-line is a strategic objective of first-class importance. It is not therefore seen how, even if retaliation by Germany were to run its full course, we should be worse off for the action now proposed. On the contrary, we have more to gain than lose by a German attack upon Norway or Sweden. . . .[301]

But this last minute shows an ominous overconfidence in the ability to retain a hold on Norway in the face of German air power, for the truth is that Britain had neither the resources nor the plans to give her air force the mobility which the Luftwaffe displayed during the Norwegian campaign. All concerned were taken by surprise by the speed with which the Norwegian airfields were taken over and converted into effective, defended bomber bases—all by the use of transport aircraft.

In March 1940 the Cabinet approved a plan for mining the Leads. On 25 March the Supreme War Council decided that the date should be 5 April, and it was agreed to hold small military forces in readiness to occupy Narvik, Stavanger, Bergen and Trondheim so as to forestall the expected German reaction to the mining. Shortly afterwards the start was postponed to 8 April and the scene was then set.

Unfortunately, and unknown to the Allies, the Germans had also been considering the Norwegian problem since the start of the war and their plans were far advanced. The High Command believed that the Allies would take some action in the area and the German Navy was anxious to secure bases on the coast. Hitler ordered planning to start in December, and on 1 March he signed a directive ordering the occupation of both Norway and Denmark. After some delays the date of execution was fixed for 9 April. The concept was bold and relied on surprise, which it achieved in full measure. Admiral Raeder considered it 'contrary to all principles of the theory of naval warfare', but he decided to risk the whole German Navy in the operation. Ships were to storm Kristiansund, Oslo, Bergen, Trondheim and Narvik, warships carrying the troops and merchant ships the supplies. No declaration of war or warnings were to be given. Ruthless surprise was the keynote.

On the British side, the plan was hesitant and almost apologetic. The troops intended to forestall enemy reaction to the mining were kept in the Clyde and the Forth, many hours steaming from their destination. Most of the Home Fleet remained in harbour.

The disastrous course of the campaign has been often described and no attempt will be made to cover it fully. But it is as well to remind the reader of the main features which fall naturally into three phases: the minelaying and subsequent naval activity; the Allied military operations; and the withdrawal.

Phase One

Three minelaying forces, supported by a small covering force from the Home Fleet, sailed on 5 April, and the mines were laid as arranged on the 8th. But as early as the 6th reports of activity had been reaching London from the Baltic and Skaggerak, and on the 7th a report of the movements of enemy warships caused Admiral Forbes to take the Home Fleet to sea from Scapa. His mind was set on the interception of German heavy ships breaking out into the Atlantic, and he steered north-east—away from the area at which the enemy attack was directed. The first German ships, bound for Narvik, had sailed on the evening of the 6th, and the landings on the 9th gained complete surprise everywhere; only at Oslo was there a temporary reverse when the *Blücher* was torpedoed and sunk by the forts. The Germans were soon established on shore in six harbours.

Meanwhile firm reports of the invasion had reached London on the evening of 7 April, and orders were immediately sent from the Naval Staff—not from the Chiefs-of-Staff, it should be noted—to disembark the troops waiting in cruisers at Rosyth and to send the escorts of the loaded troopships in the Clyde to sea to join the Home Fleet. Thus no military force was immediately available.

A very confused situation presented itself. There was much activity at sea. The *Renown*, which had been covering the minelaying, engaged and routed the *Scharnhorst* and the *Gneisenau*, which had been sent north to divert the Home Fleet from the landing operations in central and southern Norway. The destroyer *Glowworm* had met the cruiser *Hipper*, which was about to enter Trondheim, and had rammed and gravely damaged the German ship in a most gallant action. The Commander-in-Chief, with the main body of the Fleet, had been bombed repeatedly from the air. When he learned of the Germany entry into Bergen, he detached four cruisers and seven destroyers to attack the enemy there, but the Admiralty promptly cancelled the operation, though it was to press him to undertake a far more dangerous attack on Trondheim later on, when the Germans had had time to prepare strong defences.

274

Aircraft from the *Furious* had attacked ships in Trondheim; naval Skuas, flying at maximum range from the Orkneys, had sunk the cruiser *Königsberg* in Bergen, and the submarine *Truant* had sunk the cruiser *Karlsruhe*. Early on 10 April Captain Warburton-Lee, leading five destroyers into Narvik, had sunk two of the enemy ships in harbour and damaged others—a brave fight against heavy odds, and on 13 April nine destroyers had led the battleship *Warspite* into Narvik fjord and sunk all the ships remaining there in a most competently conducted action.

Phase One was over. The German naval forces had suffered crippling losses, and sea communications, particularly to the forces in the north, were completely cut. But the soldiers were firmly established ashore, reinforcements were being flown in, and the Luftwaffe was moving bomber squadrons to Norwegian airfields with remarkable speed. The Fleet had failed to prevent invasion—indeed, the news reached it too late—but, worse still, the troops which had been prepared for exactly such a situation were immobilized.

Phase Two

Military expeditions had then to be hurriedly improvised in order to eject the Germans from Norway. A sad story of muddle and confusion followed. On 11 April the first convoy left the Clyde bound for Narvik. While it was still on passage, some of its ships were diverted to Namsos, a small port to the north of Trondheim, with the result that many of the troops became separated from their ammunition and supplies. An advance party of seamen and marines, landed from cruisers, arrived at Namsos on 14 April and the brigade diverted from the Narvik convoy took over from them on the 16th. Reinforcements followed in troopships on the 19th.

Meanwhile, on the 14th and 15th, four sloops had sailed from Rosyth with 700 seamen and marines, hastily collected from ships refitting, bound for the area south of Trondheim. The aim was to complete a pincer movement on the city, which would be assisted—at least this was the original plan—by a frontal attack on the port by the Home Fleet supported by troops. These naval parties arrived at Andalsnes, south of

T

Trondheim, on the 17th, and were reinforced on the 18th by 1,000 troops, carried in cruisers from Rosyth. A small RAF detachment was brought across in the *Glorious* and flown ashore on to a frozen lake on the 24th.

As to the Narvik expedition, an open opportunity was presented to seize the town immediately after the second naval battle, but it was rejected and the troops of the first convoy were disembarked at Harstad, many miles away, and preparations made for a deliberate assault on Narvik later.

So by 18 April the Army was ashore in three places, but the two areas near Trondheim were already menaced by heavy air attack and the RAF fighters brought by the *Glorious* were unable to continue their operations.

On 16 April, before the landings at Namsos and Andalsnes had taken hold, it was becoming clear in London that Trondheim was the key to the campaign. The Commander-in-Chief, Home Fleet, had first been asked to consider a frontal attack on 13 April, and his reaction had been that: 'Bombing would start almost immediately . . . and to carry out an opposed landing under continuous air attack was hardly feasible.'

On 18 April, a senior officer was sent to Scapa Flow to discuss the proposal with Admiral Forbes, taking with him a letter from the First Lord, personally urging the Commander-in-Chief to agree to the operation. On 19 April the plan was cancelled* and it was decided to concentrate all effort on the pincer movement on land. Admiral Forbes was most relieved, and in the light of later knowledge of the situation and of German appreciation made at the time, there can be little doubt that the decision was right, though the cancellation was much abused both in Press and in Parliament. The truth was that only those who had experienced it could understand fully the effect of the superiority of the Luftwaffe on operations both in narrow waters and on land.

---

* Churchill made it clear later that the Chiefs of Staff had been in favour of the operation on 17 April, but had changed their minds by the 18th.[302]

Phase Three

By 28 April, several things combined to persuade Whitehall that evacuation of Namsos and Andalsnes was unavoidable, though it was hoped that Narvik could still be captured and held as an advanced base.

First, the effect of air attack was now evident. The losses and damage both to warships and to merchant ships were serious, and it was becoming increasingly difficult to transport and unload supplies. The troops ashore were being overwhelmed by the Germans with their competent air support. Secondly, it was found necessary to withdraw some heavy ships for the Mediterranean, where the probability of Italy entering the war was becoming greater. Thirdly, the German threat to the Low Countries was menacing and it was necessary to avoid dispersal of Allied force.

The evacuation of both these ports was extremely skilfully executed under heavy air attack between 30 April and 3 May. General Sir Adrian Carton de Wiart, one of the commanders, wrote: 'In the course of that last endless day I got a message from the Navy to say that they would evacuate the whole of my force that night. I thought it was impossible, but learned a few hours later that the Navy did not know the word.'[303]

Two destroyers were sunk by air attack after leaving, but the troops on board them were the only losses of the evacuation.

When the invasion of the Low Countries started on 10 May it was soon clear that Narvik, with its long sea communications and its vulnerability to air attack, could not be maintained. It was decided to capture the town on 28 May, in order to destroy the iron-ore loading-jetties and the railway to Sweden, and then to evacuate north Norway. The assault, undertaken mainly by French and Polish troops, was successful. The evacuation started on 4 June and was complete by the 8th. The operation went smoothly, except for one serious incident when the *Scharnhorst* and *Gneisenau*, which had been sent out to attack the ships in the anchorage at Harstad—the Germans being ignorant of the evacuation—met and sank a troopship, a tanker and finally the aircraft-carrier *Glorious* and her two escorting destroyers. The escort made a gallant torpedo attack and one torpedo severely damaged the *Scharnhorst*. The action took place in broad daylight, and it will always remain a mystery why the *Glorious*, with six serviceable Swordfish aircraft embarked, allowed herself to be surprised by the German ships.* Her enemy report was made on low power on an auxiliary radio set and was not received ashore, and the German radio claims brought the first news of the sinking to the Admiralty. So ended a campaign which, though illuminated by many successful actions and much gallantry, had brought ignominious defeat. It is true that the German Navy ended it with no major warship fit for sea (the *Gneisenau* was damaged by a torpedo from the submarine *Clyde* on her way back to Germany after the *Glorious* action, and the *Lützow* was torpedoed and damaged by the *Spearfish*), but this did not compensate for the failure first to prevent and then to defeat invasion.

Direction of naval operations

In the course of controlling operations, there were a number of serious mistakes, many of which were due to unnecessary intervention by Whitehall.

First of all, it may seem surprising that the Home Fleet should not have been at sea in position to counter the expected reaction to the minelaying on 8 April, particularly since the Norwegian Government had been warned formally of the proposed action on 5 April, and such news was likely to spread. It is true that the enemy reaction proved, by chance, to be simultaneous instead of consequential, but to have had the Fleet at sea would appear to have been a wise precaution. Indeed, as a military force had been assembled, perhaps it would have been better to have it also poised at sea, ready for action, instead of lying in the Clyde and the Forth.

Secondly, there was a reluctance to accept the implications of the Intelligence reports which started to flood into London

---

* I remember returning to Scapa from the Narvik area in the damaged destroyer *Cossack* in mid-April. The mast of a capital ship was seen over the horizon one morning and 'Action Stations' at once ordered. Fortunately it proved to be the *Warspite*, but we had the *Scharnhorst* and *Gneisenau* very much on our minds.

on 6 April. A correct and clear appreciation of the German operations was sent to the Commander-in-Chief on 7 April, but its effect was spoiled by the conclusion that 'all these reports are of doubtful value and may well be only a further move in the war of nerves'. This reluctance to grasp the enemy intentions stemmed from the obsession with the danger of a break-out by German heavy ships into the Atlantic. This in turn communicated itself to the Commander-in-Chief, and it was unlucky that the Naval Staff, which made some unhappy interventions in operations, did not, as was suggested by some of its members, advise Admiral Forbes that he was steering too far to the north when he left harbour on the evening of the 7th. His course was set so as to cut off any German ships breaking out into the Atlantic, and by steering in this direction he left the central North Sea, where the invasion was taking place, uncovered.

Thirdly, once the Germans had moved, there seems to have been an urge to get every warship to sea as soon as possible, often with no clear idea as to what they should do when they got there. To have removed the troops from the cruisers at Rosyth and the escorts from the transports in the Clyde was surely impetuous; if the troops had sailed they might have been able to evict the Germans from Trondheim and Bergen before the defences had been prepared. Certainly they would have been ready to land at Narvik after the second battle. Similarly, to have sailed the *Furious* from the Clyde before she had had time to embark her fighter squadron was unwise.

Fourthly, the force which had mined Vestfjord was ordered to leave its patrol and join the *Renown* only just before the Germans passed on their way to Narvik. Four minelaying destroyers and their four escorts would have given a good account of themselves against the ten enemy destroyers. The directions to Captain Warburton-Lee before the first battle of Narvik bypassed Admiral Whitworth in the *Renown*, who was considering strengthening Warburton-Lee's force, and he did not so proceed. But it can be argued that a stronger force would have destroyed the Germans in Narvik, made the second battle unnecessary and allowed the town to be occupied at once. The Admiralty decision to cancel the attack on Bergen

which Admiral Forbes had ordered on 9 April was also unfortunate, and it is now known that the shore batteries were
not yet back in service and a good chance presented itself.
This cancellation contrasted sharply with the strong persuasion
of Admiral Forbes to attack Trondheim several days later,
when the defences were stronger and the danger from air
attack far worse.

Fifthly, the loss of the *Glorious,* and the general lack of
satisfactory arrangements for the safety of the convoys
evacuating the Narvik area in early June must also be mentioned. No air searches were laid on, and the heavy ships of
the Home Fleet were not disposed to give cover. The secret
of the evacuation has been held to be partly responsible for
these errors, but the excuse is not convincing.

It is not possible to say now how blame should be allocated
for these mistakes; the evidence is not yet available. It is
known that Admiral Pound was convinced of the merit of
strong Admiralty control of operations at sea, and it was he
who ordered the troops out of the cruisers at Rosyth on 7
April. Yet he had assured Admiral Forbes in November that
'Commanders-in-Chief should normally be left free to conduct
their own operations without constant intervention from
Whitehall'.[304]

Churchill later agreed that '. . . the Admiralty kept too close
a control upon the Commander-in-Chief, and after learning his
original intention to force the passage into Bergen we should
have confined ourselves to sending him information'.[305] But
this was a comment on the cancellation of the Bergen attack
and not on the conduct of the campaign as a whole.

In the planning of the Trondheim operations the First
Lord became deeply involved, and used all his powers of
persuasion to urge the Commander-in-Chief to attack. There
can be no doubt that, as has been so often noted, neither he
nor his Naval Staff advisers appreciated the difficulties faced
by ships in narrow waters dominated by the Luftwaffe. His
natural urge for action and his strategical sense that Trondheim, which commands the narrow neck of Norway and thus
the approaches to Narvik and the north, was the key to the
campaign, combined to force him to exert great pressure on

the senior officers at the scene of action. It was fortunate that the Chiefs-of-Staff eventually convinced him that the possible gains were not worth the probable losses.

It must also not be forgotten that Churchill was the chairman of the Military Co-ordination Committee during the campaign, a duty of which he had relieved Admiral Chatfield on 3 April. Nevertheless, it is not possible to place the blame on one man or on one service.

An experienced military historian has written:

> Of all the political and military miscalculations, that the Germans would not be able to land effective forces on the western seaboard of Norway in the face of a British fleet at Scapa Flow was the most damaging. To this more than to any other error may be traced the subsequent story of defeat. The estimate must primarily have been one of the naval staff, but it was very acceptable to the general and air staffs, the latter especially wishing to give no encouragement to avoidable commitments in Scandinavia. So the estimate was not effectively challenged by those who might have presented the other side of the case and insisted that adequate land and air forces must be sent if Britain was to engage in a campaign in Scandinavia.[306]

One can agree with every word, for if realistic views had been held the Admiralty and the Fleet would not have been so mesmerized by the dangers of a break-out of enemy heavy ships and thus would have been more ready to deal with invasion. There can be no dispute that if the early indications had been correctly interpreted and the Fleet had been sent to the central North Sea the invasion would have been smashed.

But, if mistakes were made during the Norwegian Campaign, once it had started, and in the assumptions of planners of all services before its start, the primary responsibility must be traced to earlier periods and particularly to that between the wars, when inter-service co-operation was so ineffective, and when, with the shadow of the Dardanelles hanging over them, the services, starved and neglected, sank into comparative apathy towards amphibious warfare.

A force of amphibious ships and craft, manned by trained experts and directed by staffs well versed in the technique of land/sea/air warfare, would have transformed the situation in

Norway. And, in Whitehall, a harmonious machinery for directing events, such as was devised later when Churchill was Minister of Defence, would have avoided the divided counsels and contradictory orders, the muddle and the improvisation which led to the humiliating defeat of the British expedition to Norway. Thus it is on those in power before the war, and particularly after the menace of Hitler was so clear, that the main share of the blame must be laid.

In the second volume of his memoirs, dealing with the war years,* Mr Macmillan reflects on his deep anxiety in May 1940, when the Chamberlain Government was falling, lest Mr Churchill's loyal support of Chamberlain to the very last and his involvement in the Norwegian campaign should prevent him becoming Prime Minister. It was fortunate for the country that sense prevailed.

Churchill brought, like a storm, his immense energy and his powers of vivid imagination to the Admiralty. He did much to marry technological development with tactical thought and to ensure that no scientific idea which could be useful in the war at sea was neglected.

He helped to maintain the confidence of the Navy in itself. The service was proud of its First Lord and watched with satisfaction his growth in stature as, almost imperceptibly, he became the spokesman for defence in the higher councils of the nation and its main co-ordinator in Whitehall. But his restlessness, his insatiable quest for the offensive, and, I am afraid, some bad advice from his Naval Staff, led him into mistakes. During the twilight war, at least, he was obsessed by the past. I have noted some examples already. Another was his recall to high command of elderly retired officers like Lord Cork, Lord Keyes and Admiral Evans. These men were *his* contemporaries and had made their names in *his* war. Perhaps subconsciously, he believed that they were more aggressive and more likely to seize an initiative than the new generation of sea captains. But he was wrong. Men like Cunningham, Somerville, Horton, Vian and many others possessed all the qualities of aggression and initiative of the older men, combined with a far deeper

* *The Blast of War* (Macmillan, 1967).

comprehension of modern developments, especially in the air.

Of course, Churchill did tremendous work for the Navy. He helped to bring order, realism and urgency to the ship-building programme. He galvanized the scientific departments. He drove the Admiralty machine as it had not been driven for a quarter of a century. But when the final judgement can be made, I believe that his period as First Lord in 1939–40 will be regarded as a preparation for the great role of national leader which lay ahead, rather than as an achievement outstanding in its own right.

12

PRIME MINISTER, MAY 1940—JUNE 1945

The immense scale of events on land and in the air has
tended to obscure the no less impressive victory at sea. The
whole Anglo-American campaign in Europe depended upon
the movement of convoys across the Atlantic. . . . In spite of
appalling losses to themselves they [the U-Boats] continued to
attack . . . Even after the autumn of 1944, when they were
forced to abandon their bases in the Bay of Biscay, they did
not despair.[307]

WSC

THE months of the summer and autumn of 1940 will
surely rank as the supreme period of Winston Churchill's
life. At a time of desperate peril he inspired the nation
to tremendous effort, and embodied in his own personality the
highest qualities of the British people. Tributes are numerous.
To me, the judgement of Lord Normanbrook, a man of selfless
wisdom, expresses simply and shortly the essence of his
achievement. He had mentioned to Lord Moran that there was
much defeatism after Dunkirk, and Moran had replied that he
did not remember people being jumpy—'Extraordinarily
phlegmatic they seemed to me'. Normanbrook said, 'I agree
about the public, but there were a lot of jitters among those at
the top. . . . If it had not been for Winston anything might
have happened.'[308]

On forming his administration, Churchill chose A. V.
Alexander (later Lord Alexander of Hillsborough) as First
Lord. A Labour MP, with previous experience of the Admiralty,
he was devoted to the Navy and proved a loyal and faithful
friend over many years, but it would be wrong to pretend that
he was a strong man, and the Prime Minister continued,
especially for the first three years when the result of the war
at sea still hung in the balance, to take a close interest in
naval matters and even to behave as though he was still First
Lord.

The combination of Alexander and Pound, and later of
Alexander and Cunningham, however, ensured that interference was kept at a reasonable level—interest in naval

284

matters was to be welcomed, of course—and only once did the Prime Minister overrule his advisers on a vital issue: the dispatch of the *Prince of Wales* and the *Repulse* to Singapore.

Now that he was Prime Minister, Churchill's 'daily prayers' continued to bombard the Admiralty, exhorting, inquiring, criticizing and proposing on subjects ranging from the important to the trivial. The appendixes to the six volumes of *The Second World War* are filled with these missives; the ship-building programme in particular received keen attention. The Army also received many minutes; the Prime Minister's military background urged him to probe the details of tanks, guns and other technical matters, and the swollen number of supporting arms required to maintain a fighting division in the field was a constant target for criticism.

The Royal Air Force was not let off lightly, but it seemed that the Prime Minister was ready to admit that his grasp of the war in the air was less firm than it was of the war in the other two dimensions, and he did not interfere in the technicalities of Air Force administration.

Opinions still differ as to the value of these 'prayers'. Many of those who worked in Whitehall at the time would contend that they added unnecessary burdens to men already over-strained. Indeed, later in the war, when the Prime Minister was tired or ill, it is certain that he did not even read some of the answers which had been prepared with such care and at such inconvenience. But, on balance, the advantages outweighed the disadvantages. Many of his ideas—and those of his staff and his friends—were of great value. Many abuses, stupidities and scandals were corrected and many false accusations or claims were refuted. Above all, complacency was impossible with the thought that a 'Pray-inform-me-on-one-sheet-of-paper-why . . . ' might descend at any moment.

The new Prime Minister also became Minister of Defence, a post with neither a department nor a directive, but by using the military members of the Cabinet Secretariat as his staff and by making their leader, General Ismay, a member of the Chiefs-of-Staff Committee, he achieved from the start a remarkably close partnership with the service chiefs which avoided completely the damaging and shameful struggles between 'Frocks and Brass Hats' of the First World War.

Mr Macmillan quotes the Prime Minister as having said, when congratulated on the lack of friction between the Government and the professional heads of the services, that the Chiefs-of-Staff Committee represented the 'sum of the fears' of its members and produced only indecision.[309] But Mr Macmillan has also wisely observed that Churchill regarded conversation as a method not so much of doing business as of having some fun after the day's work, or else of testing the strength of his companion's views or character. Business was conducted strictly on paper, and Churchill's remark can be discounted.

By taking the chair at many Chiefs-of-Staff Committee meetings he was able to exercise a personal supervision of the war effort unknown in the past, which President Roosevelt neither attempted nor achieved. But these arrangements inevitably led to the eclipse of the operational functions of the three service ministers, who were thus able to concentrate on the formidable administrative problems of their departments —a demotion which was loyally accepted.

One problem might have been a source of friction: the Prime Minister insisted on his right to issue directives to the Joint Planning Committee and to demand from it appreciations and plans of his pet schemes. This issue was amicably resolved, however, by his agreement that any replies to his requests should first be sent to the Chiefs of Staff for their consideration. When one reads in the reports of the Führer's Conferences and other German sources of the muddles and misjudgements caused by Hitler's methods of dealing with his admirals and generals, one is still more grateful for the smooth-running machine which operated in 'Storey's Gate'.*

The Prime Minister's relations with the Navy were strengthened by his trust in and affection for Admiral Pound, whom he found a tower of strength in many times of trouble, and any naval study of these momentous times would be incomplete without reference to Pound's failing health. As early

---

* The Headquarters of the Chiefs of Staff and the Planners.

as 1941 it became clear that he was a tired man. He never spared himself and he was ready to see Churchill at any time of night or day. He was known to doze at Cabinet and Chiefs-of-Staff meetings, though it was always said that when the words 'ships' or 'Navy' were mentioned he at once became alert. Many memoirs refer to this decline in the strength of the First Sea Lord, and Sir Stafford Cripps, according to Lord Moran, told the Prime Minister in September 1942 that Pound was 'past his work'.

Pound fell ill during the Quebec Conference of August 1943, and his interview with Churchill on that occasion is movingly recounted. ' "Prime Minister, I have come to resign. I have had a stroke and my right side is largely paralysed. . . . I am no longer fit for duty." I at once accepted the First Sea Lord's resignation, and expressed my profound sympathy for his breakdown in health.'[310]

Churchill had always resisted attempts to get Pound relieved. He hated changes in his trusted advisers and personal staff, and Pound himself, though ready to go, was dismayed by the rumoured choice of a successor and so was persuaded to stay on.[311]

In the clear light of hindsight, it would seem that Pound was suffering from the first symptoms of the malady from which he later died, and that it would have been wiser if he had been relieved much earlier, for some serious mistakes were made which could only be explained by the decline in his faculties. But one hesitates to criticize the loyalty of a leader who wished to keep his old friend by his side, or the devotion to duty of a faithful servant of the nation who refused to quit his post.

The choice of a successor as First Sea Lord was found difficult. For reasons which the Navy were at a loss to understand, the Prime Minister did not then have complete confidence in Admiral Cunningham, whose exploits in the Mediterranean rate in retrospect as high as any in our long naval history. Admiral Fraser, the Commander-in-Chief of the Home Fleet, was offered the post, but with typical modesty he declared that although he thought he had the confidence of his own fleet he knew that Cunningham had the confidence of the whole Navy. He added that he had yet to fight and win a battle,* and he asked to be allowed to decline.

Thus Cunningham's assumption of office was fraught with suspicion on both sides, for the Admiral had been infuriated by the prodding signals with which he had been bombarded in the Mediterranean, the answers to which a devoted and able staff had with difficulty succeeded in converting into polite refusals.

But after a short time mutual confidence was gained. In 1944 Moran records Churchill's saying, 'I like Cunningham very much. I am very lucky to get such a successor to dear old Pound.'

This remark followed a violent disagreement on policy with the First Sea Lord. It is not suggested that there was always perfect harmony, for Churchill would goad Cunningham and make him extremely angry, but he admired his staunch opposition.

On Cunningham's side, it is clear from his *Sailor's Odyssey* and from many other sources that the initial suspicion was soon replaced by admiration and devotion, tinged, it must be added, with some considerable irritation. One observer of many U-boat Committee meetings has recorded that Cunningham was sometimes too angry to reply to the Prime Minister and would pass on the question to one of his subordinates to answer.

One final comment on the Prime Minister's method of work may be allowed. As a chairman of a meeting, he seldom behaved in the same way twice and while he always dominated the proceedings he would sometimes be brooding and taciturn and at other times ebullient and provocative. He paid little regard to the agenda and was easily sidetracked. All reports agree that Attlee or Cripps, with their sharp concentration, gained the best results from the more technical committees; yet it was the Prime Minister who singled out the vital issues at stake and carried them forward with the force of his personality.

---

* He soon had his wish—on Christmas Day 1943, when he sank the *Scharnhorst*.

The invasion threat

In June 1940 one of the first major decisions to be faced by the new Cabinet was to approve the plans for resisting invasion by the German armies poised on the French coast. There was a wide difference of opinion between the Commander-in-Chief Home Fleet and the Admiralty on the naval measures to be taken. The Admiralty wished to mass a striking force of cruisers and destroyers based on the Thames Estuary, with the aim of protecting the coast from Newhaven to the Wash. Each major port was to have similar forces, and this could only be done by dividing the Home Fleet and by stripping the Atlantic convoys of their escorts.

Admiral Forbes held that the correct strategy was to keep the main Fleet at Scapa to cover an expedition against either England or Ireland, and also to make frequent sweeps of the North Sea. He also wished to leave the escorts with the convoys. While the RAF was in control over England, he did not believe that any invasion force could hope to succeed, and he was confident that he could quickly destroy any expedition which managed to approach our coasts.

The Admiralty view prevailed, however, and the depleted Home Fleet 'lolled' in Scapa or Rosyth throughout the summer. The detached cruisers and destroyers achieved little success in the Channel and the southern North Sea, while the Atlantic convoys suffered very heavy losses.

It is difficult to understand why the Prime Minister supported the Admiralty view, for he had always agreed in 1914 that the Fleet must remain intact, ready to challenge the German Fleet and then to destroy the invasion supply forces. In 1940 there was no German Fleet and it was surely just as important to keep our forces concentrated in order to massacre any expedition which the Germans were rash enough to dispatch.

The U-boat attack on merchant shipping in the Atlantic

We have seen in the last chapter that, despite some mistaken views on the tactics of U-boat-hunting and the defence of shipping, Churchill was alive to the dangers and constantly warned the Admiralty Staff that Germany would soon increase her U-boat strength and that complacency at our early success was very dangerous. His warnings proved true in the summer and autumn of 1940, for during these months sinkings by U-boats were very many and the escorts seemed helpless. The measures taken to decrease the slaughter included the routeing of ships north of Ireland, the closing of the English Channel to all but the smallest coasters and finally, in October, the recalling of the escorts from invasion patrols. But losses continued, as did the patrolling of U-boat probability areas instead of the close escorting of convoys.

The Navy was also surprised by the operation of 'wolf-packs' of U-boats which attacked convoys at night, steaming at high speed on the surface and often outstripping the escorts. This tactic had been forecast by Doenitz in a book in 1939, but surprise was complete and hasty improvisations of little value.

During this period, the Prime Minister's greatest achievement was to obtain the loan of fifty old American destroyers. The agreement was ratified on 2 September 1940, and the ships started to arrive soon afterwards. They required modernization and alterations before they could enter service, but despite some defects they performed useful work. The story of the negotiations which preceded this deal is fascinating.[312] One of the points of dispute was the future of the Fleet if Britain was successfully invaded, and Roosevelt demanded a pledge that the ships would sail across the Atlantic to continue the fight. Churchill would not agree to any public disclosure of such defeatism and it took some time to evolve a satisfactory formula.

> As regards an assurance about the British Fleet . . . We intend to fight this out here to the end, and none of us would ever buy peace by surrendering or scuttling the fleet. But in any use you may make of this repeated assurance you will please bear in mind the disastrous effect from our point of view, and perhaps also from yours, of allowing any impression to grow that we regard the conquest of the British Islands and its [sic] naval bases as any other than an impossible contingency.[313]

Churchill also took the initiative in moving the Headquarters of the Western Approaches Command from Plymouth to

Liverpool, where it was better placed to direct convoy operations. There was a temporary respite in shipping losses at the end of 1940, caused by the arrival of the American destroyers, the commissioning of new British escorts and finally by the surprising fact that the Germans had only twenty-one U-boats operational, for their emergency building programme was not yet in full production and new construction had not replaced losses.

However, the respite was brief. In early 1941 attacks on ships in the Atlantic by aircraft from Norway and from France were frequent, disguised surface raiders claimed many victims, and in March a renewed U-boat offensive sank over 200,000 tons of shipping. The Prime Minister issued, on 6 March, his 'Battle of the Atlantic' directive, which was intended to spur on not only the sailors and airmen engaged at sea but also the bombing crews which attacked the building yards, the dockers who unloaded the ships—indeed everyone who was concerned with the battle. The directive started:

1. We must take the offensive against the U-boat and the Focke-Wulf [long-range reconnaissance aircraft] wherever we can and whenever we can. The U-boat at sea must be hunted, the U-boat in the building yard or in dock must be bombed. The Focke-Wulf and other bombers employed against our shipping must be attacked in the air and in their nests.

2. Extreme priority will be given to fitting out ships to catapult or otherwise launch fighter aircraft. . . .

3. All the measures approved and now in train for the concentration of the main strength of the Coastal Command upon the North-Western Approaches, and their assistance on the East Coast by Fighter and Bomber Commands, will be pressed forward. . . .

One part of the directive (Paragraph 5—'The Admiralty will re-examine, in conjunction with the Ministry of Shipping, the question of liberating from convoys ships of between 13 and 12 knots . . .') was soon shown to be wrong by the work of the Operational Research teams under Blackett, and here we find Churchill's antipathy to convoy again emerging.

The rest of the directive discussed the measures necessary to protect the ports from air attack, to speed the turn-round of shipping, to accelerate repair of merchant ships and to improve transport arrangements in the docks.[314]

Churchill was then obsessed by the use of bombing as a war-winning weapon. Unfortunately, as was soon shown, the results of bombing U-boat bases and building yards were extremely disappointing and expensive in gallant and valuable aircrews. Today it is clear that the directive would have been better interpreted if our bombers had been employed to give air escort to the convoys or else to lay mines in enemy-controlled waters. But, like convoy escort work, the laying of mines gained the stigma of 'defensive operations'. Minelaying was carried out reluctantly and by newly formed crews to gain experience for the bombing of cities. But statistics now show that the minelaying had very serious effects—not only by sinking or damaging ships and U-boats, but also by inter-fering with U-boat training and with shipping movements generally.

The Prime Minister also formed, in March 1941, the Battle of the Atlantic Committee, at which he presided every week in order to review the course of the struggle. The remainder of 1941 produced more activity of surface ships, aircraft and U-boats, and also two political events of the greatest import-ance. First, Hitler attacked Russia in June, and at once the Prime Minister decided that material help to Russia must take first priority. Thus started the first of the Russian convoys which were later to cause so much bitter fighting and so many tragic losses. Fortunately the enemy took time to deploy his forces, and convoys to Russia were unscathed in 1941. Secondly the meeting between the American President and the Prime Minister at Argentia in August produced an important agree-ment whereby the American Navy would escort convoys across the western half of the Atlantic.

During the last quarter of 1941 there was a decrease in sink-ings due, as we now know, to Hitler's diversion of U-boats to Norway and to the Mediterranean. But the lull was not to last long. In December the Japanese War started and: 'I do not pretend to have measured accurately the martial might of Japan, but now at this very moment I knew the United States was in the war, up to the neck and in to the death. So we had won after all!'[315] But there were many crises to be faced in the Atlantic before victory was gained.

The year 1942 started with a series of heavy sinkings on the eastern seaboard of the United States. The American Navy had ignored the lessons which the British had learnt so painfully, and Admiral King did not start a convoy system until May. In addition, the co-operation between the aircraft and the warships which were searching for U-boats was most unsatisfactory, and the Germans had one of their 'happy times', a small number of submarines achieving great success without loss. By June the convoys had reduced the sinkings, so the U-boats moved to the Caribbean where they found new and easy targets. In the first six months of 1942 the U-boats alone sank over 3,000,000 tons; 100 new boats had been commissioned to replace the 21 lost and the prospects for the Allies were extremely gloomy. To add to the difficulties, Doenitz then deployed strong forces against the convoys in the middle of the Atlantic.

There was now a formidable controversy between the Admiralty and the Air Ministry. The Admiralty contended— rightly, as post-war analysis has shown—that the air escort of convoys paid better dividends than the bombing of U-boat bases and building yards. The Air Ministry were most reluctant to reduce the weight of the bombing offensive and the Cabinet was called in to adjudicate. After prolonged discussion the Prime Minister eventually decreed a compromise which aimed to increase the resources of Coastal Command 'without as far as possible causing any decline in the bombing of Germany'.[316] This unsatisfactory decision was responsible for a considerable delay in attaining victory in the Atlantic and caused the loss of many ships. Churchill regarded bombing as the only means of hurting Germany, but measures such as diverting the anti-submarine aircraft of Coastal Command to join a 'thousand-bomber raid' on Germany were grave misuses of valuable aircraft and trained aircrew.

Sinkings in the Atlantic continued to be very heavy throughout 1942, and in November 700,000 tons of shipping were sunk by U-boats alone and another 100,000 by other causes. These losses could not be allowed to continue. So the Prime

Minister convened a new body—the anti-U-boat Committee—to consider the measures needed, and it was soon evident that the most important requirement was the long-range aircraft for convoy escort. Some were obtained from America, some were extracted from Bomber Command, and the airfields at Newfoundland and Labrador were converted into bases for anti-submarine operations.

By then, the fruits of Professor Blackett's operational research were being gathered. Only ships of high speed were allowed to sail independently, convoys were made larger, escort groups were better trained, and support groups to reinforce convoys threatened or attacked. In addition, refuelling procedures allowed transatlantic escort to be started.

However, 1943 started badly, and in March, with 100 U-boats on patrol, losses were so high that some pessimists urged that the convoy system should be abandoned, though they could suggest no satisfactory substitute. So Churchill, despite the strong resistance of Stalin, who in this case was supported by Roosevelt, firmly refused to continue to run the convoys to Russia and some badly needed destroyers were released to form the Atlantic Support Groups.

Then suddenly, in a few weeks, looming defeat turned into resounding victory. Many events combined to produce this result. The support groups were invaluable, the first escort-carrier made its appearance and the escort groups themselves reached a much higher standard of teamwork. One highly efficient squadron of Liberators (No. 120), working from Iceland, covered the 'gap' where U-boats had previously had it all their own way, and co-operation between air and sea escorts improved. Better radar, accurate direction-finding sets and new anti-submarine weapons also played their part.

The disasters of March were followed by an even struggle in April, with losses on both sides, but in May sinkings of merchant ships declined sharply and the U-boats were slaughtered, forty-one being lost in that month alone.

In mid-May a slow, heavily laden convoy fought its way across the Atlantic through three wolf-packs without the loss of a single ship, while five U-boats were destroyed: this was the final blow, and on 24 May Doenitz withdrew the U-boats from the North Atlantic.

The Prime Minister followed the course of the struggle with great attention and was quick to signal his congratulations to those who had performed with distinction.

'The Battle of the Atlantic was the dominating factor all through the War. Never for one moment could we forget that everything happening elsewhere, on land, at sea, or in the air, depended ultimately on its outcome, and amid all other cares we viewed its changing fortunes day by day with hope or apprehension.'[317]

Thereafter the issue was not in doubt, though the Germans never gave up the struggle. In the autumn of 1943 they returned to the North Atlantic armed with new weapons. A little later they produced the snorkel breathing-tube, which made U-boats far more difficult to detect from the air. But they failed to interfere with the invasion of Europe in the summer of 1944, despite the magnificent targets presented. One or two ships were torpedoed, and Churchill is remembered for his displeasure, but the anti-submarine measures taken were highly successful.

At the end of 1944 reports began to be received of new types of U-boats with which the Germans hoped to regain ascendancy on the oceans. Despite the decrease in sinkings, shipping was still the main bottleneck to the many military operations being conducted all over the world, and the thought of a renascence of the U-boats was very disturbing. The Prime Minister accordingly approved the highest priority for bombing raids on the building yards, and a large number of escorts destined for the Far East were retained in Home Waters. In fact, the German U-boat force reached its highest numbers in March 1945, when no less than 461 were available, but fortunately the new types were delayed, mainly by the dislocation of transport through our bombing, and only a few appeared at sea before the end came. The narrow margin by which we avoided these new, fast submarines is sobering, for the morale of the crews was high till the last, despite the very heavy losses the U-boats had suffered.

Defensive period

After this account of the struggle against U-boats, which continued over five and a half long years, watched by Churchill with constant vigilance, we must return to 1940 and to other aspects of the war at sea.

After the French armistice, the most difficult decision which faced Churchill was the future of the French Fleet. This contained many modern and efficient units, which, if surrendered to the Germans, might change the balance at sea in favour of the Axis powers. We were now facing both Germany and Italy and our ships were hard pressed and thinly scattered.

The decision was taken by the Cabinet that the French ships must be either taken over or neutralized so that they could never sail under the German flag. Although relations between the two navies had been cordial in the first months of war, all French naval officers took a solemn oath of allegiance to the legal Government, and it was unlikely that they would comply with the British demands unless faced by overwhelming forces. In addition, Admiral Darlan, the head of the Navy, was no friend of Britain, and there is evidence that during the last days of the French struggle he refused to allow plans to be made for the Navy to continue the war overseas if France was overrun. The takeover met with mixed fortunes. In the British Home Ports a surprise coup quickly gained its object, and at Alexandria, after a skilful combination of threats and pleading by Admiral Cunningham, the French Admiral was persuaded to render his squadron unfit for sea, and so it remained for three years.

But at Oran, where the main body of the French Fleet lay, all attempts to persuade its Commander to comply with one of the several alternatives offered him failed. To the dismay of the British officers concerned, fire had to be opened, and several ships were sunk or damaged, with heavy loss of men who had been so recently our allies. It will be long debated whether the Government decision was correct. The admirals on the spot believed it to be wrong and complied with great reluctance. The chief argument in its favour is that it showed the world in unmistakable fashion that Britain, despite her isolation, was, under Churchill, utterly determined to fight on.

It is said on the best authority that the Prime Minister wrote with his own hand the signals ordering this distasteful action, because he did not wish his naval friends to be associated with a decision the responsibility for which was his alone.

Lord Beaverbook's biographer writes that Pound was firmly in favour of strong action against the French, but that the Prime Minister was horrified by the thought of bombarding the Fleet. Lord Beaverbrook's advice turned the scales, however, and the order was given; Churchill wept bitterly afterwards.[318]

During those long months before Russia and America became our allies, the Prime Minister was frustrated by his inability to take the offensive. He believed that 'the Navy can lose the War but only the Air Force can win it' and he pinned his faith on the bombing of Germany in the hope that the claims of some airmen that it would bring about the dissolution of the Reich would come true. Unfortunately these claims were unjustified. The early bombing raids were ineffective, though this was not known until Professor Lindemann made a special analysis of photographs of bombed targets. German morale was unaffected and production continued to rise until 1944.

There can be no dispute that the combined Anglo-American bombing offensive of Germany in 1944–5 was a major factor in the success of the invasion of Europe, but it can also be argued with confidence that a slower building-up of Bomber Command until the technical methods of finding and hitting the targets had been improved, and a quicker reinforcement of Coastal Command with the long-range bombers which were so essential for convoy defence in mid-Atlantic, would have saved millions of tons of shipping and gained an earlier victory.

In the summer of 1940, Churchill was urging that small-scale raids on Europe should be started, and he insisted on the development of landing-ships and -craft for the eventual re-entry to the Continent, as well as setting up a combined-operations organization to study amphibious techniques and to prepare for and execute raids on occupied territory.

The Middle East was the only active theatre of land operations, and Churchill took tremendous risks to denude the Home base of men and material to build up our forces in Egypt. There were many battles with the Admiralty over the transport of reinforcements through the Mediterranean, particularly of tanks, for the lessons of Norway had so impressed the naval staff that the pendulum had swung from over-confidence to pessimism about the air threat to warships. Certainly while the Mediterranean Fleet faced only the Italian Air Force, Churchill was proved to be right, and it was only the arrival of the German Stuka dive-bombers which made the central Mediterranean untenable for supply ships unless in very heavily escorted convoys.

During the years of the siege of Malta, the Prime Minister was fully alive to the interaction between the fortunes of the island and the progress of the battle in the desert. Only when Malta was supplied with stores and defended by fighters, could aircraft, submarines and occasionally cruisers and destroyers bring the transport of supplies to the Axis armies in North Africa to a standstill. But the nourishing of Malta depended greatly on airfields sited well to the westward of Alexandria in order to provide protection for the convoys bringing in food, fuel and ammunition. Fortunately, none of the many German plans to invade Malta were executed and the gallant island remained, with varying fortunes, to carry out its vital role. There were many disagreements, both with the naval staff and the Commander-in-Chief, but the importance of Malta was never one of them.

Reference has already been made to the unhappily worded telegrams sent to Admiral Cunningham, urging him to further efforts, and the most unhelpful suggestion of all was made in April 1941, when the Prime Minister suggested sinking the battleship *Barham* as a blockship in Tripoli harbour. Cunningham refused this impractical proposal, and instead bombarded Tripoli with his whole fleet. Churchill had a fetish for the suicidal use of battleships, for later in the war he would have run one aground on the Normandy beaches to act as a fort during the invasion, but Cunningham, by then First Sea Lord, was again able to veto the venture.

Probably the most testing times ever endured by British naval forces came during the evacuation of Greece and Crete

HMS *Ark Royal* under attack

On the bridge of HMS *Kimberley* watching Operation 'Dragoon'

A kamikaze hit on **HMS** *Formidable*

Admiral Sir Andrew Cunningham

in the early summer of 1941. The decision to strip the Army and Air Force in the desert to come to the defence of Greece was a political act, made against the advice of the naval staff, and especially of Admiral Phillips, who was at that time a close associate of the Prime Minister.

Historians will long argue whether it was right to risk disaster to aid an ally, but no one can dispute that the fears of the naval staff were only too real and the results were igno-minious evacuations and defeat in the desert. And historians will never forget, I trust, the remark made by Cunningham when asked to send out his exhausted and battered ships for one more journey to Crete to take off the soldiers: 'It takes the Navy three years to build a ship. It will take three hundred to build a new tradition.' And the ships sailed.

In the summer of 1941, plans had been made to send a strong force to the Far East station, which was very vulnerable and which the Japanese were evidently planning to attack. But the heavy losses, both at home and in the Mediterranean, reduced the number of ships which could be spared and eventually it was decided to send only the new battleship *Prince of Wales*, the old battle-cruiser *Repulse*, and the new carrier *Indomitable*. The Admiralty wished these ships to be based in the Indian Ocean, where they would be well placed to operate in any direction, but the Prime Minister insisted that they must go to Singapore, where he believed they would serve as a de-terrent to Japanese adventures. Then a serious navigational error put the *Indomitable* out of action, and the naval staff's opposition to the move to Singapore increased. The tragic results are only too well known. The *Prince of Wales* and *Repulse* met, without fighter protection, the crack Japanese torpedo and high-level naval bombers, and were swiftly sunk. This was the only major matter on which the Prime Minister overruled his naval advisers—he wore down their opposition by constant pressure until they were forced to agree.

There were many unhappy aspects of the disaster—the lack of the *Indomitable*, the absence of the few shore-based fighters which were available in Malaya, the unfortunate decision to delay the squadron's return to Singapore by investigating

299

what proved to be a false report of a Japanese landing. The comments of Admiral Cunningham are also of great interest for at the end of a chapter which describes many air attacks on his battle-tested fleet he says: 'The loss of the *Prince of Wales* and *Repulse* . . . had a profound effect upon our sailors, who rather took the view that these two ships, because of their inexperience of aircraft attacks, should never have been sent out. However, that is not for me to discuss.'[319]

The Period of the Offensive

The Navy was fully extended throughout the Second World War and there were none of the complaints of inaction which followed the Kaiser's War. But after the victory in the Atlantic in May 1943, the Prime Minister, while never forgetting the war at sea, concentrated more on the bombing offensive, on land operations, and above all on the formulation of strategy with our American allies. Thus one must omit mention of many stirring occasions, the brilliant work of our submarines, and many successful combined operations, because the Prime Minister was not now so directly involved; but I have chosen three examples for comment because of his profound influence on their inception. These are the convoys to Russia, the operations for re-entry into Europe, and the dispatch of the British Fleet to the Pacific.

Russian convoys

The decision that material aid must be sent to Russia's northern ports was taken soon after the German attack in June 1941, and by the end of the war 720 ships, most of which sailed in 40 convoys, delivered over 4,000,000 tons of cargo, 5,000 tanks and 7,000 aircraft. But 92 merchantmen and 18 warships were lost in these hazardous operations which threw a heavy burden on the Home Fleet and diverted escorts from the Atlantic convoys. After a quiet start in 1941, each Arctic convoy became a major fleet operation with a close escort, a supporting force of cruisers and a covering force of capital ships and aircraft-carriers. Every element combined to make these convoys the most testing of the war. The dreadful weather and the ice in winter, the perpetual daylight in summer, all helped the enemy. The convoys were always within range of air attack. The water conditions made A/S detection of U-boats difficult, and battleships, cruisers and destroyers lurked in the Norwegian fjords—an ever-present menace. At the end of each journey the Russian welcome was cool, and the assistance offered sparse. There was no gratitude expressed, and communication consisted chiefly of complaints when convoys had to be suspended.

The Prime Minister took the brunt of these wearing exchanges with Stalin. He pressed the Admiralty very hard, and some of the convoys were sent with great reluctance, but more than once he affirmed Admiralty policy to suspend convoys, notably in the early spring of 1943 when the Home Fleet destroyers were needed for the crisis of the Battle of the Atlantic, and also in the summer of 1942, after the disaster to convoy PQ 17, when only thirteen ships out of thirty-six reached Russia.

The cause of the tragedy was the withdrawal of the escort cruisers and destroyers and the order to scatter the ships of the convoy, a signal made under the mistaken belief in the Admiralty that the battleship *Tirpitz* was about to attack the convoy. The dispersed ships were then set upon at leisure by both U-boats and aircraft and the few survivors had harrowing experiences before reaching safety.

The repercussions of this massacre were widespread. In addition to the suspension of the convoys until the autumn, the merchant seamen temporarily lost confidence in the willingness of the Navy to protect them, and it was some time before mutual trust was restored. In addition, after hearing the reports of the American warships which at that time formed part of the Home Fleet, Admiral King, the Chief of Naval Operations, was so horrified by this disastrous example of control from Whitehall that he quickly transferred his ships to the Pacific. To quote Admiral Nimitz: 'Henceforth King viewed U.S.-British naval operations with disfavor,' which accounts for many of the difficulties with King over further operations and in particular his opposition to the participation of the British Fleet during the last stages of the war in the Pacific in 1945.[320]

It has been said, wrongly, that the Prime Minister was responsible for the order to scatter the convoy, but the evidence is conclusive that Admiral Pound, against the advice of his staff, personally sent the signal. Moreover, in a telephone conversation with the Commander-in-Chief before the convoy had sailed he had indicated that he might scatter the ships in an emergency and the Commander-in-Chief had protested vigorously, pointing out that it would be contrary to all recent experience.[321]

Thereafter the Russian convoys fought hard against great odds, but they won through with comparatively light losses, especially when escort carriers sailed with most of the convoys, their aircraft performing great work in defence against both aircraft and U-boats. On one occasion in December 1942 a convoy was attacked by the battleship *Lützow*, the cruiser *Hipper* and six large destroyers, but the close escort and the supporting cruisers drove them off. Hitler was so angry at this failure that he ordered Admiral Raeder to pay off all his heavy ships because they were so useless. However, Raeder resigned and his successor Doenitz persuaded Hitler to reconsider the decision. Then a year later, during the passage of another convoy, the *Scharnhorst*, which had made a sortie to attack the convoy, was found and sunk by the Home Fleet.

Except for convoy PQ 17 the story of the Russian convoys is one of which the Navy can be very proud, for the naval staff always believed that if the roles had been reversed we would have destroyed each convoy which passed the Norwegian coast. But fortunately Hitler's directives severely hampered German operations, which were relatively unsuccessful.

The invasion of Europe

The Prime Minister made three important interventions in the planning for the invasion. The first was the idea for artificial harbours; the second was his refusal to agree to American proposals to invade in 1942 and 1943; and the third was his disagreement with the proposal to attack in the south of France simultaneously with the Normandy invasion. He describes how in 1917 he had suggested the idea of building a natural harbour at Borkum and at Sylt for destroyers and submarines.[322] Lighters would be towed across and then filled with sand and sunk. Fortunately he did not describe this plan in *The World Crisis* for reasons of lack of space, and the idea was resurrected and used with great success in the 'Mulberry' harbours off Normandy. In this same paper of 1917 he produced the idea of lighters to carry tanks which would run up the beaches.

When the USA entered the war, there was a natural enthusiasm to attack the Germans as soon as possible. The dangers and difficulties of a cross-Channel invasion were not fully appreciated, and plans for a lodgement in 1942 and a full-scale invasion in 1943 were in turn proposed. Our Chiefs of Staff were convinced that both schemes were impossible, because neither the ships nor the craft were available and amphibious training had hardly started. So Churchill used his personal influence with the President to persuade the United States leaders to agree to an invasion of North Africa in 1942 as a first step, and from this stemmed the attacks on Sicily, Salerno and Anzio.

With hindsight, knowledge of the difficulties and delays of Operation 'Overlord' and the struggle to break out of the initial lodgement, it is clear that 1944 was the earliest practicable date for an invasion and that a failure in 1943 would have been a disaster which would have much prolonged the War.

Historical judgements of the value of the invasion of the south of France—Operation 'Dragoon'— are not yet final. The Prime Minister did not wish to reduce the forces fighting in Italy, and claimed that a victory there would help 'Overlord' more than any advance up the Rhone Valley, but the Americans disagreed violently, stressing the need for Marseilles as an entry port for the vast US armies still waiting to sail for Europe. They suspected Churchill of sinister imperialistic designs, though in fact he was thinking more of forestalling a direct Soviet takeover of the whole of eastern Europe.*

This time he was unable to persuade the President, and the

---

* When Churchill sent a British Division to help the Greek Government quell a Communist rebellion at the end of 1944, Admiral King refused to allow American ships to be used to transport men or materials to Greece.

invasion of the south of France took place nine weeks after 'Overlord'. Characteristically, once the decision was final, he supported it fully and even witnessed the landing from the destroyer *Kimberley*.

The British Pacific Fleet

During the early months of 1944, there was much disagreement over the strategy of the war against Japan. The Prime Minister disagreed with his own Chiefs of Staff, the Supreme Commander, Admiral Mountbatten, produced alternative proposals and the Americans disagreed generally with each and all because they believed that the British effort should be mainly devoted to opening the land route through Burma to China. In March 1944 Churchill, having been told by the President that no British naval contribution would be required in the Pacific until the summer of 1945, decreed that a 'Bay of Bengal' strategy should be adopted. However, the constantly changing situation required constantly changing plans. By the time of the Quebec Conference in September 1944, the operations in Europe were proceeding well and there were some—though not including the Prime Minister—who thought that Germany might be defeated by the end of the year. Churchill describes his thoughts while preparing for the Quebec Conference on passage in the Queen Mary.

Over 160,000 British prisoners and civilian internees were in Japanese hands. Singapore must be redeemed and Malaya freed. For nearly three years we had persisted in the strategy of 'Germany First'. The time had now come for the liberation of Asia, and I was determined that we should play our full and equal part in it. What I feared most at this stage of the war was that the United States would say in after-years, 'We came to your help in Europe and you left us alone to finish off Japan.' We had to regain on the field of battle our rightful possessions in the Far East, and not have them handed back to us at the peace table.

Our main contribution must obviously be on the sea and in the air. Most of our Fleet was now free to move eastwards, and I resolved that our first demand on our American Allies should be for its full participation in the main assault on Japan. The Royal Air Force should follow as soon as possible after Germany was defeated.[323]

In his review of the war which the Prime Minister delivered at the start of the Conference, after describing the plans for the operations to capture Rangoon, he offered the British Main Fleet—'a powerful and well-balanced force'—to join in the operations against Japan under United States Supreme Command. Roosevelt said at once 'no sooner offered than accepted', an intervention which did not please Admiral King, but, despite King's efforts to frustrate the plan—for he wished the United States Navy to finish off the Japanese unaided—he was overruled, and plans for the dispatch of the British Pacific Fleet went ahead.

Preparations were on a vast scale, for one condition of acceptance was that the Fleet should be self-contained logistically, and this involved the collection of a large 'Fleet Train' of merchant ships to carry the fuel, stores, provisions and ammunition needed. When the time came, however, the United States Navy in the Pacific made the Fleet extremely welcome and helped to ease some logistic difficulties, and the relationship between the two navies at sea was excellent.

After two preliminary raids on oil refineries in Sumatra, the Fleet left the Indian Ocean and arrived in mid-February at Sydney, where Admiral Fraser, the Commander-in-Chief, had his headquarters. After some high-level discussions on the conflicting claims of General MacArthur and Admiral Nimitz, both of whom wanted to use the Fleet, it was assigned to Nimitz, who in turn placed it under the command of Admiral Spruance for the operations against Okinawa in March 1945. By then the Japanese *kamikaze* bombers were making heavy suicidal attacks, and the British aircraft-carriers with their armoured decks emerged very creditably from the ordeal. During the first two periods of operations, each of which lasted about a month, no less than four carriers were hit, but they were quickly able to continue operations, whereas the American ships with their light decks were gravely damaged.

Further plans for the British Pacific Fleet to join the United States Fleet were made, but on 11 August, soon after the operations had started, the Japanese surrendered—a surrender which was accelerated by the explosion of the atomic bombs but which had been already inevitable owing to the total blockade which was fast bringing the Japanese war-making machine to a complete halt.

That the contribution of the British Pacific Fleet had been useful was generously acknowledged by our American allies. Churchill, who was rejected by the British electorate on 26 July, must have had the consolation of pride and satisfaction that his demand for the Royal Navy to play its part in the final defeat of Japan had been so splendidly fufilled.

13

RETROSPECT 1911-55

*The leader of the nation, the saviour of our people and the
symbol of resistance in the free world.*[324]

IN 1955 Winston Churchill laid down the burden of
governmental office. It is of interest to consider the state
of the Royal Navy at that time and to attempt to judge
whether he could be satisfied that the reforms which he had
initiated over forty years ago, when he became First Lord of
the Admiralty for the first time, had been fully carried out.

The Navy had emerged from the Second World War with
great confidence. Despite some disasters, it had fought
valiantly and successfully, and it was proud of its record and
believed that the country shared this pride.

To compare the states of the Navy at various epochs is a
fascinating but delicate operation. Traditionally, the Golden
Age had been regarded as the Nelson era—an era illuminated
also by such men as St Vincent, Howe, Duncan and Collingwood. Certainly it was then that the great victories over the
French, the Spanish and the Dutch were obtained, when
Nelson himself established a tradition which, contrary to some
cynical opinions, encouraged change and progress and banished
reaction and sloth.

But a closer look at the history of these stirring times pro-
duces a less perfect picture. Flag Officers were promoted solely
on seniority, and, though there were some great Admirals,
there were a number of duds, who had to be sent to lesser
commands or put on half-pay in order to let the competent
officers take control in the most important fleets. Sir John
Orde, not a dud by any means but not a great Flag Officer,
was 'passed over' in favour of Nelson for the command of the
squadron which was detached from the main fleet for service
in the Mediterranean in 1798. He challenged the Commander-
in-Chief, St Vincent, to a duel because of this decision, and a
most undignified squabble continued for years. Admiral Parker,
too, was another rejected in favour of Nelson, and all in

x

all there was little harmony among the senior officers of the fleet.

Even the Captains' List was patchy. Nelson chose, or had chosen for him, an unsurpassed team which quickly became the band of brothers which brought so many triumphs. But when Nelson was detached by St Vincent for the campaign which led to the victory of the Nile, there was much anxiety at the weakness of the Fleet which he left with St Vincent— not because of the physical loss of the ships of the line so much as the loss of captains like Troubridge, Foley, Ball, Miller, Louis, Hood and Saumarez. There were not enough other captains of that calibre—men with initiative, zeal and a burning eagerness to attack the enemy; there were too many dull, inactive men who had to be prodded into action and who were reluctant to seize any initiative which was presented, and Nelson and his band were the exception rather than the rule.

The Navy of 1914–18, the Navy that Churchill helped mould, achieved much, and its morale remained high under very difficult conditions. After the Battle of Jutland in May 1916 the defects in the safety arrangements of the magazines of the big ships, which had resulted in the loss of three battle-cruisers and the near-loss of Beatty's flagship, the *Lion*, had been corrected, but the senior Admirals (and no one else, for it was a well-kept secret) were severely handicapped by the knowledge that British shells were useless when fired at long range and broke up on the armour of the German ships instead of penetrating it. The Fleet would not be fully supplied with efficient shell until 1918, and, not unnaturally, action with a German fleet known to be equipped with extremely effective shell was not an attractive prospect. Even so, Beatty, who became Commander-in-Chief of the Grand Fleet in December 1916 when Jellicoe took over as First Sea Lord, was determined to seek action, and planned to try to meet the enemy at dawn so as to give himself the whole day to close the range and pound the enemy into defeat.[325]

But Jellicoe was no Nelson, despite his many virtues, and Beatty had Nelson's spirit but lacked his technical genius. After the First World War, the number of senior officers with a 'fighting' reputation was small. Beatty, Keyes, Tyrwhitt and Goodenough spring to mind, but by contrast there were others who were dull and unimaginative and who failed dismally to grasp some splendid opportunities.

The senior officers of the Second World War, who, unlike their predecessors of 1914, started in 1939 with war experience of 1914–18, were of an altogether higher standard, At the start there were a few who inevitably were not equal to the strain, but they were soon put ashore without indignity. The only shameful episode—the desertion of convoy PQ 17—was a direct Admiralty responsibility ordered by a sick man against the advice of the Commander-in-Chief and against the wishes of the officers at sea.

Admiral Sir Andrew Cunningham's leadership of his fleet during those first two years of the war in the Mediterranean will bear favourable comparison with any of Nelson's campaigns, and the harmony among his staff and his captains was complete. The names of Fraser, Somerville, Burroughs, Vian, Oliver and Troubridge can equally be compared with the best leaders of the Nelson era, while the skill and leadership with which Admiral Horton directed first the British submarine operations and then the Battle in the Atlantic against the German U-boats, and the way Admiral Ramsay planned and directed the Dunkirk evacuation and then the invasions of North Africa, Italy and Normandy, were unequalled.*

More specifically, the work of the Captains of the Fleet destroyers,† which fought in the Norwegian campaign, which took part in the evacuations from Dunkirk, Greece and Crete, which escorted convoys both to Murmansk and Malta (often one immediately after the other), and which operated so efficiently in the Indian Ocean and Pacific, cannot ever be bettered in Britain's long naval history. Names like Mack, Warburton-Lee and Armstrong, who were lost, and Sherbrooke,

---

* Admiral Lord Mountbatten achieved greatness as a Supreme Commander, and it is not possible to place him in the 'handicap stakes' for lack of a comparison in earlier wars.
† I should make it clear that I was a junior officer throughout the war, and never commanded a 'Fleet' destroyer.

Stokes, Onslow and Tyrwhitt, who survived, to mention only a few, will always be remembered.

Similarly, the exploits of the Submarine Service were unsurpassed and many triumphs were obtained despite very heavy losses, especially in the Mediterranean; while the naval aviators flew their ancient machines with skill and determination and later operated the new aircraft from America with great success. Many convoy escort commanders gained distinction, but here again, there were no comparable personalities in the First World War with whom comparisons can be drawn.

As to the men on the Lower Deck, it was no longer necessary to 'coal ship' on return to harbour and living conditions aboard were better than in 1914–18. But the improvements were small, and the ships spent more time at sea and were involved in many more actions. In both wars, the sailor and the marine were the salt of the earth and behaved as such.

The best of the Navy of 1939–45 was as good as the best of Nelson's time; while the general standard of competence among the Admirals and Captains was higher. The fleets which fought in the Second World War were better than any other in our history.

One of the main reasons for Churchill's arrival at the Admiralty in 1911 was to form a Naval Staff. In 1955 there was nothing left of the inter-war-years distrust of the Staff Officer, and without the need for Staff training becoming a fetish as in the Army, its advantages were known and recognized. The staffs of the Commanders-in-Chief, both ashore and afloat, had performed admirably during the Second World War, and, with some exceptions in the field of defence of trade and anti-submarine warfare, the Admiralty machine had operated well. The modern senior officer who graduates from the Naval Staff College to the Joint Services Staff College, and later to the Imperial Defence College, should be well equipped both for high command in the Navy and for co-operation with the other Services.

Just as social conditions and living standards had changed ashore, so there had been a similar radical transformation in the condition of the personnel of the Navy by 1955. Progress had been accelerated by the war and, a point often overlooked, by close contact with the American Navy.

The service had been strengthened and invigorated by the retention of a number of reservists and other non-regulars after the war, and today, the Flag List contains the names of Admirals who started their careers in the Royal Naval Reserve, the Royal Naval Volunteer Reserve, the Royal Air Force and even the Polish Navy. Such promotions could never have been even considered in the years between the world wars.

The entry of officers had by 1955 become independent of the parents' income, as Lord Fisher had pleaded in 1905. The age of entry had been raised to 17–18—a more debatable reform—and the artificial distinctions between the different branches of the Navy had been swept away. The presence of an engineer specialist on the Admiralty Board as Fourth Sea Lord in 1965 provided an excellent proof of continued progress.*

The training of junior officers had been revolutionized—not invariably for the better, as the time spent at sea as a midshipman had been reduced to only one year. But they were treated as officers and not punished as schoolboys as had been the case fifty years earlier.

Paradoxically, the need for promotion from the lower deck had decreased because the new system of entry allowed able boys from every walk of life to enter as cadets; but the opportunity remained in order to allow the late developer to be rewarded. In addition the number of what used to be called 'warrant officers' (renamed 'special duties officers') was increased.

The standard of education of the lower deck had continued to rise as was necessary if the sophisticated equipment in the new ships was to be maintained and operated correctly. Routine had become less rigid and the number of parades and musters much reduced. The relationship between officers and

---

* In the case of officer reforms, 1956 is the important date when the new system was introduced, but the difference in timing is very small.

men was close and cordial without loss of discipline—the reverse in fact. There was much more mixing at games and sports; cricket, hockey and rugby were no longer the prerogative of the officers. Everything was not perfect, of course; there were bad officers and they still produced bad ships, but these were remarkably few.

Pay and living conditions had been much improved, and in the new shore establishments, especially, the standards were very high. Food was excellent. Marriage allowances* were paid and married quarters provided. Periods of service abroad with separation from families had been reduced in length though not in frequency. All these improvements were indeed needed if recruits were to be obtained and, what is even more important, if trained men were to be persuaded to volunteer to stay on for further periods of service after their first engagement had expired. In a welfare state, with a high standard of living and a policy of full employment, these problems are very real.

In 1949 a comprehensive investigation into the administration of justice in the Navy was carried out by a Committee under the chairmanship of Mr Justice Pilcher. The Committee's two reports make interesting reading, the number of changes recommended being remarkably few and the criticisms remarkably mild.

There were three important changes. First, the inclusion of Non-Executive officers as members of Courts Martial; secondly the tidying-up of the rather informal procedure for investigating offences likely to need summary punishment; and thirdly the reduction in the severity of the summary punishments which the Captain could award, by removing dismissal with disgrace from the list of summary punishments—a sensible change and one which was already followed in practice.[326]

The other changes were unimportant and the outcome had been an improvement in a system which needed little modification. Certainly Churchill seemed satisfied, for when he found

---

* Marriage allowance for officers was introduced in 1937, but the method did not commend itself to the bachelors, for every officer had his pay cut by half a crown and the married officers were granted five shillings a day with the proceeds!

a proposal to amend the Naval Discipline Act* in the legislative pipeline on relieving Attlee as Prime Minister, he is said to have remarked that 'the Royal Navy has won two great wars with the present Act, if necessary it can win a third', and the bill was dropped from the programme.[327] The fruits of his battles to reform the system in 1912 had endured well.

As the result of a recommendation of an earlier Committee which investigated the administration of justice in the Army and Royal Air Force in 1946,[328] a recommendation which was supported by the Pilcher Committee, a Court Martial Appeal Court was set up in 1952. But for many reasons, the most important being that the naval commanding officer has greater powers of summary punishments than the commanding officer in the other two services, the number of courts martial in the Navy is small in comparison. As a result, to date, out of 186 naval applications for leave to appeal only 9 cases have been heard by the Court, and not one has succeeded: a most satisfactory tribute to the system.†

As to discipline generally, a direct comparison of statistics between 1911 and 1955 is interesting. The number of officers and men borne was 118,000 and 100,000 respectively, reflecting the reduction in the number of ships. In addition a greater proportion of the latter figure was based ashore.

The number of courts martial in 1955 dropped to one-third of the number in 1911, which reflects the social and educational progress both of the country and of the Navy. Summary punishments—those awarded by the Captain—were about the same, the numbers being 1·1 per man in 1955 and 1·0 per man

---

* The Naval Discipline Act was eventually rewritten in 1957 (HMSO 58913), but the end product was very similar to the original Act, except that the wording had been clarified.

† I gave verbal evidence to some members of the Pilcher Committee in 1949 and surprised them by averring that the system of naval courts martial was strikingly unjust. I spoke from the bitter experience of acting as the *ex officio* prosecutor at numerous courts martial in 1946–8 when I was Executive Officer of a large naval barracks. I explained that I had had no legal training nor advice on how to conduct a case. The defendant was often represented by a courteous but sharp local solicitor. As a result, a number of guilty men were acquitted. The Pilcher Committee recommended that prosecutors in tricky cases should have legal training.

in 1911. But the number of 'warrant' summary punishments, which involve the more serious offences and require the approval of a Flag Officer before being awarded, dropped by half.

The other summary punishments, comprising 95 per cent of the whole, were awarded for such matters as returning from leave late or drunk, bad language, absence from place of duty and other breaches of naval manners which would not be considered 'crimes' in civilian life. The drop in the number of serious offences and the remarkable similarity in the frequency of the minor offences shows, I think, that the improvement in discipline had been accompanied by no fall in the standards of smartness which are so important in a service like the Navy.

Perhaps I may be forgiven for introducing into the text, for the first and last time, the evidence of my personal experience. When 'Flag Officer, Sea Training' in 1960–1, I was lucky enough to embark at sea in no less than seventy-two ships and submarines of every class in the Navy—in some for a few hours, in others for a few days.

I was deeply impressed by the interest and keenness shown by the ratings of all branches, whether operators, maintainers or members of the 'logistics' departments. I thought that they were superior to the men whom I had known and liked so much in the thirties. They were better educated, more highly trained and they were kept far more busy, whether at sea or in harbour.

The officers were about the same as in the thirties. Some were very good indeed, there was a mass of average, competent, but not very inspiring men, and there were a few duds who were unsuited to naval life. In general, I think, the technical competence of the average officer was higher than in the thirties, but his qualities of leadership were somewhat lower.

But taking the Navy as a whole, I believe that the standards in the fifties were as high as at any time in our peacetime history and I see no sign of any deterioration today.

Strategy

By 1955, owing to the spread of nuclear weapons, naval confidence had diminished and was being replaced by doubts as to the future. Some people—not sailors—said that nuclear air power was now supreme and that the need for Navies was past. Korea had already proved them wrong and a series of other conflicts on a minor scale reinforced the proof; but in political circles the doubt remained whether sea power still had a part to play in keeping the peace of the world.*

Churchill played only a shadowy role in these questions. He was mesmerized by the new atomic bombs, both megaton and kiloton, and he believed that the Royal Air Force was the most important arm. His belief in the need for a large Navy seemed to decrease, though his confidence in the service was undiminished and he fought like a tiger at Washington in 1952 to obtain the post of Supreme Allied Commander Atlantic for a British officer, wrongly, in my opinion, because of the disparity of the forces involved; and as Prime Minister, he was very ready to use the Navy, not only in the Korean war but also in many minor operations.

Since the end of the War, the Admiralty had made some mistakes in policy—hindsight is easy—but even so I believe that in 1955 the Navy was more ready for conflict, whatever form it might take, than ever before in peacetime—although this may not be considered a great tribute.

At the time of the massive rearmament programme started during the Korean War, too much emphasis was laid on the needs of a war with Russia and too much money spent on minesweepers and on preparations for a 'general' war. Yet Korea itself showed the future pattern. Nuclear weapons would prevent 'general' wars and limited conflicts and guerrilla operations would be the order of the day.

We were very slow to build up a competent Amphibious Force—the commando carrier and the assault-ship of 1965 were not new ideas and could have been available in 1955. What a difference they could have made to the Suez operations!†
As it was, the Amphibious Force was old and slow, with many

---

* Mr Duncan Sandys was especially dogmatic, and his White Paper of 1957 is now remarkable only for the number of its forecasts which have proved unsound.
† At Suez the *Theseus* carried helicopters, but was not specially fitted as a commando carrier.

of the ships lying in reserve; it could be used neither quickly nor flexibly.* Just as Trade Defence had been the Cinderella of the Navy between the wars, so in 1955 amphibious warfare was not entirely respectable, and the Amphibious Warfare Squadron did not receive the attention it deserved. Equally, naval aviators were inclined to concentrate on purely naval problems and to forget the importance of co-operation with the Army, though Suez, Kuwait and many other operations were soon to show that the main purpose of the aircraft-carrier was to support amphibious operations. But the importance of gaining control of the air over the sea was fully appreciated and the carrier had become, rightly, the core of the Fleet.

The Navy of 1955 was over-stretched. Responsibilities exceeded capabilities, but for this Governments must be blamed although the traditional attitude of the Navy that there was nothing beyond its resources, nothing it could not do, must bear some responsibility. A time must come when it has to be said firmly: 'No, it cannot be done.' Today, there is still over-stretch but at least the new construction frigates and destroyers have arrived and the older ships have been scrapped.

In the tactical field, the comparison between 1911 and 1955 was startling. There was a well-run tactical school where an electronic tactical table allowed problems to be studied with imagination. Perhaps the great difficulty was to decide what tactical situation was most likely to be met, and there was a natural tendency to 'fight the last war'. In the purely anti-submarine field, theoretical problems were studied at the Joint Anti-Submarine School at Londonderry and then put into practice at sea off the north of Ireland. In the fleets at sea, realistic exercises were frequent, and a Sea Training Command was shortly to be set up to look after newly commissioned ships and to ensure that time was not wasted on elementary weapon training in the fleet.

At sea, as opposed to the corridors of Whitehall, relations with the Royal Air Force were excellent and co-operation with

---

* I am discussing the techn¹cal operation, not the political wisdom of the Suez affair.

Coastal Command and, where relevant, with Fighter Command worked smoothly.

Technical matters

Our close contacts with the United States Navy during the War had produced a shock in many technical fields, particularly those of propulsion machinery, anti-aircraft weapons and naval aircraft, and in the techniques of replenishing ships with fuel and supplies while under way. It was clear too that we had a lot to learn about ship construction generally.

The inferiority of our propulsion machinery reflected the stagnation of the marine engineering industry in Britain and it was the Navy which after the War led the way in introducing high-temperature, high-pressure boilers at sea and new techniques for diesel engines. But both processes took some time to take effect.

In the field of replenishment at sea, with the help of close co-operation with the USN, which has always been most generous in offering technical information, our capability was much improved, and by 1955 task forces were able to remain at sea for very long periods—a return to the times of Nelson. During the Beira patrol of 1966–7 this was to prove most useful.

In anti-submarine warfare, the wartime lead had been just retained in 1955, though the vast expenditure of the USN was fast reducing the gap; in the field of radar and in the techniques of operation rooms, I think that we were ahead of our allies and these matters provided some exchanges for the technical information received.

Perhaps the greatest contrast between Churchill's early days and 1955 was in the state of naval aviation. By 1955 the Fleet Air Arm had recovered from the crippling inter-war years and was extremely efficient. British naval aircraft were no longer far inferior to their counterparts abroad, and in many aspects of the operation of aircraft we led the world. Britain produced the steam catapult, the angled deck and the mirror landing-sight, inventions which so greatly improved the operation of aircraft from carriers. In the direction of aircraft in the air, too, we were unmatched.

In the development of guided weapons, both for anti-aircraft use and against surface ships, progress had been slow, and I believe personally that the intervention of a Ministry of Supply or of Aviation between the Admiralty and the manu-facturers was mainly responsible for the delays.

On re-reading this chapter, I had a suspicion that I had painted too rosy a picture of the Navy of 1955. But further reflection convinces me that, while by no means perfect, the Admiralty had done more than in any period in its history to learn from its mistakes, and that the outcome compared well with any other Navy in the world.

My soldier and airman friends whom I have interrogated on this delicate question sometimes complain of naval arrogance and an inclination to resent having to work with the other services. Perhaps there is something in what they say, though it is not so bad as in 1911. In any event, naval officers believe that, given a job to do, the Navy will do it better than anyone else, and if that is arrogance then we must plead guilty.

This book started with the words 'Winston Spencer Churchill played a great part in shaping the Navy of today'. It should now be possible to judge whether they were true, and further-more, whether Churchill was satisfied with the results. The part he played in 1911–15 in building up a modern fleet and in introducing modern concepts of staff work, of discipline and of social conditions was both unique and most effective; in 1939, he made certain that progress in all these fields con-tinued. He was well aware that a great service with a long history is liable to resist change and he ensured that change was not obstructed by the traditionalists. On balance, there can be no dispute that his influence on the service during both his periods of office as First Lord was wholly good. On the other hand, it is difficult to be certain of his own opinion on the outcome of his labours, for there is little evidence on which to draw.

Except in his history, he wrote little about the Navy after the Second World War and his references to it in Parliament were few. In 1948, however, when Mr Thomas was ill during the debate on the Naval Estimates, Churchill took his place as spokesman for the Opposition. Early on in his speech he said: 'In war, it [the Navy] is our means of safety—in peace it sustains the prestige, repute and influence of this small island, and it is a major factor in the cohesion of the British Empire and Commonwealth.' However, much of the speech consisted of criticisms of the policy of scrapping the old pre-war battleships. His references to the Fleet Air Arm were few and one now gets the impression that he was not in touch with reality on such technical matters.

In 1952 his pride in the Navy was still undiminished, though it was now shared with the Royal Air Force, and he fought hard for what he believed were the Navy's rights in the Command structure of the North Atlantic Treaty Organization. What little he wrote or said indicates that he was well pleased, and there seem to be no signs of disappointment or dissatisfaction.

Sir Winston Churchill, the greatest Englishman who ever lived, saved the world from Nazi domination in 1940 and continued to lead the nation with skill and devotion till final victory was won. He also had more influence on the condition of the Royal Navy in two world wars than any other civilian, and, in a long life of remarkable accomplishments, the state of the Navy in 1955, which reflected so many of the reforms for which he had fought and had been responsible, must have given him much satisfaction.

SOURCES

1. WSC, *Lord Randolph Churchill* (Odhams, 1951), 24.
2. WSC, *Savrola* (Longmans, 1900).
3. WSC, *London to Ladysmith via Pretoria* (Longmans, 1900).
4. WSC, Speech to the House of Commons, 10/7/35.
5. WSC, *The World Crisis, 1911–1918* (Odhams, 1938, 3 vols.), I, 14.
6. Admiral Sir Percy Scott, *Fifty Years in the Royal Navy* (Allen & Unwin, 1919).
7. *London to Ladysmith*, 310.
8. Lord Randolph Churchill in evidence to the Hartington Commission (1900).
9. Lady Violet Bonham Carter, *Winston Churchill as I Knew Him* (Eyre & Spottiswoode and Collins, 1965), 154.
10. *World Crisis*, I, 53.
11. Professor Arthur J. Marder, *From the Dreadnought to Scapa Flow* (OUP, 1961–6, 3 vols.), I, 106–7.
12. *Dreadnought to Scapa Flow*, I, 121.
13. *Dreadnought to Scapa Flow*, I, 131–2.
14. M. V. Brett (ed.), *The Journals and Letters of Reginald Viscount Esher* (Nicholson & Watson, 1934, 2 vols.).
15. P. de Mendelssohn, *The Age of Churchill* (Thames & Hudson, 1961), 407.
16. Esher.
17. E. P. Hesian, *W. S. Churchill*.
18. *World Crisis*, I, 24.
19. Marder, *Fear God and Dread Nought, the Letters of Lord Fisher of Kilverstone* (Cape, 1952–9, 3 vols.), II, 226.
20. *World Crisis*, I, 23–4.
21. *World Crisis*, I, 25.
22. Sir Sidney Lee, *King Edward VII* (Macmillan, 1925–9, 3 vols.).
23. Royal Archives, XII/21.
24. Royal Archives, X6/34.
25. *Fear God and Dread Nought*, II, 313.
26. Frank Owen, *Tempestuous Journey: Lloyd George, His Life and Times* (Hutchinson, 1954), 213.
27. *Dreadnought to Scapa Flow*, I, 243.
28. *World Crisis*, I, 47.
29. General Sir Frederick Maurice, *Haldane, 1856–1915* (Faber, 1937–9, 2 vols.), I.
30. *World Crisis*, I, 47.
31. R. B. Haldane, *An Autobiography* (Hodder & Stoughton, 1929), 232.
32. Dudley Sommer, *Haldane of Cloan: His Life and Times, 1856–1928* (Allen & Unwin, 1960), 249.
33. Stephen McKenna, *Reginald McKenna, 1863–1943* (Eyre & Spottiswoode, 1948), Chapter VII.
34. *Dreadnought to Scapa Flow*, I, 6.
35. Navy Records Society, Fisher Papers, II, 208.

36. Barbara Tuchman, *August 1914* (Constable, 1962), 57.
37. Admiral Sir Edward Bradford, *Life of Admiral of the Fleet Sir Arthur Knyvet Wilson* (Murray, 1923), 199.
38. Admiral Mark Kerr, *Prince Louis of Battenberg, Admiral of the Fleet* (Longmans, 1934).
39. *Dreadnought to Scapa Flow*, I, 199.
40. Vice-Admiral K. G. B. Dewar, *The Navy from Within* (Gollancz, 1939), 158.
41. Lord Hankey, 'Government Control in War' (11th Haldane Memorial Lecture, Birkbeck College, London, 1942).
42. *Dreadnought to Scapa Flow*, I, 370.
43. *Dreadnought to Scapa Flow*, I, 389.
44. Kerr, 164.
45. Admiral Duncan, *The Earl of Camperdown* (Longmans).
46. Dewar, 137.
47. Filson Young, *With the Battle Cruisers* (Cassell, 1921), 10.
48. Admiral of the Fleet Lord Cork and Orrery, *My Naval Life* (Hutchinson).
49. Captain Lionel Dawson, *Gone for a Sailor* (Rich, 1936), 108.
50. Cork and Orrery, 33.
51. Dawson, 102.
52. Fisher, II.
53. Dewar, 110.
54. PRO Adm. 1/8268.
55. Lionel Yexley, *Our Fighting Seamen* (Stanley Paul).
56. *Dreadnought to Scapa Flow*, I, 10.
57. Admiral Sir William James, *The Eyes of the Navy* (Methuen, 1955), 17.
58. *Dreadnought to Scapa Flow*, I, 205.
59. *The Navy*, November 1911, 286.
60. *World Crisis*, I, 52.
61. *World Crisis*, I, 56.
62. Sturdee Papers.
63. Frewen Diaries.
64. Bonham Carter, 237.
65. *World Crisis*, I, 92.
66. *The Navy*, November 1911.
67. *The Navy*, March 1912, 66.
68. Admiral James, 'Churchill and the Navy' in *Churchill by his Contemporaries*, ed. Neade (Hutchinson, 1953), 141.
69. *Dreadnought to Scapa Flow*, I, 254.
70. *Dreadnought to Scapa Flow*, I, 253.
71. Bonham Carter, 273.
72. Admiral Sir Reginald H. S. Bacon, *The Life of Lord Fisher of Kilverstone* (Hodder & Stoughton, 1929, 2 vols.), II, 104.
73. Kerr.
74. Haldane.

75. 'Etat-Major', 'The Coming Naval War Staff' in *The Navy*, January 1912, 3.
76. PRO Cab. 37/108/135.
77. Naval Staff History, Admiralty Library.
78. Bradford.
79. Asquith Papers.
80. Royal Archives, GV G286/2.
81. *World Crisis*, I, 65.
82. Rear Admiral W. S. Chambers, *The Life and Letters of David, Earl Beatty* (Hodder & Stoughton, 1951).
83. *World Crisis*, I, 68.
84. *World Crisis*, I, 70.
85. Royal Archives, GV G285/43.
86. Royal Archives, GV G285/9.
87. Royal Archives, GV G285/12.
88. Royal Archives, GV G285/27.
89. Royal Archives, GV G285/25.
90. Royal Archives, GV G406/1.
91. Royal Archives, GV G406/5.
92. Royal Archives, GV G775/1.
93. Royal Archives, GV G775/2.
94. Royal Archives, GV G775/3.
95. Admiral Bacon, *Life of Jellicoe* (Cassell, 1936), 181–3.
96. Admiral Sir Dudley de Chair, *The Sea is Strong* (Harrap, 1961), 151.
97. Kilverstone MSS.
98. *Dreadnought to Scapa Flow, I*, 258.
99. *Dreadnought to Scapa Flow, I*, 259.
100. Royal Archives, GV G414/15.
101. Royal Archives, GV G414/1.
102. Royal Archives, GV G414/15.
103. Royal Archives, GV G414/9–10.
104. Royal Archives, GV G414/15.
105. Royal Archives, GV G414/14.
106. Royal Archives, GV G414/25.
107. Randolph S. Churchill, *Winston S. Churchill: II, The Young Statesman, 1901–1914* (Heinemann, 1967), 643.
108. *Navy League Annual*, 1915–16, 30. Written in 1916, some months after Balfour had relieved Churchill at the Admiralty.
109. PRO Adm. 116/1278.
110. *The Navy*, 1912, 313.
111. *The Navy*, 1913, 2.
112. Royal Archives, GV G414/4.
113. PRO Adm. 397/2.
114. *Dreadnought to Scapa Flow*, I, 269–70.
115. *From Sea to Sky* (Bles, 1947), p. 30.
116. Letter to author.

117. 'The Oil Engine and the Submarine' (1914) in Asquith Papers.
118. C. E. Fayle, *The Official History of the Great War: Seaborne Trade* (Murray, 1920, 3 vols.).
119. *Life of Jellicoe*, 181.
120. *The Naval Memoirs of Admiral of the Fleet Sir Roger Keyes* (Eyre & Spottiswoode, 1934–5, 2 vols.), I, 43.
121. PRO Adm. 116/1278.
122. Brassey's *Naval Annual*, 1913, 20.
123. Brassey, 1914, 4.
124. Peter Padfield, *Aim Straight: a Biography of Sir Percy Scott* (Hodder & Stoughton, 1966).
125. Rear Admiral Sir Murray F. Sueter, *Airmen or Noahs* (Murray Fraser, 1928), 132.
126. PRO Cab. 38/20/1.
127. 116th, 120th, 121st and 122nd meetings of the CID.
128. Sueter, 417. Unfortunately, like all the enthusiasts, he omits the mistakes and thus much lessens the value of the evidence.
129. PRO Cab. 38/20/1.
130. C. F. S. Gamble, *The Story of North Sea Air Station* (O.U.P., 1928).
131. Bell Davies, *Sailor in the Air* (Peter Davies, 1967), 181. The *Furious* conversion in 1917 was not successful, despite brave efforts by the pilots.
132. PRO Cab. 38/20/1.
133. PRO Cab. 38/26/22.
134. PRO Case 5762, Air Policy.
135. 121st meeting.
136. Captain Donald Macintyre, RN, *Wings of Neptune* (Peter Davies, 1963), 6.
137. Jones, *The War in the Air* (O.U.P., 1920), I, 207.
138. Jones, I, 270.
139. Gamble, 24.
140. PRO Cab. 38/27/22: 2nd report on the Royal Flying Corps.
141. Longmore.
142. Asquith Papers.
143. Samson, *Fights and Flights* (Ernest Benn)
144. October 1914, 287.
145. *World Crisis*, I, 119.
146. *Dreadnought to Scapa Flow*, I, 358.
147. *World Crisis*, I, 121n.
148. *World Crisis*, I, 120.
149. 100th meeting of the CID.
150. *World Crisis*, I, 118.
151. Bonham Carter (Chapter XIX) gives a delightful account of this cruise.
152. Royal Archives, GV G393/5.
153. PRO Cab. 37/105/27.
154. 118th meeting of the CID.

155. Asquith Papers.
156. *Navy League Annual*, 1913–14, 86 and passim.
157. PRO Cab. 37/109/32.
158. 118th meeting of the CID.
159. PRO Cab. 37/109/34.
160. E. L. Woodward, *Great Britain and the German Navy* (O.U.P., 1935), 406.
161. *The Navy*, April 1913, 105.
162. *The Navy*, August 1913, 217.
163. Royal Archives, GV G775/1–7.
164. Royal Archives, GV G775/5.
165. World Crisis, I, 140.
166. Royal Archives, GV G775/4.
167. Asquith Papers.
168. Randolph Churchill, II, 681.
169. Royal Archives, GV G682a/3.
170. I, 147.
171. Sir James Fergusson of Kilkerran, *The Curragh Incident* (Faber, 1964).
172. Admiral Sir Lewis Bayly, *Pull Together!* (Harrap, 1939), 155.
173. De Chair, 152–3.
174. Letter from Vice Admiral H. T. Baillie-Grohman to author.
175. Royal Archives (Hopwood to Stamfordham, 21/3/14).
176. *World Crisis*, I, 155.
177. Richmond Diaries.
178. *World Crisis*, I, 171.
179. See also: Admiral of the Fleet Lord Chatfield, *The Navy and Defence* (Heinemann, 1942), 122.
180. Sir Julian Corbett and Sir Henry Newbolt, *History of the Great War: Naval Operations* (Longmans, 1923–30, 5 vols.), I, 34.
181. PRO Adm. 137/47.
182. *World Crisis,* I, 261.
183. *World Crisis*, I, 261.
184. PRO Adm. 137/47.
185. Marder, *Portrait of an Admiral: The Life and Papers of Sir Herbert Richmond* (Cape, 1952).
186. Corbett, I, 441.
187. PRO Adm. 137/47, 389–90.
188. PRO Adm. 137/47, 393.
189. PRO Adm. 137/47, 392.
190. PRO Adm. 137/47, 386.
191. *Portrait of an Admiral.*
192. *World Crisis*, I, 265.
193. *Dreadnought to Scapa Flow*, II, 87.
194. *Dreadnought to Scapa Flow*, II, 86.
195. *Dreadnought to Scapa Flow*, II, 88.
196. Esher.

197. *Dreadnought to Scapa Flow*, II, 88, quoting Admiral Oliver.
198. *World Crisis*, I, 371.
199. *World Crisis*, I, 367.
200. Captain G. M. Bennett, *Coronel and the Falklands* (Batsford, 1962). The Engineer Officer had found the strain of war too much, and was suffering from nervous exhaustion. The ship could manage sixteen knots.
201. *World Crisis*, I, 373.
202. *Dreadnought to Scapa Flow*, 211n.
203. PRO Adm. 137/304.
204. *World Crisis*, I, 398.
205. *World Crisis*, I, 414–30.
206. Jellicoe Papers.
207. 'A Reply to Criticism', Jellicoe.
208. WSC to Fisher, 23/12/14, quoted in *Fear God and Dread Nought*, III, 109.
209. *World Crisis*, I.
210. *World Crisis*, I, 498.
211. *World Crisis*, I, 559.
212. PRO Adm. 137.
213. PRO Adm. 137.
214. *World Crisis*, I, 455.
215. PRO Cab. 137/551.
216. *National Review*, August 1923, 838.
217. *The Eyes of the Navy*, 81.
218. Jellicoe Papers.
219. Naval Staff monograph.
220. *Gallipoli* (Batsford, 1965).
221. WSC to Asquith, 31/7/14.
222. WSC, *Great Contemporaries* (Thornton Butterworth, 1937), 339.
223. WSC to Asquith, 29/12/14.
224. Admiral James, *A Great Seaman: the Life of Admiral of the Fleet Sir Henry F. Oliver* (Witherby, 1956), 144.
225. *Dreadnought to Scapa Flow*, II, 189.
226. *Life of Jellicoe*, 188.
227. *World Crisis*, I, 482.
228. PRO Cab. 25/107.
229. Mitchell Report on the Dardanelles, 1919 (Admiralty Library).
230. Mitchell Report.
231. *Dreadnought to Scapa Flow*, II, 201.
232. PRO Cab. 19/29.
233. I have relied on: *Dreadnought to Scapa Flow*, I; Rhodes James; Corbett, II; *World Crisis*; the report of the Dardanelles Commission; and the report of the Mitchell Committee of 1919 (convened by the Admiralty and containing members from all three services) for my facts. The judgements are my own.
234. PRO 19/29.

235. Lord Hankey, *The Supreme Command, 1914–1918* (Allen & Unwin, 1961), 264–5.
236. *World Crisis*, I.
237. *World Crisis*, I. Date incorrectly given as 27 rather than 26 January.
238. *Dreadnought to Scapa Flow*, II, 210.
239. Dardanelles Commission Report.
240. Dardanelles Commission.
241. *Dreadnought to Scapa Flow*, II, 227.
242. Dardanelles Commission.
243. *World Crisis*, I, 669.
244. Dardanelles Commission.
245. *Dreadnought to Scapa Flow*, II.
246. Asquith Papers.
247. Mrs Churchill to Asquith, 20/5/15 (Asquith Papers).
248. *World Crisis*, 'The Aftermath', 459
249. Bonham Carter, 448.
250. David Lloyd George, *War Memories* (Nicholson & Watson, 1933, 6 vols.), I, 636–8.
251. PRO Cab. 21/27, 4–6.
252. PRO Cab. 21/27, 4–6.
253. PRO Cab. 21/27, WC 233, 14.
254. Sir Basil H. Liddell Hart, in *Encounter*, April 1966.
255. A Boyle, *Trenchard* (Collins, 1962), Chapters XII–XV.
256. Chalmers, 371.
257. WSC, *The Second World War* (Cassell, 1948–54, 6 vols.), I, 143.
258. *Second World War*, I, 608–9.
259. *World Crisis*, 'The Aftermath', 423–4.
260. 137th meeting of the CID; second meeting of subcommittee.
261. 148th meeting of the CID.
262. 137th meeting of the CID.
263. L. S. Amery, *My Political Life* (Hutchinson, 1953, 3 vols.), II.
264. PRO Cab 27/164. Report of the committee appointed to examine the report of the Geddes Committee on National Expenditure.
265. Arthur Swinson, *Action for Libel*.
266. *Second World War*, I, 45–6.
267. *Second World War*, I, 46.
268. Liddell Hart, *Memoirs* (Cassell, 1965, 2 vols.), I, passim.
269. Chalmers.
270. WSC, *Marlborough: His Life and Times* (Harrap, 1933–8, 4 vols.), 11.
271. *Second World War*, I, 162.
272. Admiral of the Fleet Lord Fraser of North Cape, 'Churchill and the Navy' in *Winston Spencer Churchill: Servant of Crown and Commonwealth*, ed. Sir James Marchant (Cassell, 1954), 78.
273. *Second World War*, I, 371.
274. *Second World War*, I, 147.

275. *Second World War*, I, 315.
276. *Second World War*, I, 317.
277. *Second World War*, I, 343–4.
278. *Second World War*, I, 344–5.
279. *Second World War*, I, 386.
280. Macintyre, in US Naval Institute Proceedings, September 1967.
281. *Second World War*, I, 692–3.
282. *Churchill by his Contemporaries*, 151.
283. *Second World War*, I, 626–8.
284. Captain S. W. Roskill, *The War at Sea* (HMSO, 1954–61, 3 vols.), I, 69.
285. *Second World War*, I, 416. Churchill gravely overestimates the approval of the First Sea Lord and the DCNS.
286. Fraser, 85.
287. *Second World War*, I, 668–9.
288. *Second World War*, I, 669.
289. *Second World War*, I, 669n.
290. Roskill, I, 134.
291. Roskill, I, 106.
292. *Second World War*, I, 387.
293. *Second World War*, I, 383.
294. Führer's Conference on Naval Affairs, 1939.
295. Führer's Conference.
296. *Second World War*, I, 474.
297. Roskill, I, 152.
298. Major General J. L. Moulton, *The Norwegian Campaign of 1940* (Eyre & Spottiswoode, 1966), 42. This provides the latest and best account of the campaign.
299. *Second World War*, I, 479.
300. *Second World War*, I, 490.
301. *Second World War*, I, 491–2.
302. *Second World War*, I, 561–3.
303. Lieutenant General Sir Adrian Carton de Wiart, *Happy Odyssey* (Cape, 1950).
304. Roskill, I, 202.
305. *Second World War*, I, 537.
306. Moulton, 296.
307. *Second World War*, VI, 472.
308. Lord Moran, *Winston Churchill: The Struggle for Survival, 1940–1965* (Constable, 1966), 700.
309. Harold Macmillan, *The Blast of War* (Macmillan, 1967), 424.
310. *Second World War*, V, 118.
311. Admiral of the Fleet Viscount Cunningham of Hyndhope, *Sailor's Odyssey* (Hutchinson, 1951), 573.
312. Philip Goodhart, *Fifty Ships that Saved the World* (Heinemann, 1965).
313. *Second World War*, II, 360.

314. *Second World War*, III, 107–9.
315. *Second World War*, III, 539.
316. Roskill, II, 370.
317. *Second World War*, V, 6.
318. Kenneth Young, *Churchill and Beaverbrook: a Study in Friendship and Politics* (Eyre & Spottiswoode, 1966).
319. Cunningham, 436.
320. C. W. Nimitz et al., ed., *Triumph in the Atlantic* (Prentice-Hall, 1964), 91.
321. Roskill, 11, 136.
322. *Second World War*, II, 216.
323. *Second World War*, VI, 129.
324. Young, 230.
325. Chatfield, 153–8.
326. CMD 8094 (Considered Court-Martial Procedure) and 8119 (Considered Summary Punishments).
327. Letter from the Hon. Ewen Montague, QC, to author.
328. CMD 7608 (Lewis Committee).

INDEX

Index

Churchill (Sir), Winston L. S. —*cont.*
France, 132–3; his Mediterranean policy consistent, 137; surveys whole naval position (1912), 138; his '*Luxus Flotte*' speech, 143; on the German *Novelle*, 144; his speech on Naval Estimates (1912), 145–6; on competition in armaments, 145–6; criticized by Navy League, 148–9; warns of increased expenditure on ship-building (Oct.–Nov. 1913), 149; and the small states' warships and Lloyd George (correspondence, Jan. 1914), 151–2; his speech on Naval Estimates (1914–15), 153–4; and Home Rule for Ireland, 155; and the Curragh incident, 155–9 *passim*; his three years of achievement, 159–61; De Chair on, 128 *n*, 160; Kitchener on, 161; the Naval Review (July 1914) and tactical exercises, 162–3; Fleet at war stations: How to fight the war?, 164; initial war aims, 164–5; and War Staff Group, 165; and the BEF to France, 165; Sir John French, and the RN Division, 178; and Antwerp, 179; and Coronel, 181; restrains Fisher's dismissals, 191–2; and Grand Fleet to Firth of Forth, 195; his versatility, 196; and 'command', 197; and honours and awards, 197; his methods of work, 197–8 & *n*, 198–200; his facility in discussion, 198; his restlessness and offensive spirit, 201–15; his appreciation of the situation on the Western Front and in Russia, 203–4; and the Dardanelles, 207–21 *passim*, 240–1, 246; and Turkey, 207; and Gallipoli, 207; and his 'experts', 214–15, 219; his 'indictment', 219–20; and Fisher (an uneasy partnership), 221–2; circumstances of his leaving the Admiralty, 223; his faults and merits, 224; Chancellor of Duchy of Lancaster, 224; resigns from Government, 224; Mrs Churchill on, 224; author's comments on him as First Lord, 225; on 'negative admirals' and on convoys, 225–6; influence of this on war at sea, 1939–45, 226; his resignation speech, 227–8; in the trenches in France, 228 *bis*; attacks Admiralty in debate on Naval Estimates, 228; returns to politics, 229; and journalism, 229–30; Minister of Munitions, 230–4; and Smuts Report on Air Organization, 232; and an Air Ministry and independent air force, 232–3; Minister for War and Air, 234–7; and Trenchard, 234, 237, 239; his Memorandum on control of aircraft, 235–6; Colonial Secretary, 237–40; and Turkish crisis (1922), 237 & *n*; and joint staff training and Imperial Defence, 237–8, 239; and the future of capital ships, 238–9; and Beatty, 238–9; saves Navy from disaster

through economy cuts, 239; his electoral defeat (1922), 240–1; and Douglas libel case, 241–2; on Battle of Jutland, 242; Chancellor of the Exchequer, 242–5; disastrous effect on the Services of his economies (1925–9), 242–5; 'in the shadows' again, 245–50; and India, 245; and Abdication crisis, 246; and Marlborough's strategy, 246; and air defence and radar, 247; and re-armament, 247; and guns for new battleships, 247–8; and anti-submarine training, 248; and Abyssinian crisis (1936), 250; and Munich crisis (1938), 250; and Mediterranean and Home Fleets, 250–1; and France and the Maginot Line, 251; and atomic and nuclear energy, 251; back to the Admiralty, 252–3; his 'daily prayers', 259, 260, 285 *bis*; and Dudley Pound, *q.v.*, 253, 287, 288; his impact on the administration, 259–61; and cadet-ships, 260; his energy and industry, 260–1; and Courts Martial for losing a ship, 261; his broadcasts, 261; his quests for offensive operations (1939–45), 261–6; and trade defence and the convoy system, 263–6; exaggerates figures of U-boat sinkings, 266; his actions in 1914–15 and 1939–45 compared, 267–83; and Norwegian campaign, 271–81; his work as First Lord in 1939–40, 282–3; Prime Minister (1940–5) and Minister of Defence, 284–306; and Chiefs of Staff Committee, 286; and Cunningham, *q.v.*, 287–8; his methods of work (as PM), 288; and impossibility of defeat, 290; and anti-U-boat operations, 291–5 (*see also* Battle of the Atlantic *and* U-boats); and bombing of Germany, 292, 293, 295, 297, 300; and disposal of French fleet, 296–7; and 'Overlord', 297, 302–4; his inventiveness, 303; resigned Premiership, 307; his reforms surveyed, 307–19; on the Royal Navy (in 1948), 318–19

Coastal Command, RAF (*formerly* Coastal Area): 233, 234, 236; the 'Cinderella', 256; in 1939–45, 291, 293, 297; and the Navy, 316–17

Command of the sea (naval supremacy): 35, 51

Committee of Imperial Defence (CID): 14, 22, 25 & *n*, 36, 39 & *n*, 46, 47, 49 *bis*, 92, 116 & *n*, 131 *ter*, 133, 134, 137, 207; history, duties and composition of, 47–8; on naval supremacy and home defence (1908), 50; meeting of (23 Aug. 1911), 53; and naval aviation 117–18; and airships, 119, 120, 121; and a 'National Corps of Airmen', 122; Report of Aviation Sub-Committee (29 Dec. 1912), 122–4; and the Air Committee, 125; meeting of (4 July 1912), 134–7; WSC's efforts and the

Index

Index